HISPANIC AMERICAN VOICES

HISPANIC AMERICAN VOICES

Deborah Gillan Straub, *Editor*

AN IMPRINT OF GALE

DETROIT • NEW YORK • TORONTO • LONDON

Hispanic American Voices

Deborah Gillan Straub, *Editor*

Staff

Sonia Benson, *U•X•L Senior Developmental Editor*
Carol DeKane Nagel, *U•X•L Managing Editor*
Thomas L. Romig, *U•X•L Publisher*

Edna M. Hedblad, *Permissions Associate*

Shanna Heilveil, *Production Associate*
Evi Seoud, *Assistant Production Manager*
Mary Beth Trimper, *Production Director*

Michelle DiMercurio, *Art Director*
Cynthia Baldwin, *Product Design Manager*

Library of Congress Cataloging-in-Publication Data
Hispanic American Voices/Deborah Gillan Straub.
       p. cm.
    Includes bibliographical references and indexes.
       ISBN 0-8103-9827-3 (alk. paper)
       1. Hispanic Americans–Biography. 2. Hispanic Americans–History. 3. Speeches, addresses, etc., American–Hispanic American authors. I. Straub, Deborah Gillan.
    E184.S75H564 1996
    973'.0468–dc20

    96-42019
    CIP

Contents

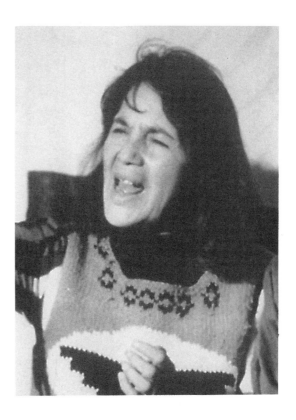

Dolores Huerta

Speech Topics at a Glance

Tony Bonilla

Reader's Guide

Antonia Hernández

Hispanic Americans have played a major role in shaping the history and culture of the United States since the European conquest of the New World. A highly diverse group with roots in Spain or the Spanish-speaking countries of South and Central America, Mexico, Puerto Rico, or Cuba, Hispanic Americans descend from people who became U.S. citizens for a variety of reasons throughout history. Some were early explorers and pioneers of North America; others were Mexican citizens living in territory that was ceded to the United States by Mexico. Puerto Ricans were granted U.S. citizenship in 1917. Civil wars in Latin American countries caused many to flee north, while others entered the United States to work during labor shortages created by World War II and the Korean War. In any case, within the Hispanic American community there is a large population with roots that go back to the European-based founders of North America as well as many who have recently arrived from other nations. In 1996 the U.S. Census Bureau reported that Hispanic children were the largest group of U.S. children after non-Hispanic whites. It is anticipated that Hispanics will be the nation's largest minority group early in the twenty-first century.

Despite a history as long and eminent as that of any American group, Hispanic Americans have often faced discrimination in the United States. To receive equal treatment in areas as basic as employment, voting rights, and education, many Hispanic leaders have struggled against harsh odds in all levels of government, as well as in the courts, union halls, farm fields, and factories, in the media, and on the streets. Together their disparate voices present a vivid portrait of the ongoing fight for justice in this nation of immigrants. *Hispanic American Voices* is a collection of excerpted speeches delivered by sixteen Hispanic American leaders who have spoken out on vital issues from the late nineteenth century to the present.

Voices includes historical oratories, such as the powerful "Our America" speech, in which the exiled Cuban freedom-fighter José Martí imparts his dream of a united, independent Latin America, and the 1945 radio broadcast of Puerto Rican governor Luis Muñoz-Marín, in which he asks the American public to support the cause of self-government for his island. The speeches of César Chávez and Dolores Huerta, co-founders of the United Farm Workers, and U.S. Representative Henry B. Gonzalez invoke the tremendous struggle for basic human rights among farm workers in this country. More current moments of history are captured by Housing and Urban Development secretary Henry G. Cisneros in his piercing depiction of Los Angeles after the 1992 riots (the "urban apocalypse in smoky smelly orange"), Antonia Hernández's debunking of anti-immigrant propaganda disseminated to promote California's Proposition 187, and Linda Chavez's argument against state-sponsored multicultural education.

It is not possible in this first edition of *Hispanic American Voices* to include all of the many prominent Hispanic Americans who have contributed to U.S. culture. Due to the unavailability of certain materials for publication, some important speeches were regretfully omitted from this volume. *Voices* does, however, provide a compelling array of perspectives, with first-hand insight into key issues, events, and movements in Hispanic American history.

The entries in *Hispanic American Voices* are arranged alphabetically by speaker. Each begins with introductory material, providing a brief biography of the speaker and the historical context of the speech that follows. Informative sidebars expand on topics mentioned within the entry. A "Sources" section, directing the student to further readings on the speechmaker and his or her speeches, concludes each entry.

Hispanic American Voices also contains approximately eighty black-and-white photographs, a subject index, a listing of speeches by major topics, and a timeline. Words and phrases are defined in the lower margin of the page on which they appear.

Related Reference Sources

Hispanic American Almanac explores the history and culture of Hispanic America. The volume is organized into fourteen subject chapters including immigration, family and religion, jobs and education, literature, and sports. The volume contains more than seventy black-and-white photographs and maps, a glossary, and a subject index.

Hispanic American Biography profiles ninety Hispanic Americans, living and deceased, prominent in fields ranging from civil rights to athletics, politics to literature, entertainment to science, religion to the military. A black-and-white portrait accompanies most entries, and the volumes conclude with an index listing all individuals by field of endeavor.

Hispanic American Chronology explores the significant social, political, economic, cultural, and educational milestones in Hispanic American history. Arranged chronologically, the volume spans from 1492 to modern times and contains more than seventy illustrations, extensive cross references, and a subject index.

Acknowledgments

The editor wishes to thank the following people who served as advisors on this project: Wil A. Linkugel, Professor of Communication Studies, University of Kansas, Lawrence, Kansas; Rhonda Rios Kravitz, Head of Access Services, Library, California State University, Sacramento, California; and Hilda K. Weisburg, Media Specialist, Sayreville War Memorial High School, Parlin, New Jersey.

Your Suggestions Are Welcome

The editor welcomes your comments and suggestions for future editions of *Hispanic American Voices*. Please write: The Editor, *Hispanic American Voices,* U•X•L, 835 Penobscot Building, Detroit, Michigan 48226-4094; call toll-free: 1-800-877-4253; or fax: (313) 961-6347.

Introduction

Traditions in Hispanic American Oratory

Eloquence of expression has become ingrained in Hispanic culture through education and oral tradition since the emergence of the Spanish language in the Middle Ages. Much of the university curriculum at that time consisted of lecture and oral debate in Latin, and this tradition passed into Spanish when it became the official tongue of Spain during the Renaissance. Spanish subsequently became the language of governmental, educational and religious institutions throughout Spain's colonies in the Americas.

Educational methodology in Hispanic countries has been criticized for relying too much on oral recitation. But few outsiders have understood the value that the culture places on the oral performance itself and on improvisation. The product of an Hispanic education is expected to be able to compose and deliver extemporaneously [without rehearsal] a beautiful, enlightening and precise speech on any topic.

The same is true in folk culture, where improvisation and

Henry B. Gonzalez

elegance of expression have always ranked very high in the creation of epics, songs and stories. Hispanic audiences of all kinds—students in university classes, townsfolk at a patriotic celebration or churchgoers listening to a sermon—have typically expected and delighted in long compositions that reflect in both style and content the weightiness of the subjects under discussion.

It is, however, in the political realm that Hispanics have produced their most memorable and celebrated oratory. What may be considered the golden age of Spanish oratory began during the nineteenth century, when the Spanish American countries sought freedom from Spain. The powerful speeches of Venezuela's Simón Bolívar, Argentina's José San Martín, Mexico's Benito Juárez and scores of others who led independence movements and founded republics live on in legend and in history, and they are still studied throughout the Americas as examples of both literature and oratory.

Hispanics in the United States not only inherited these oratorical traditions but participated in their development. Of course, those areas that were once part of Spanish America—Puerto Rico, Florida and the Southwest—were directly involved in the political discourse of Mexico and Spain. But as early as the first decade of the nineteenth century, expatriates [people who left their native country to live elsewhere] from Spain established themselves in New York [New York], Philadelphia [Pennsylvania] and Boston [Massachusetts] and used their oratorical prowess to raise funds for the effort to oust French invaders from the Iberian [Spanish] peninsula. Later, various Spanish American independence movements—particularly the century-long struggle to win freedom for Cuba and Puerto Rico—were financed and planned in part in New York, Philadelphia, Tampa [Florida], New Orleans [Louisiana] and other cities.

Of all of the orators who have articulated the needs and aspirations of the Hispanic communities in the United States, probably the most famous was José Martí, the lawyer, poet and leader of the Cuban independence movement during the late nineteenth century. He spent much of his life in the United States working as a journalist and lining up support for his cause among members of Hispanic communities from New York to New Orleans. The topics of Martí's speeches ranged from the right of the Cuban people to self-determination to an examination of the cultural conflicts between Anglo Americans and Hispanics. He also spoke out against racism and prejudice in the United States and around the world. One of his most important speeches—one that has become mortar in the building of Latin American identity in the hemisphere—is "Nuestra America" ("Our America"), which he delivered in New York around 1891.

Like many of the important addresses given by Hispanic leaders in the United States, Martí's speeches were originally transcribed and published in local Spanish-language newspapers; some have since been reprinted in history books and textbooks. In general, however, Spanish-speaking orators in the United States have not been well served by schools, libraries, publishers, and other institutions. Most of the speeches Hispanic Americans have given over the last two centuries have been lost to us forever, sometimes because they were never recorded, and sometimes because librarians and archivists failed to save newspaper accounts of an address or the speaker's personal notes. Even publication in a Spanish-language newspaper did not guarantee that a speech would be preserved, for out of an estimated 4,000 Hispanic periodicals published in the U.S. between 1800 and 1960, only incomplete runs of some 1,300 have been located to date.

Despite the loss of this rich heritage, the spirit of José Martí and others like him live on in today's Hispanic expatriate and immigrant communities across the United States. It is a pattern that also repeats itself among public servants and the leaders of various civil rights organizations. The eloquent and forceful declaration of organizing principals for the community, the call for unity and solidarity, the appeal to divine or human rights for inspiration, and the motivation to take action all figure prominently in the speeches of activists such as Henry G. Cisneros and César Chávez.

As in most European cultures, women in Latin America historically were not encouraged to pursue higher education or participate in public life. Nevertheless, Hispanic culture is replete with the names of women who emerged as leaders in education, politics, unions, the arts and many other areas, and in doing so they became outstanding orators. While their accomplishments were modest given the patriarchal make-up

of Hispanic society in general, their activism and public oratory help us to understand the contemporary leadership of such
women as Nicaragua's Violeta Chamorro, Puerto Rico's Felisa
Rincón de Guatier, and even Argentina's Evita Perón, all of
whom became leaders of their people through the force of
their impassioned reasoning and public speech. Today, Hispanic American women such as Nydia Velásquez of New York and
Ileana Ros-Lehtinen of Florida are establishing a new tradition
of eloquence as members of the United States Congress.

Dr. Nicolás Kanellos
Professor and Founding Publisher of Arte Público Press
University of Houston
Houston, Texas

Suggested Readings

Conte Aguero, Luis, *José Martí y la oratoria cubana,* Tribuna de
Educación Popular (Buenos Aires), n.d.

Cruz Sesoane, María, *Oratoria y periodismo en España del siglo
XIX,* Fundación Juan March (Madrid), 1977.

Melián Laíño, Alvaro, *La oratoria argentina, 1810–1910,* Ministe-
rio de Educación y Justicia (Buenos Aires), 1963.

Mora, Magdalena, and Adelaida R. Del Castillo, editors, *Mexican
Women in the United States: Struggles Past and Present,* UCLA Chicano Studies Research Center, 1980.

Credits

Federico Peña

Grateful acknowledgment is made to the following sources who have granted us permission to reproduce material in this volume of *Hispanic American Voices*. Every effort has been made to trace copyright, but if omissions have been made, please contact the publisher.

Bonilla, Tony. From a speech delivered in February 1983, in Chicago, Illinois, upon winning an award presented by Jesse Jackson. Reproduced by permission of the author.

Chávez, César. From a speech at a Greater Washington Central Labor Council luncheon, 1974. Reproduced by permission of the César E. Chávez Foundation. / *Catholic Mind*, October 1975 for "Saying 'Yes' to Man's Dignity" by César Chávez. Reproduced by permission of the César E. Chávez Foundation.

Chavez, Linda. From a speech delivered in October 1992, "Fostering Appreciation for Cultural Diversity: Recognizing America's Changing Complexion," at the National Preservation Conference. Reproduced by permission of Linda Chavez.

Fernandez, Joseph A. From a speech delivered on September 7, 1993, to the National Press Club. Reproduced by permission of the author.

Hernández, Antonia. From a speech delivered on October 5, 1994, "Are We Compassion Fatigued?," at the Temple Isaiah in Los Angeles, California. Reproduced by permission of the author.

Huerta, Dolores. *Delano Record,* April 28, 1966, "Speech at Capital Rally," by Dolores Huerta. Reproduced by permission of Dolores C. Huerta. / From a keynote address delivered on October 21, 1974, at the Annual Convention of American Public Health Association in New Orleans, Louisiana. Reproduced by permission of Dolores Huerta.

Yzaguirre, Raul. From a speech delivered on May 31, 1994, at Mercy College, White Plains, New York. Reproduced by permission of the author.

The photographs and illustrations appearing in *Hispanic American Voices* were received from the following sources:

Cover: César Chávez, **The Library of Congress**

Timeline: UPI/Corbis-Bettmann: p. xxi, xxiii (bottom), xxiv (top); © **Archive Photos:** p. xxii (bottom); **The Bettmann Archive:** p. xxiii (top); **Reuters/Corbis-Bettmann:** pp. xxiv (bottom), xxvii (bottom); **AP/Wide World Photos:** pp. xxv; xxvi (top and bottom), xxvii (top), xxviii.

Text: AP/Wide World Photos: pp. 1, 13, 17, 22, 33, 49, 57, 58, 61, 65, 80, 90, 99, 121, 124, 140, 145, 160, 182, 201, 215; **UPI/Corbis-Bettmann:** pp. 4, 15, 43, 103, 107, 134, 137, 157, 168, 171, 190, 196, 210, 230, 237; **Corbis-Bettmann** pp. 26, 148, 221; **The Library of Congress:** p. 36; **Arizona Historical Society Library:** p. 41; **Reuters/Corbis-Bettmann:** pp. 72, 73, 175, 213, 225; **Arte Público Press Archives, University of Houston:** pp. 86, 187; **Hernández, Antonia, photograph by George Rodriguez. Reproduced by permission of Antonia Hernández:** p. 110; **Reuters/Lou Dematteis/Archive Photos:** p. 115; **Impact Visuals/Mev Puleo. Reproduced by permission:** p. 118; **Magnum Photos:** p. 127; **Reuters/Zoraida Diaz/Archive Photos:** p. 179; © **Archive Photos:** pp. 193, 198.

Timeline of Important Hispanic American Events

1800–1996

Boldface indicates speakers featured in this volume

Antonio López de Santa Anna

1810 Hispanic colonists in New Spain (a territory encompassing Mexico as well as large portions of the present-day southwestern United States) proclaim their independence from Spain.

1821 New Spain gains its independence and renames itself the Republic of Mexico. Anglo American settlers begin to move into Mexican territory, especially Texas.

1833 Antonio López de Santa Anna is elected president of Mexico. He will rule as dictator for most of the next twenty years.

1836 Anglo American settlers in Texas resist Santa Anna's military rulers. A battle erupts at the Alamo between the Anglo-Texans and Santa Anna's troops. All of the Anglos are killed. Six weeks later Anglo-Texans defeat the Mexican army at the Battle of San Jacinto. They declare their independence from Mexico and form the Republic of Texas.

1845 The United States officially annexes Texas.

1846 The United States declares war on Mexico.

1848 The Treaty of Guadalupe Hidalgo ends the war between the United States and Mexico. Mexico cedes territory in what is now California, Arizona, New Mexico, Texas, Colorado, Wyoming, and Nevada. The treaty gives Mexican nationals one year to choose U.S. or Mexican citizenship.

1803
Louisiana
Purchase

1812–15
War of 1812

1819–30
Simón Bolívar unites
newly independent
South American republics

1821
United States
purchases Florida
from Spain

• • **1800** • • **1810** • • **1820** • • **1830** • • **1840** • • **1850** • •

José Martí

1848–49 The California gold rush begins. Large numbers of Anglo American settlers arrive in the former Mexican territory.

1853 Santa Anna sells to the United States the area from Yuma (Arizona) to the Mesilla Valley (New Mexico).

1862 Congress passes a law allowing "any alien" who is honorably discharged from the military to apply for naturalization.

1868 Congress ratifies the Fourteenth Amendment, which recognizes blacks as citizens with certain constitutional guarantees and declares all people of Hispanic origin born in the United States as citizens.

1868–78 The Cuban War for Independence (also known as the Ten Years' War) forces many Cubans into exile, with most choosing to flee to Europe and the United States.

1892 The Cuban Revolutionary Party is created to organize the Cuban and Puerto Rican independence movements.

1895 Led by **José Martí**, Cuban revolutionaries begin a war for independence from Spain.

1897 Spain grants Cuba and Puerto Rico some measure of independence and home rule.

1898 The United States and Spain clash over their influence in Latin America, beginning the Spanish-American War. Spain quickly meets with defeat and is forced to give up Puerto Rico and Guam to the United States. The United States agrees to pay Spain $20 million for the Philippines. Cuba achieves independence from Spain but remains under U.S. military control until 1902.

U.S. troops in the Spanish-American War

1850	1861–1865	1870	1877
California admitted to Union	Civil War; slavery abolished	Fifteenth Amendment grants all male citizens right to vote	Reconstruction Era ends in South

• • **1850** • • **1860** • • **1870** • • **1880** • • **1890** • • **1900** • •

1900	Mexican ambassador protests brutal lynchings and murder of Mexican Americans in the southwestern United States.
	Congress establishes a civilian government in Puerto Rico under which islanders can elect their own House of Representatives.
1910	The Mexican Revolution begins as an attempt to overthrow Porfirio Diáz's leadership, which favors large landowners who take land from *campesinos* or peasants. As Mexico passes from one leader to the next, rebels continue to fight, under the command of Pancho Villa and others in the North and under Emiliano Zapata in the South. Many civilians are killed in this brutal war, which lasts nearly ten years. Thousands of people flee north, with most settling in the southwestern United States.
1917	Congress grants citizenship to all Puerto Ricans.
	Congress passes the Immigration Act, which imposes a literacy requirement on all immigrants.
1921	The United States imposes limits on the number of immigrants allowed to enter the country in a single year.
1925	Congress establishes the U.S. Border Patrol.
1929	The League of United Latin American Citizens (LULAC) is founded to secure greater opportunities for Mexican Americans.
1943	To help deal with the wartime labor shortage, the U.S. government reaches an agreement with the Mexican government to allow temporary workers known as *braceros* to enter the country.
1946	**Dennis Chávez** tries but fails to gain approval in the U.S. Senate for antidiscrimination legislation known as the Fair Employment Practices Act.

Emiliano Zapata

Mexican American soldiers sing after a day of training, World War II

1903
Orville Wright flies
first airplane

1914–18
World War I

1920
Nineteenth
Amendment grants
vote to women

1929
Stock market
crashes; Great
Depression begins

1939–45
World War II

• • **1900** • • **1910** • • **1920** • • **1930** • • **1940** • • **1950** • • •

*Puerto Rican and U.S. flags fly
over San Juan, Puerto Rico, 1952*

1950   Due in large part to the efforts of **Luis Muñoz-Marín,** Congress changes Puerto Rico's status from protectorate to commonwealth.

Puerto Rican nationalists try to assassinate President Harry Truman.

1954   The Supreme Court issues its *Hernández v. Texas* decision, establishing Hispanics as a separate class of people suffering from discrimination and therefore entitled to the protection of the Fourteenth Amendment. It is the first Mexican American discrimination case to reach the nation's highest court and the first argued by Mexican American attorneys.

Puerto Rican nationalists shoot at members of Congress from the spectators' gallery, wounding five legislators.

1954–58   Operation Wetback results in the deportation of nearly four million people of Mexican descent from the United States, often without hearings.

1959   In Cuba, revolutionary leader Fidel Castro assumes control after President Fulgencio Batista resigns and flees the country.

1961   The United States severs diplomatic relations with Cuba.

Cuban exiles—aided by the United States— stage the Bay of Pigs invasion of Cuba.

1962   In California, **César Chávez, Dolores Huerta,** and other activists form the National Farm Workers Association, later known as the United Farm Workers (UFW).

In a series of events known as the "Cuban Missile Crisis," the Soviet Union abandons its plans to establish missile bases in Cuba in exchange for a promise from President John F. Kennedy that the United States will not attempt another invasion of Cuba.

Fidel Castro

1950–1953
Korean War

1954
The Supreme Court prohibits public school segregation

1955–1956
Martin Luther King, Jr., leads bus boycott in Montgomery, Alabama

1959
Hawaii becomes the fiftieth state

1964	Due to the efforts of Representative **Henry B. Gonzalez** of Texas and other legislators, the *bracero* program ends.

Congress passes the Civil Rights Act of 1964, which prohibits discrimination in hiring and employment practices and paves the way for various affirmative action programs.

1965	Fidel Castro allows Cubans with relatives in the United States to leave—if their relatives come and get them. The policy prompts many Cuban Americans in South Florida to set out by boat to pick up family members.

César Chávez at picket rally

The Immigration Act of 1965 is approved, allowing for much higher levels of non-European immigration to the United States, especially from Latin America, the Caribbean, and Asia.

Congress passes the Voting Rights Act of 1965, which bans states from denying the right to vote to people unable or unwilling to pay a poll tax and to those unable to read or write English.

1966–73	More than 250,000 Cubans—about 10 percent of the island's population—immigrate to the United States under the terms of a special airlift program.
1968	**César Chávez** undertakes the first of many fasts on behalf of the farm workers movement.

Chicano student organizations spring up around the country amid a general atmosphere of dissent and rebellion.

1973	The Supreme Court rules in *Espinoza v. Farah Manufacturing Company* that nothing in the Civil Rights Act of 1964 prohibits discrimination on the basis of citizenship or alien status.
1974	Congress passes the Equal Educational Opportunity Act, making bilingual education available to public school students whose primary language is not English.

1965–73
U.S. troops fight in
Vietnam War

1968
Student protest
demonstrations hit
221 U.S. campuses

1974
President Richard Nixon resigns
after Watergate investigation

• • **1960** • • **1963** • • **1966** • • **1969** • • **1972** • • **1975** • •

Vilma S. Martinez

1975 Congress extends the Voting Rights Act of 1965 for seven years and specifically adds protection for Hispanic voters as well as for black voters. **Vilma S. Martinez** of the Mexican American Legal Defense and Educational Fund (MALDEF) is instrumental in persuading Congress to extend the law to cover Hispanics.

1976 The Supreme Court rules that blacks and other minorities are entitled to retroactive job security.

1978 In a serious blow to affirmative action, the Supreme Court issues its Bakke decision declaring racial and ethnic quota systems in college admissions unconstitutional.

1980 More than 125,000 Cubans immigrate to the United States as part of the so-called Mariel boat lift.

Jorge Mas Canosa co-founds the Cuban American National Foundation.

The Refugee Act of 1980 abandons the definition of "refugee" as someone who flees a communist country.

1981 **Henry G. Cisneros** wins the San Antonio, Texas, mayoral election to become the first Hispanic mayor of a major U.S. city.

1985 **Antonia Hernández** is named head of the Mexican American Legal Defense and Educational Fund (MALDEF).

1987 President Ronald Reagan signs into law the Immigration Reform and Control Act in an effort to curb illegal immigration by prohibiting the hiring of illegal aliens. The act allows aliens who can prove that they were in the United States prior to January 1, 1982, to apply for temporary status and eventually become citizens.

1989 The Supreme Court rules that workers who are negatively affected by court-approved affirmative action plans may file lawsuits charging discrimination.

Cuban refugees board U.S. Navy warship

1980
Serious racial disturbances erupt in Miami, Florida

1981
First report on AIDS is published

1988
Jesse Jackson places second in Democratic presidential primary

1990	**Antonia C. Novello** becomes the first woman and the first Hispanic surgeon general of the United States.

Antonia C. Novello becomes the first woman and the first Hispanic surgeon general of the United States.

Joseph A. Fernandez is named head of the New York City public school system.

1993   **César Chávez** dies.

Henry G. Cisneros becomes U.S. Secretary of Housing and Urban Development.

Voters in Puerto Rico reject statehood.

Federico Peña becomes U.S. Secretary of Transportation.

1994   Thousands of Cubans attempt to make their way to the United States on makeshift rafts and other unseaworthy vessels, sparking a refugee crisis in south Florida.

Antonia Novello

President Bill Clinton announces that he is ending the special status enjoyed by Cuban immigrants for 28 years, which granted them U.S. residency if they made it to American shores. Cuban refugees are picked up at sea and detained at Guantánamo Bay, a U.S. naval base on the southeastern coast of Cuba.

The United States and Cuba reach a new agreement on the refugee issue. In return for Fidel Castro's pledge to discourage Cubans from trying to flee on rafts and other vessels, the United States promises to accept a minimum of 20,000 refugees a year through normal channels.

Demonstrators protest Proposition 187

California voters pass Proposition 187, which denies state education, medical, and welfare services to undocumented immigrants.

1990–91 Persian Gulf War	**1991** Dissolution of the Soviet Union: Cold War ends	**1993** Congress approves the North American Free Trade Agreement (NAFTA)	**1994** Republicans gain majorities in Congress

Immigrants take oath of citizenship at Ellis Island

1995 Activists in several states mount efforts to end affirmative action.

United States sends Cuban refugees picked up at sea back to Cuba. Angry Cuban Americans in Miami react with marches and other protests.

California Governor Pete Wilson signs an executive order ending some state affirmative-action programs.

The Supreme Court declares unconstitutional the practice of using race as the major factor in drawing legislative districts.

1996 Cuban fighter jets shoot down two small civilian planes belonging to an anti-Castro Cuban exile group based in Miami. Four people are killed.

In Riverside County, California, sheriff's deputies are videotaped beating several illegal Mexican immigrants who had led them on an eighty-mile chase. Mexican authorities criticize U.S. treatment of immigrants.

The U.S. Census Bureau reports that Hispanics have become the largest group of children in the country after non-Hispanic whites. (Non-Hispanic blacks rank third.)

President Bill Clinton delays enforcing legislation that grants U.S. citizens the right to sue foreign companies that use formerly American property (such as factories or mining operations) seized by the Cubans back in 1961. Canada, Mexico, and European nations that do business with Cuba had promised to take strong action against the United States if the lawsuits were allowed.

Federico Peña agrees to head the U.S. Department of Energy.

1995
Million
Man March

1995
Supreme Court limits federal affirmative-action programs.

1996
Welfare Reform Bill; welfare decisions pass from federal government to states

Tony Bonilla

1936–

*Mexican American attorney and
civil rights activist*

Tony Bonilla was just a child when he first experienced the sting of discrimination in his rural hometown of Calvert, Texas. There Hispanics and blacks lived and worked together, separated by a highway and a set of railroad tracks from the whites, most of whom shunned both groups. As a result, Bonilla has always felt a special bond with African Americans, which has fueled his ongoing efforts for unity among Hispanics and blacks as they seek social, economic, and political justice.

Bonilla's education after high school began at Del Mar College in Corpus Christi, Texas. He earned his associate's degree there while on a football scholarship. He then received his bachelor's degree from Baylor University in 1958 and his law degree from the University of Houston two years later. Bonilla has been in private practice for many years with one of his brothers and several other partners. His specialty is personal injury litigation (lawsuits involving people who have been hurt and want those they hold responsible to help pay for medical expenses and other costs).

"IF WE'RE GOING TO TALK ABOUT COALESCING BETWEEN BLACKS AND HISPANICS, THEN AT SOME POINT ... WE HAVE TO BITE THE BULLET AND SHOW ... THE REST OF THE BLACK AND HISPANIC COMMUNITY IN THIS NATION THAT IT *CAN* BE DONE, THAT IT *WILL* BE DONE, AND THAT IT *MUST* BE DONE."

Outside the courtroom, Bonilla has devoted a great deal of his time to various political and civil rights causes. During the mid-1960s, for example, he served for three years in the Texas state legislature. Since then he has been appointed to several special posts in the state government, including the Coordinating Board for Texas Colleges and Universities, the Texas Constitutional Revision Committee, the Governor's Select Committee on Public Education, and the Advisory Committee on the Spanish-Speaking Population for the 1980 Census.

Leads Two Major Hispanic Organizations

But Bonilla's most significant marks were as a key leader of two important Hispanic organizations. From 1972 until 1975, he was executive director of the League of United Latin American Citizens (LULAC). He followed this with a stint as the group's president from 1981 until 1983. More recently, he has served a number of terms as president of the National Hispanic Leadership Conference (NHLC).

When he was with LULAC, Bonilla was a national spokesperson for the Hispanic community on social, political, and civil rights issues, economic affairs, and education. He also broke new ground by encouraging more cooperation between Hispanics and blacks in the belief that together they could create a much more powerful force for political and social change. Working with him on many occasions during this period was African American clergyman and civil rights activist Jesse Jackson.

In February 1983, during his first campaign for the Democratic presidential candidacy, Jackson presented Bonilla with an award for the many bridges he had built between LULAC and Jackson's Operation PUSH (People United to Serve Humanity), an organization dedicated to economic, social, political, and educational development for underprivileged Americans. Bonilla accepted the honor at a ceremony held in Chicago, Illinois, during Harold Washington's historic campaign to become the city's first black mayor. Besides emphasizing his continued support for Washington, Bonilla delivered a lively speech on the benefits of forming relationships such as the one between LULAC

Jesse Jackson and the Rainbow Coalition

When he campaigned for the Democratic presidential nomination in 1984, Jesse Jackson ran on a platform of racial unity with his National Rainbow Coalition, Inc., a coalition of minority group organizations.

"Our flag is red, white, and blue, but our nation is a rainbow—red, yellow, brown, black, and white—and all are precious in God's sight," Jackson declared. "America is not like a blanket, one piece of unbroken cloth—the same color, the same texture, the same size. It is more like a quilt—many patches, many pieces, many colors, many sizes, all woven and held together by a common thread. The white, the Hispanic, the black, the Arab, the Jew, the woman, the Native American, the small farmer, the businessperson, the environmentalist, the peace activist, the young, the old, the lesbian, the gay, and the disabled make up the American quilt.... All of us count and fit in somewhere. We have proven that we can survive without each other. But we have not proven that we can win or make progress without each other. We must come together...."

and Operation PUSH. The following excerpt from Bonilla's remarks was transcribed from an audiotape he provided.

Thank you very much, Reverend Jesse Jackson. And thank you, ladies and gentlemen for your presence here this morning on this very historic occasion, for it is the first time in the history of our nation that any black group has taken time out to honor a Hispanic citizen of a national level.

I have a number of things to say to you this morning, and to share some thoughts that I've wrestled with over the past several months....

When I was last here, I said that we have to practice what we preach. And if we're going to talk about **coalescing** between blacks and Hispanics, then at some point, some point, we have to bite the bullet and show our commitment and take that first step to show the way to the rest of the black and Hispanic community in this nation that it *can* be done, that it *will* be done, and that it *must* be done.

After that endorsement [of Harold Washington for mayor], I received calls from some friends in Chicago questioning my

coalescing: cooperating, joining together.

Bonilla (right) with Jesse Jackson at a LULAC convention in Detroit, Michigan, July 1, 1983

sanity. What am I doing getting involved in Chicago politics? And how could I join Jesse Jackson, Harold Washington, and others in this endeavor? In fact, at least one of them suggested that I call in sick! Well, I *ain't* sick! And I *ain't* crazy!

We know, ladies and gentlemen, brothers and sisters, when we're getting ripped off. And it's happening here in Chicago. And if we ever want to change, now's the time to do it....

Therefore, I'd like to present to you ... that I made an endorsement to support Harold Washington for mayor. That that commitment is firm. That that commitment is **irrevocable**. And that we are asking our Hispanic, our black, and other people of goodwill to join us in getting political [and] economic freedom for our people....

When I came to Chicago a couple of weeks ago and made an appearance here, people said, "Who is Tony Bonilla? Who does he think—coming into Chicago and messin' in internal

irrevocable: final, irreversible.

politics here? And what's he talkin' about dealing with blacks? Blacks are our enemies!"

And I said to myself—and perhaps the first thing I should do is tell the people here, the multitudes gathered here and those listening on the radio, that Tony Bonilla was born in Calvert, Texas. That Calvert, Texas, had a highway that ran right through the heart of the city and a railroad track that ran parallel to it. And all the blacks and Hispanics lived on one side of the track. And all the whites lived on the other side of the track. So I was raised with the black people.

When I was a senior in high school, in my hometown, I couldn't get a haircut in the white-owned barber shop. In fact, my barber was a black. My first girlfriend was a black. I picked cotton with the blacks. We hauled watermelons together. We chopped cotton together.

My dad was a Mexican national, as was my mother. And they came to this country not knowing how to read, write, or speak the English language. They worked like slaves seven days a week from sunup to sundown. And ladies and gentlemen, brothers and sisters, it was the black community in my hometown of Calvert that made it possible for all eight children to go to college, for four of us to become lawyers, for two of them to become schoolteachers, and for two of them to go into business. So I've never forgotten my roots. I'm *supposed* to be here today, Jesse Jackson. And Jesse and I are *supposed* to work together. The Lord's spirit is among us. And we know that. And there is no stopping us.

Someone shared a story with me recently. Talked about the man who was asleep. And in his sleep, he had a dream. And his whole life came upon the scene. He saw himself walking with the Master on the beach. They were walking together throughout his life. And as he looked back over his life, he noticed that there were two sets of footprints. And the Lord was always with him. But as he neared the end of his life in his dream, he saw, in looking back, that there were some times when there was only one set of footprints. And that really concerned him and he says in his sleep, "Master, Master, it worries me that during the time that I was weakest, during the time that I was the most troubled, hungry, when I was perturbed and fighting with myself and needed help, there was only one set of footprints in the sand. It troubles me, Master, that I don't see two sets of footprints."

The Master says to him, "My son, my son, I would not forget you. I love you. It was during the time that you saw that one set of footprints—that you were weak and hungry and tired and needed help—that you only see one set of footprints, my son, because that's when I was carrying you."

What we feel in LULAC and what we feel in PUSH sometimes is we travel across the country with a heavy burden of helping people whose rights have been denied, whose heads have been beaten. It's been our burden to carry our people and only leave one set of footprints....

As we travel across the country, we find our people on board a boat with no rudder. The sails are down, and the boat is floating in a sea of confusion. We don't condemn those on board that boat—we condemn the system that left us no rudder. We don't condemn our people, but the system that encourages division and confusion. You know, the system may provide us housing for our bodies but not for our souls.

So we pray, then, for understanding among our people. To learn to look at things not just from the standpoint of our own neighborhoods, but to look at a much broader picture from the standpoint of what's right for the country and our people who live in that country. To look at things not just for today and right now, but to look for the needs and concerns of the future generations of our people. To look at things not just as they are, but to look at things as how they ought to be. And it's up to us—PUSH and LULAC, black and Hispanic—to provide our own rudders, to lift up our own sails, and to steer our boat to the tranquil sea of opportunity.

When you pick up ... *Chicago* magazine and they say, "The New Majority—How Will Blacks and Hispanics Vote?" you know we've arrived because they're worried about what we're gonna do. And they *ought* to be worried!

PUSH and LULAC got together and decided to look at a few figures. We [started] thinkin', talkin', about 39,700 of the top positions in city government.... What this study shows—and we only looked at eleven departments—39,000 jobs ... [is that we've] been shortchanged.

League of United Latin American Citizens (LULAC)

400 First Street, NW, Suite 721
Washington, D.C. 20001
(202) 628-8516

Founded in 1929, LULAC has 110,000 members in 12 regional and 43 state groups. LULAC is concerned with seeking full social, political, economic, and educational rights for Hispanics in the United States. The organization supports the fifteen LULAC National Education Service Centers, offers employment and training programs, conducts research on higher education, and sponsors Hispanics Organized for Political Education (HOPE), which encourages voter registration and political awareness. LULAC publishes the *HOPE Voter's Guide,* the monthly *LULAC National Reporter,* and various reports.

You know how many Hispanics work, on the average, for the city of Chicago? Four percent. Seventeen percent population, four percent. It's *disgusting!*

You know how many blacks usually work for the city on the average? Twenty percent. If you look at the statistics, then, of the highest-paying jobs in the city, the statistics get worse and not better.

In fact, the highest number of Hispanics and blacks are working in the positions that pay nineteen thousand [dollars] or less, Reverend Jesse. You get to the positions that pay thirty-five, forty thousand—those good, nice, sweet positions—and you will not find us there by a very large number.

And it's just not employment, which is so basic. We're also talkin' about contract **procurement** and services. In '79, '80, '81, the city let 1.4 billion dollars in contracts. And the minorities, the minorities—they won't even tell us which minorities, black or Hispanic, they lumped us together then—and they said, "Minorities got 860,000 of 1.4 billion dollars." They're doin' us a big favor, takin' care of their friends in high places.

And we look at those statistics and if you look at the jobs, it should be balanced. We have forty percent black population, seventeen percent Hispanic population—there ought to be forty percent of the jobs in the city for blacks, seventeen percent for Hispanics. If you look at those statistics, we've been robbed out of a hundred and sixty million dollars! If you look at the statistics in procurement and services, His-

procurement: obtaining through one's efforts; gaining possession of.

panics should be having two hundred million dollars in contracts based on our seventeen percent. And blacks should be having somewhere around five or six hundred million dollars in contracts.

So those people in the Hispanic and black community who are supporting the other candidates, you'd better start thinkin' twice!

When we hear the politicians talk, we're reminded of the old Elvis Presley tune. You know, when they run for office, they always say, "Love me tender, love me true, never let me go." Is that right? As soon as the election's over, they put the flip side on and say, "You ain't nothin' but a hound dog."

Well, we're gonna have our own song! Our song's gonna be, "We ain't gonna play that game no more." And if there hasn't been one written, I want somebody to write it.

What does all this mean to us? Maybe I can relate it more in a biblical sense since we're in God's house and there are some ministers here and God-fearing people who are listening and in the audience. We all know the story about the prodigal son—the father who had his two sons, and one of 'em wanted all his money and wanted to take off. And he got all his money. He went off and had a good time. Went out to the best country club, we can assume. Had all kind of pretty women. Lived a wicked way, it says in the Bible. Then he lost it all. Ended up going back to feed the swine. He got to thinkin' about it. "Hey, this ain't no good. My servants back home with my daddy are doin' better than I am. I'd better go home." So what he did, then, he went back home, and we know the rest of the story—that the father killed a fatted calf and had a big feast. People asked him why, and he said, "Because my son was lost and he's been found." What we're saying, then, to our people is it's time our people came home.

Blacks and Hispanics who have been denied economic opportunity—gotta come home. Blacks and Hispanics who do not enjoy political freedom must come home. Blacks and Hispanics who are successful, who rub elbows with the big politicians and belong to the best clubs, have forgotten their roots—they've got to come home. Hispanics and blacks who have received token appointments when there are much bigger plums to pluck from that tree of opportunity—got to come home. Hispanics and blacks who have become wealthy because our people have made them wealthy have got to come home. Hispanics and blacks who are fightin' each other, even today as I stand here, have got to stop fightin' and come home. When they come home, we can have our *own* feast.

You know what Jesse said? He said, "Tony, they've been givin' us a ham all this time and we're entitled to the whole hog!" And when he told me that, he said, "You know, Tony, a hog has two hams, and I believe two shoulders and four feet." Jesse never did mention the head. Well, I want you to know, *we* want the head, because that's what we make tamales from!

When you look at the candidates for mayor who fed us these crumbs for the past many years—people fightin' each other to decide who wants to be the fair-haired buddy of the candidate, the mayor in power. You think in terms of how we've been kicked on, stepped over. We say, today, to those who are listenin'—hopefully, Mayor [Jane] Byrne and Richard Daley [are] both listenin'—I know Harold is. As far as we're concerned, Richard Daley represents a relic of the past. [The Richard M. Daley referred to here is the son of former Chicago mayor Richard J. Daley, a powerful, big-city "boss" who served as mayor from 1955 until 1976.] Mayor Byrne represents the evil of the present. And Harold Washington represents the hope of the future.

People ask, "Why do you care about what happens in Chicago?" And we say, "Because Chicago is a mirror of America. Chicago sets the tone for the way people react toward blacks and Hispanics. If they can divide us by drivin' a wedge between us in Chicago, they'll do it in Los Angeles. They'll do it in Miami. They'll do it all over the world, all over the country." You see, we recognize that in Chicago—Chicago is the straw, as Reggie Jackson says, that stirs the drink.

So it's important for us to be here. And to remind the people that the **machine** has dominated us for too long. We've given you these statistics and it shows clearly that the machine is denying us economic opportunity. One of the machine candidates has already suggested that our people go back to Mexico. Well, I tell you, if he wants us to go back to

machine: a highly organized political group run by a handful of extremely powerful people.

Mexico, we don't have to go no further than Colorado 'cause that's all ours anyway!

But you know what's happening, brothers and sisters. When you hear this man say to us, "Go back to Mexico," I'm waiting for the mayor of this great city in America to stand up and say, "I **censure** you for making a racist statement against seventeen percent of our population." I'm waiting for Richard Daley to say it. Because we can't have that kind of attitude running the government that's supposed to be our friend.

It took a lawsuit in federal court to get us—to try to get us—integration because the machine stood in the way. It took a lawsuit in federal court to try to get us representation at the city council level because the machine stood in the way of equal representation for blacks and Hispanics....

You see, the danger is that what happens in Chicago spills over. Just this week, the Justice Department announced that they're filing suit against [the town of] Cicero [Illinois] because of discrimination in housing and employment. There's going to be a lot more Ciceros if we don't stay united.

So you see, then, when people criticize me for endorsing Harold Washington, I'm here to say that Harold Washington has got my support throughout this campaign. There are some, in all **candor**, who say LULAC cannot endorse candidates. Well, LULAC can't. And LULAC hasn't said a word about endorsing Harold Washington—Tony Bonilla is. It'll be Tony Bonilla out there knockin' on doors. It'll be Tony Bonilla speakin' on radio and sending this message in Spanish, to our people, so they'll know.

What we then need, ladies and gentlemen, brothers and sisters, is more truth and love and trust and understanding. 'Cause see, people right this very moment are having meetings and scratchin' their heads saying, "How we gonna divide those people? We can't have them workin' together. That represents fifty-seven percent of the population of this city."

We've got to look back at history to see what happened. El Cid, a Spanish hero, went against the wishes of his king to try to bring the Moors and the Christians together for a united Spain, and he did it through truth and love. It was truth

censure: condemn, criticize.
candor: honesty, frankness.

and love that helped [political and spiritual leader Mohandas K.] Gandhi get independence for India. It was truth and love that helped [civil rights activist] Dr. Martin Luther King, Jr., conquer Montgomery [Alabama, a segregated southern city]. And there's going to be truth and love that will help Hispanics and blacks in the city of Chicago gain economic and political freedom.

Let me close, if I may, with a story.

There was a family out here in Kansas that made it a practice of going out and having their yearly picnic. And they were right next to a wheat field. And their little girl got lost in the wheat field. So all the people scattered out when they found out this little girl was lost and went in different directions lookin' for this little girl, and they couldn't find her. Finally, somebody came up and said, "Why don't we join hands and walk through this wheat field together, and maybe we can find her?" So what they did, then, they joined hands and they walked through that wheat field of Kansas and they found the little girl. And when they found the little girl, the father kneeled down, held her in his arms, and saw that it was too late. He looked up at the crowd gathered around him and said, "If only we had joined hands earlier!"

We don't want nobody sayin' that about blacks and Hispanics. Because we're here today to join hands. And we're gonna walk through the wheat field at Chicago! We're gonna bring hope where there's despair! Love where there's hate! Understanding where there's misunderstanding! Justice where there's injustice! Education where there's unequal education opportunities! Housing where there's indecent housing! And as we walk across Chicago holding hands, we're gonna be able to say, we're gonna be able to say, "We *shall* overcome! We *have* overcome! We're *gonna* overcome!" We can join hands right now with Jesse Jackson!

In 1983, Bonilla and several other activists founded the National Hispanic Leadership Conference (NHLC). The NHLC is a think tank, or research group, that brings together leaders from the Hispanic community and encour-

ages them to take part in the economic, political, and social affairs of mainstream Anglo society. It also encourages cooperation between the Hispanic community and other minorities as well as with various Latin American nations.

As the group's president almost since it began, Bonilla has directed projects that address a wide range of concerns. On the subject of drug abuse, for example, he and the NHLC have set up prevention programs in the Hispanic community. The group has also tried to tackle the problem at its source by discussing possible solutions with local leaders in drug-producing countries of Central and South America. In addition to these activities, Bonilla has continued to work closely with his friend Jesse Jackson and other civil rights leaders. Many of their efforts have focused on negotiating agreements with major U.S. corporations to increase minority hiring and help develop better marketing strategies. Most recently, the NHLC has been working to boost minority participation in the news media.

Sources

Books

Collins, Sheila D., *The Rainbow Challenge: The Jackson Campaign and the Future of U.S. Politics,* Monthly Review Press, 1986.

Colton, Elizabeth O., *The Jackson Phenomenon: The Man, the Power, the Message,* Doubleday, 1989.

Dictionary of Hispanic Biography, Gale, 1995.

Jackson, Jesse L., *Straight from the Heart,* edited by Roger D. Hatch and Frank E. Watkins, Fortress Press, 1987.

Periodicals

Nation, "For Jesse Jackson and His Campaign," April 16, 1988, p. 517; "Jesse Is History," June 20, 1988, pp. 15–18; "Creating a Democratic Majority," December 26, 1988, p. 705.

New Statesman and Society, "America's Great Black Hope," July 10, 1992.

Newsweek, "Does Jackson Want the Job?" June 27, 1988, p. 72.

Time, "The Jackson Problem," December 12, 1988, p. 29.

Vital Speeches of the Day, "The Rainbow Coalition," November 15, 1984, pp. 77–81.

César Chávez

1927–1993

Mexican American labor leader and activist

By most measures, César Chávez was an unlikely leader. A soft-spoken, unassuming man of short stature, simple means, and equally simple tastes, he had never even finished elementary school. Yet as the founder of the United Farm Workers (UFW) union, he unquestionably did more to improve the lives of migrant workers than any other person before him. In fact, a New York Times *reporter once described Chávez as a "David taking on the Goliaths of agriculture." He made skillful use of nonviolent protest tactics such as strikes, marches, boycotts, and fasts to challenge the exploitative practices of farmers and corporations. His efforts won him respect and support among migrant workers as well as among hundreds of sympathizers the world over.*

Early Life

Chávez's special link to the migrant workers grew out of the circumstances of his own childhood. Born near Yuma, Arizona, he spent his early years on the farm that his

"WHEN WE ARE REALLY HONEST WITH OURSELVES WE MUST ADMIT THAT OUR LIVES ARE ALL THAT REALLY BELONG TO US. SO, IT IS HOW WE USE OUR LIVES THAT DETERMINES WHAT KIND OF MEN WE ARE. IT IS MY DEEPEST BELIEF THAT ONLY BY GIVING OUR LIVES DO WE FIND LIFE."

13

grandfather had bought shortly after arriving in the United States from Mexico around 1880. When Chávez was ten, however, his life changed dramatically. The Great Depression financially devastated his family, causing them to lose their land and their house. Like thousands of others across the country, the Chávezes took to the road in search of work and ended up in California. There they joined the ranks of migrant workers, following the harvest from place to place in order to pick grapes, citrus fruits, and vegetables from dawn until dusk.

Such migrant workers typically had to put up with pitifully low wages and unbearable working conditions. "Home" was often a tiny shack made of tar paper or sheet metal without running water, electricity, or fuel for heat or cooking. Mexican American workers also faced discrimination and segregation on a daily basis. And because their families had to move wherever there was work, migrant workers' children didn't have much chance of getting the structured education they needed to escape the cycle of poverty and hard labor and inhuman living conditions.

In fact, young Chávez's formal education came to an end for the most part when he moved to California. He later recalled attending some sixty-five different elementary schools "for a day, a week or a few months" until he finally quit for good around the eighth grade. Not long after, he struck out on his own and found work in the vineyards near the town of Delano.

After serving in the U.S. Navy during World War II, Chávez returned to California to work in the fields. By this time he was not willing to quietly accept the unfair treatment that he and his fellow Mexican Americans received as farm workers. He took part in a few labor protests, but these demonstrations quickly collapsed in the face of the overwhelming power the growers exercised over their employees.

In the early 1950s, Chávez joined the Community Service Organization (CSO). The CSO had been established by well meaning non-Hispanics who wanted to empower Mexican Americans through voter-registration campaigns and numerous programs (mostly in urban areas) that offered

Great Depression: a period of severe economic crisis, from the stock market crash in 1929 to about 1940, marked by high unemployment, bank failures, factories and other businesses shrinking or shutting down in the United States and around the world.

Mexican farm workers harvest lettuce in California's Imperial Valley, 1963. Chávez objected to their working conditions: "In the days of the horse and buggy, the farm worker's dignity was equal to that of the beast. And today, in the day of mechanical harvesters, his dignity is equal to that of the machine."

poor and working-class people assistance with everyday needs such as housing and legal services.

Organizing Farm Workers

Starting out as an unpaid volunteer for the CSO, Chávez displayed a remarkable talent for recruiting new members and developing their leadership skills. As he moved up in the organization's ranks, becoming the general director in 1958, he grew frustrated by his colleagues' lack of interest in helping the rural poor—namely, the farm workers. After a time, Chávez realized that the farm workers had to create their own organization if they ever expected to improve their lives. So he resigned from the CSO and, along with **Dolores Huerta** (see entry), a fellow CSO official who shared his views, founded the National Farm Workers Association (NFWA) in September 1962.

Over the next few years, Chávez worked hard to convince people to join his new **labor union**. It was not an easy task. Most of the farm workers could not read or write; they barely made enough money to live on, let alone pay any union dues. Besides, many growers threatened to fire anyone who became involved with a union. But at countless evening meetings across California, Chávez shared his dream of launching an aggressive but nonviolent "revolution." Slowly but steadily, people signed up. By 1965, the NFWA had about two thousand members.

Feeling strong enough to take on some of the growers, Chávez and his farm workers voted in September 1965 to combine forces with a group of Filipino grape-pickers in Delano who had gone on strike for higher wages. Two of the three grape-growers—afraid they would lose their harvest— quickly agreed to raise wages and allow their workers to join the union. The third grower—the largest of the three—refused to settle, and so the strike continued.

Calls for Grape Boycott

It was not long before what was going on in California began to attract national attention to La Causa, as the farm workers' struggle had come to be known. As a result, more and more civil rights groups, liberal religious and political leaders, and other unions pledged moral and financial support to the NFWA. Chávez then decided to increase the pressure on the growers by asking all Americans not to buy California table grapes unless they carried the union label.

The strike and the boycott dragged on until 1970, a time of tremendous growth for the union. The NFWA became affiliated with the AFL-CIO (American Federation of

labor union: an association of workers who get together to improve their working conditions, wages, and benefits through collective bargaining with employers.

Labor and Congress of Industrial Organizations) in 1966 and changed its name to the United Farm Workers, or UFW. [The AFL-CIO is a federation of labor unions that, in 1992, was comprised of 88 unions and had a membership of more than 14 million people in the United States. The principal function of the AFL-CIO is to lobby on behalf of organized labor in order to promote legislation beneficial to workers and unions. Another major function of the AFL-CIO is to mediate conflicts between member unions.]

With the boycott, Chávez received international exposure as the leader of an important labor fight. More than once while he was head of the UFW, Chávez fasted (went without food) to dramatize the farm workers' plight and stress the nonviolent nature of their movement.

UFW Board members at dedication of Filipino Retirement Village, Delano, California

The boycott proved to be a spectacular success. After experiencing losses estimated in the millions of dollars, the last of the hold-outs among the grape-growers finally agreed to sign union contracts in mid-1970. This was the high point in the UFW's history. Energized by victory, it began to expand, establishing credit unions, offering medical and other forms of insurance, and lobbying legislators.

In many ways, the UFW was a unique organization in the history of the American labor movement. With its emphasis on family, on the shared Mexican background of many farm workers, and on religion, it was indeed more of a "cause" than a union. As its founder once noted, the UFW was out "to change the conditions of human life," to work on God's behalf to right the wrongs committed against the poor and minorities. Chávez himself was a devout Roman Catholic, and his beliefs shaped the spirit and direction of his organizing efforts from the start. Many priests, nuns, and other religious leaders supported both Chávez and the UFW.

In March 1974, Chávez spoke to the National Federation of Priests' Councils at the group's annual convention, held that year in San Francisco, California. The subject of his talk was "Saying 'Yes' to Man's Dignity." In his remarks, he suggested that the fight for social justice often has a deeper meaning—it is a demand to be accepted as a human being worthy of respect. Chávez also shared his thoughts on the many personal sacrifices involved in choosing a life of service. His comments are reprinted here almost in their entirety from Catholic Mind: The Monthly Review of Christian Thought, *October 1975. They were originally published in the summer 1974 issue of* Chicago Studies.

I am grateful to the priests of the United States for the continued support they have given the farm worker movement. I take this opportunity to thank particularly those priests and nuns who were with us last summer in Fresno [California]. I understand that that experience represented the largest number of religious in jail on any one social issue in the history of our country. That kind of help is very special to us. It is the help of commitment and understanding; but, even more important, it is the help of one's body—it is the help of people getting into trouble because they are helping us. It is the kind of help that is respected and appreciated by all of us. For in our struggle to change, to bring about some dignity to man—and I say to the men, the women and the children who toil in the fields—we are seeing that, throughout the ages, little—but little—dignity has come to them.

In the days of the horse and buggy, the farm worker's dignity was equal to that of the beast. And today, in the day of mechanical harvesters, his dignity is equal to that of the machine. And, so, we ask ourselves: Is that saying "yes" to man's dignity?

When priests began organizing in recent years, they also were saying "yes" to their own dignity.... We, too, in the farm movement, want to have our own federation, to be able to say "yes" to our own dignity. Saying "yes" to the farm worker's struggle is really saying "yes" to man's dignity because it is putting an ideal into action. We are blessed more than most men and most movements because we have had more men saying "yes" to our dignity in our struggle than most struggles in the history of this country have had. And I think that we have been said "yes" to by many people throughout the land because we are saying "yes" to our own dignity.

But saying "yes" to man's dignity is not something new. It has been happening in the entire history of man. Moses said "yes" to man's dignity. And so did the prophets, saints. In our lifetime [Indian political and spiritual leader Mohandas K.] Gandhi, [civil rights activist Martin Luther] King [Jr.] and others have said "yes" to man's dignity **epitomized** in Christ. Why do farm workers engage in similarly **insurmountable** odds against powerful forces—the growers, the Teamsters, those who oppose us? Why do we march and picket and face jailings, expose ourselves to physical violence, fasting and praying? I think that these things are done because we are saying "yes" to man's dignity.

Saying "yes" to man's dignity means getting into trouble. How many times when we say "yes" it becomes a controversy! And it becomes painful because in many cases the contro-

epitomized: typically or ideally represented.

insurmountable: overwhelming, unbeatable.

versy starts—it originates—among our closest friends. Saying "yes" to man's dignity means saying no to fear.

The struggle to say "yes" to man's dignity is difficult. And we often wonder why it should not be as easy as sleeping, eating and walking. But it is not. There should not be a question about saying "yes" to justice. Why should there be even a second thought? How many times in our lives do we find that we know we are right and yet we are afraid to act? The saying "yes" in the struggle for the dignity of man cannot be bought with money. Although that struggle is endless, always there is the problem that, once you say "yes," you've got to continue saying "yes." The more you say "yes" to man's dignity the more demands there are. And I think that is the way it should be. When we say "yes" to man's dignity we are saying "yes" to life because that is really what life is all about.

People who were in jail in Fresno for two weeks last summer were certainly very uncomfortable. But by their action they said "yes." And by their "yes" they stopped the arrests. They gave their bodies and they were in jail for two weeks. But they kept hundreds—God knows how many hundreds—of farm workers from going to jail. The way things stand now we may have to have more "yeses" to man's dignity this summer.

Saying "yes" to man's dignity is not only a Christian thing. We know some **agnostics** in our day who said some very **profound** things—simple but profound. [Reformer and activist] Saul Alinsky, a most controversial man, said "yes" to men—to the dignity of man—always. He once said that you really aren't free until you accept death. Once you accept death you can overcome most things. You can overcome fear which will set you free then to struggle and to do God's work in this land. And, so, the fear of struggling, the fear of material insecurity, the fear of death many times may interfere with our duty to put ourselves on the line. The conflict with the obligation of service often becomes political controversy.

Strength comes from God, and if man is created in God's image, it should come from man. The problem we have then is that when you say "yes" to man's dignity and you get elected to public office, something strange happens. The power came from the people. No sooner is power acquired than the same man who got the power from the people

agnostics: people who regard God as unknown and unknowable and who therefore follow no particular religion.

profound: intense, deeply moving.

begins to isolate himself—insulate himself—from people. Labor leaders have the same problem. The power comes from the people. There is a strange **paradox** here where we spend more time planning how not to be with people than the time we spend planning how to do the work. I understand that even some priests are not immune to this. It is that demand that we are afraid of, the demand that people know there is a good priest over there. We don't care what time or hour of the day or night it is: he'll say "yes." It is an awful thing, because that word spreads, and people come from all over and make demands. And the more he gives the more they will want.

It happens to us, too. There is a fear to put a limit. Twenty-two years ago I was working in a small community in Madeira, California, and I got myself caught in a very difficult situation. I was beginning to organize and beginning to be successful at it. The more I did, the more that was demanded of me. I was beginning to get very angry with myself and with people, because I wanted to have one Sunday off. And, after working about six months, I began to plan with my family—my wife and kids—that I was going to go to the park on that Sunday and have a picnic—and I didn't give a hoot who came. I was not going to give it up. I was just not going to be anybody's fool. I was going to take some time off. I was getting very, very upset about the whole idea. I don't mind working thirteen hours a day; but on Sunday I need a day off. And I was having difficulties living in a situation with millions of problems of people, poor and **exploited**, finding someone, some organization that was beginning to deal with their problems.

So, on Sunday I wanted to get out of the house very early. I got the kids in the car, went to very early Mass, came back home—made the mistake of coming home to pick up the picnic basket—and there was a car there with a family. Could I help them ? Their son was in jail. And could I please help him? What I wanted them to do was to go away, because although I did not want to help them, I felt very, very guilty. I did not have the courage to say "no." So I went with them and spent most of the day trying to get that man out of jail. By the time I came back, there was no way in which I could go to the picnic—and I had spent another Sunday working.

paradox: contradiction, inconsistency.

exploited: unfairly used for one's own profit.

Chávez leading UFW Grape protest, 1969

I made up my mind that day. I told my wife that I cannot continue this way. Either I get out of this work and do something else where I work forty hours a week; or, if I decide to stay here, I've got to decide that it is a pleasure to help people. And, if I cannot get that in me, really I'll be miserable the rest of my life. And I don't want to be miserable. So, I gave myself six months. That was thirteen years ago.

Saying "yes" to man's dignity when you teach means supporting them. Our union runs five or six clinics. There are nine people on the executive board of the union—seven Catholics, one Jew and one Protestant. The issues of abortion and the pill were before us. When we came to the executive board everyone said in one voice: "Oh, we don't want to get into that. We don't want to have abortions in our clinic, or the pill. We just can't have that." Easier said than done! Right away forty or fifty percent of the people working in those clinics began to rebel, and some left because we were saying "no." We thought we were saying "yes" to man's dignity by saying, "Let them live." On the other hand we were being told "no" because, if we say that, then we who are doctors and nurses can't stay here. We have to leave.

I was brought up with the liberal idea that farm workers were too poor to pay dues. And we know that, if we are going to build a movement, we have to build it ourselves, and we have to sacrifice to do it. But we did not want to ask the workers to do it because of our **paternalism.**

Several years ago, I was confronted with the decision one winter evening. I went to a man's home who was, I remember, one month **in arrears**, and the second month coming up. I went to collect the $3.50—there were no contracts then, no benefits just the idea of a union. And this man said: "I was just going to the store. I have a five-dollar bill. I will give you $3.50 if you come with me." I went to the store. He changed the five-dollar bill, gave me $3.50, and he bought $1.50 worth of groceries. I had his $3.50 in my pocket and I went home. I couldn't get over that. I couldn't sleep that night because I was asking myself: "Who am I to take $3.50 from this man for the dues, when he needed that money right last night to buy food?" But, then, saying "yes" to man's dignity means having hope. About four years later that same man was among the first workers to be hired when we got our first contract. I never forgot that. I went back to his home when he got his first paycheck. And what impressed me so much had not even made a little ripple in his memory. I reminded him, but he didn't remember. He, too, was saying "yes."

We have a duty to understand the difference between saying "yes" to man's dignity in terms of service or saying "yes" to man's dignity in terms of being a servant. I think being of service at our convenience is not really truly letting go. For, when a man says, "I will say 'yes' to man's dignity by being a servant," I think that that makes all the difference in the world—being of service on a certain day at a certain place or at a certain time as against being of service all the time, everywhere and to everyone.

Fighting for social justice, it seems to me, is one of the most profound ways in which men can say "yes" to man's dignity. And keeping silent about these issues is probably one of the most effective ways of saying "no" to man's dignity. We don't say "yes" to man's dignity by thinking that prayer is an end to things instead of a means, that saying "yes" is all we have to do instead of saying "yes, here I am, here is my body." I think that saying "yes" to man's dignity really

paternalism: a system of control under which a father-like authority supplies the needs of people and regulates their behavior to fit a specific philosophy or meet a specific goal.

in arrears: behind (in payment of a debt).

means sacrifice. There is no way on this earth in which one can say "yes" to man's dignity and know that one is going to be spared some sacrifice.

To priests of America I am happy to say: You have said "yes" to us many times. And your saying "yes" to us has meant that other people have said "yes" to us, that countless numbers of people—probably into the hundreds of thousands or even millions—have said "yes" because you have said "yes" to us. And so, dear brothers, you are then the source of hope for us—the harvesters of love and the symbol of faith.

99

By the early 1970s the UFW was facing another threat to its existence—the Teamsters, America's largest labor union. In an effort to weaken the UFW, some of the larger growers sought help from the Teamsters in negotiating with farm workers. The Teamsters, claiming to represent migrant workers, negotiated contracts with growers with whom the UFW had already formed contracts. This touched off bitter and sometimes violent confrontations as the Teamsters made major gains at the expense of the UFW. One of their most common practices was bringing in men, women, and children illegally from Mexico to replace striking UFW members.

On September 9, 1974, while the dispute between the UFW and the Teamsters still raged, Chávez was honored for his union activities at a Greater Washington (D.C.) Central Labor Council luncheon. In his address that day to fellow AFL-CIO leaders, Chávez spoke of the ongoing efforts to settle the differences between the UFW and the Teamsters. Most of the text of his speech is reprinted here from a copy held in the archives of the Walter P. Reuther Library at Wayne State University in Detroit, Michigan.

We are very happy to be here with you today to tell you that, in a very special way, we wish to thank Brother [George] Meany [president of the AFL-CIO] for his support and personal interest in the outcome of the tremendously important struggle that is taking place in California and other places in the Southwest, which will determine, eventually, whether there is going to be a union for farm workers. We want to thank him and the Federation—and all of you—for your concern, your interest, and especially for your dedication in assisting us to bring about a fair solution to the conflict in California.

Throughout the great United States, the boycott is unfolding. Many central labor councils and many state federations are really in gear....

So today is the beginning of a week of action, a week of activities that will include press conferences, parades and demonstrations, picket lines and leafleting, religious services and fund-raising, to get the message of the boycott out to the public.

We have to keep reminding the people, keep it before the public, so that they will know that the growers refuse to either recognize a union or give the workers a chance to have an election, so that they can determine for themselves which union they want.

As long as they are against these two things, we must continue to strike and boycott. The boycott, as you know, is really an extension of the strike.

You know that the farm workers are not covered by legislation. You know that the farm workers in the places where we strike are at the mercy of the courts. [You know] the awesome and total power that the growers have in small communities to get the courts to **enjoin** the union the moment there is a strike or the moment there is going to be a strike. Last year, in a period of less than sixty days, we were hit with sixty-nine **injunctions.** Right now, there are one hundred and two injunctions against our union.

The injunction is usually enforced by civil action. What they do in California is, the sheriff takes it upon himself and makes it a criminal action. The growers use the power of the district attorney and the sheriff's office to enjoin us, and enforce these injunctions—using the taxpayers' money—by making the injunction a criminal matter.

enjoin: impose an authoritative order to do or not do something.

injunctions: acts of enjoining; orders.

Chávez at picket rally: "Fighting for social justice ... is one of the most profound ways in which men can say 'yes' to man's dignity."

And then we have the "illegals." If the illegals were to be taken out of the places where we are now striking, the strike would be over tomorrow. If we could get the illegals out of the grape fields, if we could get the illegals out of the lettuce fields, the growers would have to come and meet with us within twenty-four hours. In the Delano area today, the growers are harvesting the grapes with about fifty percent of the workers that they normally need, and we estimate that about eighty-five percent, if not more, of the people working there are illegals—brand-new illegals—brought from Mexico within the last month or so.... We need to have pressure, we need to get to the U.S. congressmen and the U.S. senators and let them know what is happening, because that is the deciding factor.

We were attacked last year, this contract was stolen from us. But the concern, and the love, and the interest of the workers for our union is such that today, we have had more strikes this year than any other time in the history of our union, even though we lost those contracts and our membership was reduced by seventy percent.

If illegals were not there, we wouldn't have to have the boycott, we could win by ourselves. But we have sent wires and telephone calls and letters ... and we haven't had one answer. We try to get [U.S.] Attorney General [William] Saxbe to do something about it—no answer.

In Yuma, Arizona, which is just on this side of the Mexican border, 3,300 people work there picking lemons. They went out on strike, and they have been on strike now for two weeks tomorrow—every single worker, including irrigators, tractor drivers and pickers. Not one single lemon has been picked—not one—and it will be two weeks tomorrow. We haven't picketed, we don't need picket lines. But we have injunctions against us from the Yuma courts for having too many people out in the picket lines. That is how ridiculous things get.

We talked to the attorney that represents the growers and he said, "We are not worried, we are going to get people to do the job." So we tried to find where they were going to get the people. He said, "Well, where they usually come from."

So unless a great miracle happens, they will bring people from Mexico, just across the border—the orchards are just twenty yards from the border.

Last Friday, too, in the counties of Sutter, Yolo, Colusa, Sacramento and Solano—the five-county area that accounts for the growth of about seventy percent of all of the canning tomatoes in California—we went out on strike. The one great fear that the Teamsters have is that our union should be stopped—that our union should be terminated—because what would happen if the tomato workers went out on strike—what would happen to the canneries?

There was great expectation on the part of the workers. There was a bill proposed in California—a simple bill—to let the workers decide which union they wanted—a representation election bill.... We were able to get it through two committees of the Assembly. Finally, the whole Assembly voted for it, but when it got to the Senate, it was killed. There was tremendous pressure against the simple bill to let the people decide, by a vote, which union they wanted.

Who was campaigning against it?

The Chamber of Commerce, the Farm Bureau Federation and the Teamsters Union.

Brothers and Sisters, the boycott is having its impact, and unless great changes take place, we think that we are going to win. We are going to win, because of the concern of Brother Meany; we are going to win because of the help of the Federation; we are going to win because of the concern of all of you here.

And we are going to win because the workers have had a taste of what a union is. A group of workers who, for almost 100 years, have been struggling to have a union, when in 1970, as if by a miracle, they were able to have an idea—a taste of what a union can do for them, and even though they lost a union, they will never forget that experience. Because of that experience, we see today that we have tremendous support from the workers—their willingness to sacrifice, to go out there and struggle and do all the things that strikers must do to have a union. We see that kind of commitment....

The struggle continues. The workers continue to struggle and continue to have faith. They are no different than you and the men who built your unions—no different. They have the same ideals, the same goals, the same determination, and the same love to have a union....

99

*The rivalry between the UFW and the Teamsters lasted until 1977, when they finally reached a settlement granting the UFW sole bargaining rights among farm workers. This came on the heels of another significant victory—the 1975 passage in California of the Agricultural Labor Relations Act. This landmark piece of legislation was the first to recognize the right of farm workers to engage in **collective bargaining**. These successes, along with the farm worker-*

collective bargaining: the negotiations that take place between an employer and representatives of a labor union.

friendly administration of Democratic Governor Jerry Brown, helped bring about an increase in the UFW's membership and influence during the late 1970s.

Changing Times Deal a Blow to the Union

But the 1980s proved disastrous for the union in California and elsewhere. Beginning in 1983, the new Republican administration headed by Governor George Deukmejian tilted the balance of power toward the growers. (Many growers had contributed heavily to Deukmejian's campaign.) Changes in the makeup of the state assembly also had a negative impact on legislation affecting farm workers. On a national level, too, there was a shift toward political conservatism that did not favor unions in general or the farm workers' cause in particular. In addition, California's economy went into a slump, resulting in depressed wages and widespread unemployment.

The UFW itself was in turmoil in the 1980s. Internal disagreements and organizational problems had driven away some of the very people who had played key roles in the union's early victories. A few who commented on the situation inside the UFW blamed it on Chávez. They said he was a strict, domineering leader who would not accept any criticism. Others staunchly denied this.

By the end of the 1980s, the UFW had lost most of its contracts, and membership had dropped from its peak of nearly 100,000 in the 1970s to less than 20,000. Even a highly publicized thirty-six-day fast Chávez undertook in 1988—in order to draw attention to careless pesticide use that he felt endangered farm workers as well as consumers—failed to rekindle the old spark.

Despite these setbacks and his own increasingly frail health, Chávez continued to take the UFW's message to audiences across the country. His fund-raising efforts took him to college campuses, churches, union halls—wherever he thought he could find a sympathetic ear. Again and again, he told his listeners that what at first glance seems impossible is indeed possible, if people are willing to be creative and flexible.

Farm Workers Lose Their Champion

On April 23, 1993, Chávez—who had just ended a six-day fast—died in his sleep while in Arizona on business. His funeral procession began a few miles outside Delano and wound past farm fields before ending at the UFW compound in town. Around 35,000 mourners from all over the world attended the services.

While the union Chávez left behind had not become the nationwide organization he once dreamed of, the UFW does have members in Florida, Texas, Arizona, and Washington as well as in California. Without its charismatic founder leading the way, the union faces a rather uncertain future. Chávez's son-in-law, Arturo Rodriguez, however, made some history of his own in mid-1996, when he signed a labor contract with a large California lettuce-grower, bringing to an end a boycott Chávez had launched in 1979.

Sources

Books

Acuña, Rodolfo, *Occupied America: The Chicano's Struggle Toward Liberation,* Canfield Press, 1972.

American Orators of the Twentieth Century: Critical Studies and Sources, edited by Bernard K. Duffy and Halford R. Ryan, Greenwood Press, 1987.

Aztlan: An Anthology of Mexican American Literature, edited by Luis Valdez and Stan Steiner, Knopf, 1972.

Cortes, Carlos E., Arlin I. Ginsburg, Allan W. F. Green, and James A. Turner, *Three Perspectives on Ethnicity in America,* Putnam, 1976.

Daniel, Clete, *Bitter Harvest,* University of California Press, 1981.

Day, Mark, *Forty Acres: César Chávez and the Farm Workers,* Praeger, 1973.

Dunne, John Gregory, *Delano,* Farrar, Straus, 1971.

Hammerback, John C., Richard J. Jensen, and Jose Angel Gutierrez, *A War of Words: Chicano Protest in the 1960s and 1970s,* Greenwood Press, 1985.

La Causa Politica: A Chicano Politics Reader, edited by F. Chris Garcia, University of Notre Dame Press, 1974.

Levy, Jacques E., *César Chávez: Autobiography of La Causa,* Norton, 1975.

London, Joan, and Henry Anderson, *So Shall Ye Reap,* Crowell, 1970.

Matthiessen, Peter, *Sal Si Puedes: César Chávez and the New American Revolution,* Random House, 1969.

Meier, Matt S., and Feliciano Rivera, *The Chicanos: A History of Mexican Americans,* Hill & Wang, 1972.

Meister, Dick, and Anne Loftis, *A Long Time Coming: The Struggle to Unionize America's Farm Workers,* Macmillan, 1977.

Taylor, Ronald B., *Chávez and the Farm Workers,* Beacon Press, 1975.

Yinger, Winthrop, *César Chávez: The Rhetoric of Nonviolence,* Exposition Press, 1975.

Periodicals

Catholic Mind: The Monthly Review of Christian Thought, "Saying 'Yes' to Man's Dignity," October 1975, pp. 43–47.

Christian Century, "Viva La Causa!" August 27, 1969, pp. 115–16; "Tilting with the System: An Interview with César Chávez," February 18, 1970, p. 206.

Detroit Free Press, "Farm Workers' Chávez Is Dead," April 24, 1993, p. 2A.

Grand Rapids Press (Grand Rapids, MI), "Farm-Worker Organizer, Activist César Chávez, 66, Is Found Dead," April 24, 1993, p. A1; "Chávez Was an Inspiration to Farm Workers," April 25, 1993, p. A14; "Chávez's Last March Is 35,000 Strong," April 30, 1993, p. A3; "Farmworker Gains Slide, Union Struggles for Survival Following Death of Chávez," July 25, 1993, p. A4; "United Farm Workers Remember Chávez with 350-Mile March," April 3, 1994, p. E2.

Hispanic, "Chávez Legacy," June 1993, p. 14.

Look, "Nonviolence Still Works," April 1, 1969, p. 52.

Nation, "César's Ghost," July 26/August 2, 1993, pp. 130–35.

New Republic, "The Future of the United Farm Workers: Chávez Against the Wall," December 7, 1974, p. 13.

Newsweek, "César's Triumph," March 21, 1977, pp. 70–72; "A Secular Saint of the '60s," May 3, 1993, p. 68.

New York Times, "César Chávez, 66, Organizer of Union for Migrants, Dies," April 24, 1993.

People, "César Chávez Breaks His Longest Fast as His Followers Pray for an End to the Grapes of Wrath," September 5, 1988, pp. 52–54; "His Harvest Was Dignity," May 10, 1993, p. 71.

Time, "The Little Strike That Grew Into *La Causa,*" July 4, 1979, p. 16.

Western Journal of Speech Communication, "The Rhetorical Worlds of César Chávez and Reies Tijerina," summer 1980, pp. 166–76.

Additional information for this profile was taken from a Knight-Ridder/Tribune News Service article titled "Farm Workers' Union Rallies to Rebuild After Death of Chávez," released April 22, 1994.

Dennis Chávez

1888–1962

Spanish American member of the U.S. Senate

Dennis Chávez was the first American of Spanish descent to win a seat in the United States Senate. He served his country and the Democratic party with distinction for nearly thirty years, struggling consistently against social intolerance. During the 1940s and 1950s, he created and supported various bills designed to eliminate racial, ethnic, and religious discrimination in the workplace. In Chávez's view, this was not simply an American fight, but one that touched every nation on earth: "World peace cannot become a reality unless men are able to exercise their basic rights without discrimination because of race or creed," he once declared to a New York audience.

Early Life

A native of New Mexico who was extremely proud of his Spanish heritage, Chávez was born on ranch land that had been in his family since 1769. (His original first name was "Dionisio," which was changed to "Dennis" when he start-

"WE IN THIS NATION STAND AT A CROSSROADS IN HISTORY. EITHER WE WILL TAKE THE ROAD WHICH WILL LEAD US PAST ANOTHER GOALPOST OF HUMAN PROGRESS OR WE WILL BE FORCED INTO THE PATH RIDDLED WITH THE PITFALLS OF HUMAN HATREDS WHICH LED EUROPE INTO WORLD WAR II."

ed school.) The Chávezes were very poor, and young Dennis was forced to drop out of school after completing the eighth grade so that he could go to work to help support his seven brothers and sisters. However, he continued reading and studying on his own. His dream was to one day follow in the footsteps of his idol, Thomas Jefferson, who drafted the Declaration of Independence and later became the third American president.

In 1916, Chávez was hired to work as a Spanish-language interpreter for New Mexico politician A. A. Jones during Jones's run for the U.S. Senate. This assignment later helped him obtain a senate clerkship in Washington, D.C. There, Chávez decided to further his education. Although he had never attended high school, he passed a special entrance exam that allowed him to enroll in Georgetown University. After earning his law degree in 1920, Chávez returned home to New Mexico with an eye toward launching his own political career.

Enters Politics at the State Level

Not long after setting up a law practice in Albuquerque, Chávez ran for and won a seat in New Mexico's House of Representatives. He served in that body throughout the 1920s until winning election to the U.S. House of Representatives in 1930 and again in 1932. In 1934, he made his first try for a seat in the U.S. Senate, which he lost in a close election after a very bitter campaign.

Just a year later, however, his opponent who won the senatorial bid was killed in a plane crash. Chávez replaced him and then won election to the Senate in his own right in 1936. He was returned to office four more times over the next twenty-six years. Most of that time, he was the Senate's only Hispanic American member. Chávez distinguished himself as a tireless supporter of legislation intended to help minorities, especially Mexican Americans, Native Americans, and Puerto Ricans. He also took the lead in encouraging better relations with Latin American nations.

In general, Chávez was a quiet and soft-spoken man who rarely took part in debates with his colleagues—except when the subject was discrimination. This was especially true during the World War II years (1939–45). Chávez fully backed President Franklin Roosevelt's efforts to make jobs in the defense industry available to everyone regardless of race, ethnic background, or religion. In 1941, for example, Roosevelt established the Fair Employment Practices Committee (FEPC). The FEPC's job was to oversee the training and hiring policies of companies and unions involved in producing defense-related goods. Although a lack of money, staff, and enforcement powers, combined with strong resistance from the South, severely limited its effectiveness, the FEPC represented a significant step in the battle for justice for America's minority citizens.

Fights Discrimination in the Workplace

As one of the FEPC's most passionate supporters, Chávez continued his crusade against discrimination in the workplace after the war ended. In May 1945, he gained the approval of a Senate subcommittee for a bill (S. 101) that would have created a permanent Fair Employment Practices Commission (also known by the acronym FEPC). Its purpose was to carry on the work of the wartime FEPC as the United States shifted to a peacetime economy.

A number of southern senators were very much opposed to Chávez's bill. They predicted "trouble" (such as race riots) if whites were forced to work alongside blacks. They also argued that the bill seemed to pave the way for the government to order employers to hire a certain number of minority workers. These southern politicians—led by Senator James Eastland of Mississippi, who was later a fierce opponent of the civil rights movement—used various tactics to delay taking action on the bill throughout the rest of 1945.

A frustrated Chávez nevertheless continued his efforts to convince people of the importance of eliminating all traces of racial, ethnic, and religious discrimination in the workplace. He urged Americans not to turn their backs on those who had risked their lives defending freedom and democracy so that all might share equally in the victory.

Chávez expressed these thoughts in a speech he delivered in Chicago, Illinois, on December 1, 1945. Two days

Men outside Relief Office during the Depression. Chávez declared: "Full employment without fair employment means the fastening of religious and racial minorities to the bottom rung of the economic ladder regardless of their education, abilities, and skills."

suffrage: right to vote.

implications: consequences, effects.

later, he stood before his Senate colleagues and asked for permission to enter his remarks into the Congressional Record. *The following excerpt is thus reprinted from the* Congressional Record Appendix, 79th Congress, 1st Session, Volume 91, Part 13, *U.S. Government Printing Office, 1945.*

❝

Of all the issues confronting our country today, the issue of racial and religious discrimination is at once the most neglected and the most critical. There is no victory over [German wartime leader Adolf] Hitler and [Japanese wartime leader Hideki] Tojo which by itself will erase the injustice of economic discrimination practiced against the minority groups among our people. Full employment without fair employment means the fastening of religious and racial minorities to the bottom rung of the economic ladder regardless of their education, abilities, and skills. Unemployment compensation will not break down the barrier of prejudice. There is nothing ... which will protect the returning two millions of minority veterans from the pattern of job discrimination which exists in this country.

We in this nation stand at a crossroads in history. Either we will take the road which will lead us past another goalpost of human progress or we will be forced into the path riddled with the pitfalls of human hatreds which led Europe into World War II. We shall not be permitted to stand still. Whichever road we take will be for you, the people, to choose.

Every great crisis in American history has thus far had the moral result of increased protection and increased liberty for the individual. This country's first great crisis—the American Revolution—gave us political and religious independence. The crisis which was the Civil War gave us freedom from bondage for all men and women. Out of the crisis of the First World War came women's **suffrage**. Out of this World War II, with all its terrifying **implications**, comes: What?

The Atlantic Charter

In August 1941, just a few months before the United States entered World War II, President Franklin Roosevelt and British Prime Minister Winston Churchill met to discuss the war effort and their plans for peace. At the end of their meeting, which was held on a ship off the coast of Newfoundland, they issued a joint statement known as the Atlantic Charter. In it, they set forth the common goals and the principles they felt governments should follow after the war to ensure a lasting peace. Among these principles were the right of all peoples of the world to determine their own political future, freedom of the seas for all countries, an end to aggressive territorial expansion, and the creation of an international system of security through **disarmament.**

In addition, the charter specifically mentioned "freedom from fear" and "freedom from want" among the aims of the postwar world. These were two of the famous "Four Freedoms" that Roosevelt personally felt were essential to achieving world peace. (He had first discussed all four of them publicly as part of his State of the Union address before Congress in January 1941. The other two aims left out of the charter were freedom of speech and freedom of religion.)

In January 1942, the twenty-six countries then at war with Nazi Germany (which by that time included the United States) met in Washington, D.C. They formally pledged their support for the principles outlined in the Atlantic Charter by signing what was known as the United Nations Declaration. A little more than three years later, this same agreement formed the basis of a new international organization dedicated to settling conflicts without bloodshed—the United Nations.

This present-day crisis must at least give us true democracy, and the kernel of that is equality of economic opportunity. We must pluck down from the thin air the Atlantic Charter's (see box) freedom from fear and freedom from want and ground those freedoms not on the government **dole**, but upon the right to work and the opportunity to work for every man and every woman according to his skill, his experience, and his ability.

This is no new ideal in the development of American life. It is common knowledge that the struggle for that ideal began when the first paths were cut through the virgin wilderness by the first settlers—victims of religious and economic persecution themselves—who came to these shores. The Pilgrims in Massachusetts, the English Catholics of Maryland, the French Huguenots of the Carolinas, the Scotch

disarmament: the process of giving up or reducing the number of weapons and armed troops.

dole: the system for providing the poor with money and/or supplies.

Presbyterians of Georgia, the Quakers of Pennsylvania, the Jews, the Irish, the Dutch, the Germans, and even the poverty-stricken debtors of the English prisons came to this country as to a refuge, to a haven of new, unshackled opportunity.

The translation into law of the new concepts of religious and economic liberty was not easily achieved any more than the enactment of fair-employment legislation will be easily won. Rigid religious **conformity** was woven into the law of some of the separate colonies, and rebellious **sects** were driven forth to found new colonies where religious freedom could flourish. At one point, Catholics and Jews were not allowed to vote. For many years people without property were denied the **franchise.** But the ideal of freedom was not to be downed, and when the crisis which **precipitated** the American Revolution came about, the cornerstone of liberty upon which our country was founded was given deathless voice in the Declaration of Independence:

> We hold these truths to be self-evident, that all men are created equal, that they are endowed by their Creator with certain **inalienable** rights, that among these are life, liberty, and the pursuit of happiness. That to secure these rights, governments are instituted among men, **deriving** their just powers from among the consent of the governed. That whenever any form of government becomes destructive of these ends, it is the right of the people to alter or to abolish it, and to institute new government, laying its foundation on such principles and organizing its powers in such form, as to them shall seem most likely to effect their safety and happiness.

These words of the great leader of humanistic democracy, Thomas Jefferson, have captured the philosophy of the American ideal. Indeed, they are reechoed and restated in the American creed—the Constitution's Bill of Rights....

The people's determination to cling to this heritage of the protection of human rights under law was challenged in the **ratification** of the Constitution itself when it was discovered that that original document failed to guarantee them. It was only after amendments, constituting the so-called Bill of Rights, were agreed to that the Constitution was finally adopted. It is no accident that the first of these amendments pledged this government's protection of the individual's free-

conformity: obedience to established customs or standards.

sects: groups.

franchise: the right to vote.

precipitated: touched off, triggered.

inalienable: absolute, undeniable.

deriving: taking from a source.

ratification: approval.

dom of worship, freedom of speech and of press, and "the right of the people peaceably to assemble and to petition the Government for a **redress** of grievance." Need I remind you that it is under that right you are now here assembled?

These were rights such as the Old World had never known, and the lack of which blocked the forward march of civilization. As this country flourished and grew strong on roots fed by all its people, in other lands struggling people took them for their own and mankind moved up and onward. Nevertheless, the freedom-loving people of this nation were not yet satisfied. They saw the horror, the injustice, and the inhumanity of the institution of slavery and rose against it.

Then one of them, a Kentucky rail splitter, an Illinois and Indiana farmer, a country lawyer who was way ahead of his time [President Abraham Lincoln], came and enunciated to the whole world that this country could not exist "half slave and half free." A great war which rocked the new nation was fought between the citizens of this country to decide that question. The answer was written in the thirteenth, fourteenth, and fifteenth amendments to our Constitution—this nation's second bill of rights. [The thirteenth, fourteenth, and fifteenth amendments to the Constitution were all adopted in the years immediately after the Civil War (1861–65). Under the terms of these amendments, slavery was abolished, blacks were granted citizenship and certain constitutional guarantees, and it was forbidden to deny the right to vote to any male American citizen on the basis of race.]

These rights are now in our care to preserve and to strengthen for our children, and our children's children. How well our citizenry appreciated those rights and those freedoms was proved by their willingness to fight for them when they became endangered.... On the battlefield where suffering takes place, where men are mutilated, where men die, you do not see the attempts that are made in normal times within our own country to set aside those principles for which the soldier and the sailor have suffered.

No discrimination was shown by the Japanese enemy in his treatment of the Negro or the Jew or the Mexican or the so-called Anglo-Saxon stock—he murdered them all **irrespective** of their religion, color, or politics. On the beachheads of

redress: compensation; a way of righting of a wrong done to someone.

irrespective: regardless.

Tarawa, Okinawa, or Guam there was no discrimination. [Tarawa and Guam are small islands in the Pacific Ocean; Okinawa is one of the large islands that make up Japan. From 1943 to 1945, some of the bloodiest battles of World War II took place on those islands as U.S. troops faced Japanese forces.] Along the sandbanks of Anzio no discrimination was shown by the German or any other common enemy. [Anzio, a town in Italy, was the site of a major assault by U.S. troops on German forces in early 1944.] But here in our own country by people who should know better, and do know better, discrimination at times becomes **rampant**. Even now, the ugly head of racial and religious prejudice shows itself too vividly to be ignored.

To outlaw the discriminatory employment practices stemming from racial and religious bigotry is the new task which must now engage us. We have seen, in wartime, the effectiveness of a Fair Employment Practices Committee. It gave hope and courage to those on the battlefields and new opportunities for those at home to test their **mettle** on the production lines. Aircraft plants were persuaded to upgrade Mexican Americans; white workers to cooperate with colored workers. Government agencies accepted in new positions qualified minority workers referred by Civil Service. Trade unions policed their own nondiscrimination policy among their locals. Employers rearranged work schedules to permit **Sabbatarians** and orthodox Jews opportunity to observe religious customs. The theory of fair employment became a successful practice.

For that reason, some of us in Congress have determined that now we must have a basic law to carry out the **purport** of the Declaration of Independence and the Constitution. That is why Senate bill 101 and House bill 2232 were introduced. The bill to establish a permanent Fair Employment Practices Commission is designed to have but one function—to eliminate unfair employment practices based on discrimination on grounds of race, color, creed, national origin or ancestry.

Under the bill, management continues free to set its own hiring, training, and upgrading practices: to adjust its internal plant policy; and to discharge according to any standard it may adopt so long as there is no **arbitrary** discrimination because of race, color, creed, national origin, or ancestry. In the same way, organized labor continues free to manage its

rampant: widespread, out of control.

mettle: strength, ability to do one's best.

Sabbatarians: people who strictly observe Saturday rather than Sunday as the Sabbath.

purport: intention.

arbitrary: determined by personal preference rather than logic or reason.

Dennis Chávez

Mexican American women working for the Southern Pacific Railroad during World War II

internal affairs according to its own lights, except that it cannot deny any of the advantages or opportunities of union organization and collective bargaining to any person because of race, color, creed, national origin, or ancestry. The bill covers all federal agencies, firms having federal contracts, and firms in or affecting interstate commerce having six or more employees. The agency cannot enforce its own orders, but it is empowered to go to the courts to request enforcement when firms or unions coming under its **jurisdiction** refuse to discontinue discriminatory employment policies.

Of course, there are those who say, "Why not just investigate discrimination and educate those who persist in erecting barriers of prejudice?" But experience has shown that education is not enough. Even on the basic principles of nature

jurisdiction: control or authority to apply laws.

and the **Mosaic laws**, murder is **denounced**, but nevertheless, every civilized nation in the world has laws against murder. We are instructed to love our fellow men, but we still take the precaution of establishing laws to protect them from **fraud** or violence.

It was my privilege to serve as chairman of the subcommittee which held hearings on S. 101. Representatives of every faith, every race, every walk of life testified on this measure. I think I lean to the side of conservatism when I estimate that sixty million Americans were represented in those hearings. That is an amazing expression of popular interest in any legislation....

After those hearings, the Senate Committee on Education and Labor recommended S. 101 to the full Senate for favorable action by a 12-to-6 vote. This bill is now high on the Senate calendar ready for debate and vote. It is also on the president's [Harry Truman] must-list of legislation [and] I think I am safe in saying that the majority of the Senate body is favorably **disposed** toward this legislation. What, then, keeps the bill from the Senate floor?

Unfortunately, there are men in the Senate who are **adamant** and, I believe, mistaken in their opposition to the enactment of this measure. These senators, recognizing that the tide of human progress has out-paced them, would try to stem its onrush by the extreme tactic of **filibustering** the bill. To meet that kind of opposition we need not only a majority of senators to support the bill—we must have, in addition, the **cloture vote** of two-thirds of the entire Senate to successfully counterattack the threatened filibuster....

What we want most now is action. We know that practices growing out of discrimination and intolerance, which are thoroughly un-American, must not be allowed to continue. The American way of protecting human rights against such practices is by law. We have the backing of our president. We have the commitment of the Republican party. Therefore, whether you are a Democrat or a Republican, you have the right and the responsibility to remind your leadership that these promises are yet to be fulfilled. You have it in your hands to get such a law. Make your voices heard.

In doing this you will be promoting Americanism. You will perform a service to your country by **eradicating** an evil that

Mosaic laws: the biblical Ten Commandments that Moses received from God.

denounced: condemned, criticized.

fraud: cheating, deception, trickery.

disposed: inclined.

adamant: stubborn; inflexible.

filibustering: using extreme stalling tactics to prevent action on a piece of legislation.

cloture vote: a special vote calling for the end of a debate in a legislative body.

eradicating: eliminating, getting rid of.

is foreign and un-American, an evil that smacks of the racial theories of Hitler and [his propaganda minister Josef] Goebbels and not of the four freedoms of the Atlantic Charter. You will be performing further service to our country by thus furnishing proof to fellow peoples throughout the world that we mean to live the letter and the spirit of our American creed and that our nation is sincere in championing the cause of the democracies and the rights of man.

We have just fought a great war to a successful conclusion. It would be a national disaster and humiliation if those who have fought valiantly abroad to defend the freedom and dignity of the individual against racial **barbarism** should now come home to find that the bringing of peace meant a wiping out of the antidiscrimination policy that we achieved in

Mexican American soldiers in training, 1943. Chávez commented: "Some persons think that it was all well and good to use such men and call upon them to make the supreme sacrifice in foreign fields ... but that they are not good enough to receive equal treatment in our country."

barbarism: savagery, cruelty.

wartime. Today we stand embarked upon the task of reconversion for peace. Shall we reconvert to racial prejudice, national bigotry, and religious discrimination, or shall we reconvert to full peacetime employment based on the American principle of equality of human rights?

Let me give you an example of what I mean. During this war, 245 Congressional Medals of Honor—the highest honor our nation can give its war heroes—were awarded. Six of these were given to servicemen who in ordinary times would be referred to as "these Mexicans." They were Joe Martinez, who died from Japanese bullets at Attu [in the Aleutian Islands of Alaska]; Ysmael Vellegas, who gave his life at Luzon [in the Philippines]; Jose Calugas, who distinguished himself at Bataan [in the Philippines]; Joe Lopez, who saved his entire company in Belgium; Cleto Rodriguez, who with one other overcame three hundred Japanese soldiers at Manila [in the Philippines]; and Macario Garcia, who singlehanded[ly] assaulted two enemy machine-gun emplacements in Germany. Honors and awards of every description—the Distinguished Flying Cross, the Purple Heart, the Silver Star, the Air Medal, etc.—were given to members of all the minorities who make up the American people. Would it be their just due, when these heroes apply for a job, to have them turned down on account of the accident of their birth or their religious belief?

Do you remember the timeless words uttered by [Abraham] Lincoln at Gettysburg at the close of the Civil War? Let me repeat just two sentences to you, for they **epitomize** the spirit in which we must put our shoulders to the wheel if we are to move forward:

> It is rather for us (the living) to be here dedicated to the great task remaining before us—that from these honored dead we take increased devotion to that cause for which they gave the last full measure of devotion—that we here highly resolve that these dead shall not have died in vain—that this nation, under God, shall have a new birth of freedom—and that government of the people, by the people, for the people shall not perish from the earth.

epitomize: typically or ideally represent.

99

On January 17, 1946, Chávez finally succeeded in intro-
ducing the Fair Employment Practices Act (S. 101) on the
Senate floor. Again, he faced resistance from several of his
southern colleagues. In fact, Mississippi's James Eastland
proposed sending the bill back to committee so that the
Senate could avoid having to deal with it at that time.
Chávez argued passionately against the idea, declaring on
the Senate floor:

❝

We love to talk about liberality and about saving the world.
We sent our boys to Europe, to China, and to the Pacific. The
only decoration which thousands of them received was a
white cross surmounting a grave. So we should look at the
record; we should look at the casualty lists. On them there
will be found the name of McGinty, an Irishman; the name of
Michael, an Armenian; the name of Levine, a Jew; the name
of Chávez, a Mexican; and the names of many others....

It is most regrettable that some persons think that it was all
well and good to use such men and call upon them to make
the supreme sacrifice in foreign fields, to land on a deadly
beach at Okinawa or Guam or elsewhere, but that they are
not good enough to receive equal treatment in our country. I
say to my colleagues that they had better place themselves in
the correct position. Those boys did not die in vain. We must
make sure that it can never be said that our boys who went all
over the world and conquered many other nations in order to
achieve freedom and victory, died in vain....

If senators think that the proposed legislation is political, I
assure them that it is not. It is not being offered in the interest of the Democratic party or in the interest of the Republican party. It is being offered in the interest of America, and
in the interest of fairness and decency. If the Constitution
(U.S.) is worth anything, if the Declaration of Independence
is worth anything, if the boys who died on the field of battle
did not die in vain, fair-employment practices are correct and
necessary....

I do not find anything in the Constitution which says that
only those whose ancestors happened to be from the British

Isles may be Americans. The Constitution says nothing at all like that. I have known some pretty good Americans who were not of British extraction, and when the country was in the midst of an emergency, when the shooting started, we found the Levines, the Gallaghers, the Negroes, the Assyrians, the Jews, and others doing their part in the war effort....

I have been fighting for the so-called underprivileged all my days, because I was one of them. I was reared in that atmosphere, and I am proud of the chance I had in America under the government of the United States, and I want my fellow beings to have the same chance I had....

Because I happen to have been rather fortunate, and when I go home I have a fairly good meal, or, at any rate, plenty to eat, it does not make me happy to reflect that possibly there are thousands and millions throughout the country who do not have anything to eat. Others may feel happy, others may be content when there are poor people in this country as a result of discrimination. I cannot be contented with such a condition. It is not American....

99

Chávez's efforts that day were not enough, however. Southern Democrats filibustered for eighteen days, until February 9, when a vote was taken to end the debate. Forty-eight senators voted in favor of the motion, and thirty-six voted against it—far short of the two-thirds majority needed to break the filibuster. The defeat led Chávez to withdraw the Fair Employment Practices Act from consideration. In doing so, he noted:

It took the crucifixion of Christ to redeem the world. It took **intestinal fortitude** to bring about the Declaration of Independence. It took ordinary American decency to bring about the Constitution of the United States. It took the death of Americans during the Civil War to find out that this was one country. It took this vote today to find out that a majority cannot have its will....

intestinal fortitude: guts, courage.

Notwithstanding what has happened today and heretofore, America will go forward. This is only the beginning. Please believe me, this is one country, as Lincoln said. We cannot have it divided. We cannot have one country for the South and another country for the other states of the United States.

"

Even though it meant battling his own party, Chávez continued to sound the call for an end to racial intolerance. But he soon began to use a somewhat different tactic to reach his audiences. Failing to pass antidiscrimination laws was not just unfair, he declared, it was also a threat to national security. Chávez warned that disunity and bitter controversies within the United States would make it easier for communism to gain strength throughout the world. (Communism is a system of government in which the state controls the means of production and the distribution of goods. It clashes with the American ideal of capitalism, which is based on private ownership and a free market system.) And he noted that purely from a practical standpoint it was foolish to hold back the minority population from contributing all it could to the country's well-being.

But Chávez's pleas had little influence where it counted—in the U.S. Senate. Although new legislation surfaced several times during the late 1940s, the 1950s, and the early 1960s regarding fair employment practices, these proposals always met with strong resistance from southern lawmakers. In many instances, bills never even made it to the Senate floor for a vote. Antidiscrimination measures were finally passed in 1964—two years after Chávez died of cancer while serving his fifth term in office—as part of the landmark Civil Rights Act.

Sources

Books

Congressional Record, 79th Congress, 2nd Session, Volume 92, Part 1, U.S. Government Printing Office, 1946.

notwithstanding: despite.

Congressional Record Appendix, 79th Congress, 1st Session, Volume 91, Part 13, U.S. Government Printing Office, 1945; 80th Congress, 2nd Session, Volume 94, Part 11, U.S. Government Printing Office, 1948.

Periodicals

New York Times, "Senator Chávez, 74, Is Dead in Capital," November 19, 1962.

Linda Chavez

1947–

Spanish American political leader and writer

Linda Chavez is a self-described "stubborn" person who often goes "against the grain." She has, in fact, created a stir among political liberals and some members of the Hispanic American community for challenging their views on topics such as affirmative action (giving special consideration to ethnic minorities and women to overcome the effects of past discrimination), bilingual education, and immigration policy. She is also an outspoken opponent of efforts to encourage multiculturalism (the celebration of social, racial, ethnic, and religious differences) instead of assimilation (the process of blending in with the dominant culture), especially when the government becomes involved. Chavez believes that such efforts divide rather than unite the country. As she once declared, "The more diverse we become racially and ethnically, the more important it is that we learn to tolerate differences—and also to celebrate what we all have in common."

"TOO OFTEN THOSE WHO PROPOSE MULTICULTURAL EDUCATION ARE SO OBSESSED WITH THE EXCESSES OF ANGLO CONFORMITY THAT THEY FAIL TO SEE THE BENEFITS OF A SHARED, COMMON CULTURE—NOT ENTIRELY WHITE, ANGLO-SAXON, AND PROTESTANT—BUT COMMON NONETHELESS."

Early Life

Chavez was born in Albuquerque, New Mexico, in the same general area where her father's ancestors had lived for nearly four hundred years after their arrival from Spain. (Her mother's family is of English and Irish descent.) When she was nine, she moved with her parents and younger sister to Denver, Colorado. There Chavez experienced racial discrimination for the first time in her life. But she overcame the sting of prejudice by remembering some words of advice from her father—to always be proud of her heritage and to continue to strive for success.

After graduating from high school, Chavez attended the University of Colorado and earned her bachelor's degree in 1970. She then went on to pursue graduate studies in English literature at the University of California at Los Angeles (UCLA). Chavez arrived at UCLA during a time of tremendous social unrest both on and off campus. Along with many other student demands, pressures mounted for developing a Chicano studies program. Chavez was drafted to develop a course in Chicano literature, even though she felt that there wasn't enough material to teach the subject.

What Chavez experienced as a professor of Chicano literature left her disgusted. Her more radical students "didn't believe they had to read books at all, much less any book that was written by a non-Hispanic," she later recalled. Some of her students literally turned their backs on her in protest of her assignment of non-Hispanic commentary on the Hispanic experience. Outside class, she experienced acts of vandalism against her personal property and threats on her life after she failed students who didn't complete the required course work. In addition, Chavez believed some of her fellow professors encouraged students to defy authority rather than to work and learn in school.

Embraces Conservative Politics

A disappointed Chavez headed for Washington, D.C. in 1972. She worked in several jobs with politically liberal objectives, including six months at the Department of Health, Education, and Welfare during the administration of Democratic President Jimmy Carter. While working as the editor of the American Federation of Teachers publication American Educator, however, Chavez first caught the eye of Washington-area conservatives who were impressed with a series of articles she wrote on the need to return to "traditional values" in the schools. In 1981, she received an invitation to serve as a consultant to the administration of Republican President Ronald Reagan.

In 1983, Chavez became staff director of the U.S. Commission on Civil Rights. (See box on page 52 for more information.) She immediately ruffled some feathers when she issued a memo calling for an end to the kinds of programs and practices typically supported by liberals because they falsely assume that "racism and sexism are ingrained [inborn] in American society." She was especially critical of **affirmative action**, maintaining that it lowers people's dignity and self-esteem by reducing them to an ethnic category. In addition, Chavez raised some eyebrows when she declared that "a general decline in academic standards coincided with the advent [coming, beginning] of affirmative action in higher education."

In 1985, Chavez became the highest-ranking woman in the Reagan administration when she accepted the post of director of the White House Office of Public Liaison. This assignment involved promoting the president's policies among members of Congress and various public groups. (Around this time, Chavez officially declared herself to be a Republican rather than a Democrat.) She left her White House job ten months later and in 1986 ran for the office of U.S. senator from Maryland. It was an especially hard-fought and bitter campaign that promoted Chavez, a married mother of three, as the "family values" candidate. Her opponent was liberal Democrat Barbara Mikulski, who was unmarried and childless. Chavez lost by a large margin.

Chavez then withdrew from public office—but not from the public eye. She became the head of U.S. English, an organization that supports making English the official national language. A year later, however, she resigned in protest of what she felt were the "anti-Hispanic" and "anti-Catholic" attitudes the founder of the group had expressed in a private memo that was made public.

affirmative action: programs designed to remedy the effects of past discrimination and to end such discrimination by improving the employment and educational opportunities of women and members of minority groups.

The U.S. Commission on Civil Rights

Established in 1957, the U.S. Commission on Civil Rights (CCR) was intended to be an independent, nonpartisan government advisory group that would monitor how federal agencies enforce civil rights laws banning discrimination in employment, education, housing, and politics. Commissioners would investigate complaints, report their findings to the president as well as to Congress, and recommend corrective actions when necessary.

Beginning around 1970, however, during the administration of President Richard Nixon, the CCR accused the government of ignoring their reports and backing away from a commitment to eliminate discrimination. The relationship between the White House and the commissioners continued to deteriorate throughout the administration of President Gerald Ford (1974–77) and worsened even further under President Ronald Reagan (1981–89).

Shortly after Reagan entered office in 1981, he fired the chairperson of the CCR for supporting affirmative action, voting rights, and busing to achieve school desegregation. The former chairperson was replaced with a conservative black Republican who had backed Reagan in the 1980 election. It was the first time in the CCR's history that an incoming president had made such a bold attempt to shape the group's membership.

The conflict between the CCR and the Reagan administration came to a head in 1983, when the president fired three Democratic commissioners. He explained his decision by saying that the commissioners did not share his views on affirmative action and busing. A public outcry followed, and Congress cut off the group's funding. Finally, in November 1983, the president and Congress reached an agreement on restructuring the CCR. The number of commissioners was increased from six to eight, and the president and Congress were each allowed to name four members to serve staggered six-year terms. Furthermore, they agreed that commissioners could only be removed from their jobs for just cause, not for their political beliefs.

Joins Conservative Think Tank

*Chavez then became associated with the Manhattan Institute, a conservative **think tank** located in Washington, D.C. There she was a senior fellow and head of the Center for the New American Community. In that position, she carried out the center's mission to "foster a renewed commitment to a common American civic culture and shared identity among the many diverse people who built this nation and live in it today."*

In 1995, the Center for the New American Community broke away from the Manhattan Institute and changed its

think tank: a group organized to research a variety of different but related topics.

name to the Center for Equal Opportunity (CEO). Chavez serves as president of the new organization, which is a project of the Equal Opportunity Foundation, a nonprofit research institution that focuses on racial preferences, immigration and assimilation, and multicultural education. The CEO's goal is to promote "colorblind equal opportunity and racial harmony."

Chavez contributes frequently to a variety of publications, and in 1991 she wrote the book Out of the Barrio: Toward a New Politics of Hispanic Assimilation. *In it she discusses topics such as bilingual education, voting rights, immigration policy, and affirmative action. She also emphasizes Hispanic progress and achievement in an effort to overturn what she believes are stereotypes about Hispanics as a poor and disadvantaged underclass. In fact, Chavez thinks the current anti-immigration feeling is a direct result of such images and attitudes. "If we are constantly telling everyone through our Hispanic leaders that we can't make it in America," she explains, "well, then, we shouldn't be surprised when people say maybe we don't want so many of you here."*

In addition to appearing on radio and television news and public-affairs programs to discuss her views, Chavez is often called upon to share them in person with various groups. In October 1992, she spoke in Miami, Florida. The occasion was the forty-sixth annual National Preservation Conference, sponsored by the National Trust for Historic Preservation. The theme of Chavez's talk was how to encourage appreciation for cultural diversity in the United States without losing sight of what should be the ultimate goal of all newcomers—assimilation. An excerpt from her speech is reprinted here from Historic Preservation Forum, *January/February 1993.*

The face of America is changing—becoming more diverse and complex than at any time in our history. We're no longer a white-and-black society struggling to integrate two major groups of people who have been in this country for nearly four hundred years, but a multiracial, multiethnic society in which newcomers are arriving in record numbers every day. The 1980s will be remembered as a period of one the highest levels of immigration in our nation's history. Some ten million persons immigrated to the United States in the last decade, a number as great as that of the peak decade, 1900 to 1910.

Unlike the immigrants of the early part of this century who were primarily from Europe, the great bulk of the last decade's immigrants—approximately eighty percent—were from Asia and Latin America. Much has been made of this phenomenon and many who favor restricting immigration suggest that these new Asian and Latin immigrants will be less successfully absorbed into the fabric of American society....

But, in fact, when we look at one of these groups, we find that most Hispanics are assimilating the social, educational, economic, and language norms of this society despite the image of Hispanics portrayed in the media and **perpetuated** by Hispanic leaders. Let me just acquaint you with a few facts about the Hispanic population with which you may not be familiar:

- Mexican-origin men have the highest labor-force participation rates of any group, including non-Hispanic whites and Asians.

- U.S.-born Hispanics have rapidly moved into the middle class. The earnings of Mexican-American men are now roughly eighty percent of those of non-Hispanic white men.

- Mexican-Americans with thirteen to fifteen years of education earn, on an average, ninety-seven percent of the average earnings of non-Hispanic white males.

- Most differences in earnings between Hispanics and non-Hispanics can be explained by educational differences between the two groups, but at the secondary-school level, young Mexican-Americans are closing the gap with their non-Hispanic peers. Seventy-eight percent of second-generation Mexican-American men aged twenty-five to thirty-four have completed twelve years of school or more, compared with approximately ninety percent of comparable non-Hispanic whites.

- English proficiency is also key to earnings among Hispanics, but here, too, conventional wisdom about Hispanics

perpetuated: maintained, made to last indefinitely.

is mostly invalid. The overwhelming majority of U.S.-born Hispanics are English-dominant, and one half of all third generation Mexican-Americans—like most other American ethnics—speak only one language: English.

- What's more, Hispanics, with the exception of Puerto Ricans, have marriage rates comparable to those of non-Hispanic whites. Three quarters of Mexican-origin, Cuban, and Central and South American Hispanics live in married-couple households. And nearly half own their own homes.

If these facts come as a surprise to you, it's largely because most of the analysis of Hispanics fails to note that nearly half of the adult Hispanic population is foreign-born. And like new immigrants of the past, Hispanic immigrants will take at least one generation to move up the economic ladder and into the cultural mainstream.

Perhaps a little history lesson is in order. The current period is not the only time in our history during which we have viewed new immigrants with distrust and suspicion. We tend to forget that Italians, Greeks, Jews, Poles, and others—whom some people lump together as "Europeans"—were considered alien to the white Americans of the early twentieth century, most of whom were of British, German, or Scandinavian descent.... For anyone who believes that immigrants of an earlier day lived in a **halcyon** time of tolerance and acceptance among their fellow white European-descended Americans, I recommend a few hours of reading through the reports of the 1921 Dillingham Commission, which in 1924 ultimately recommended a quota system to keep out southern and eastern European immigrants and Asians. [See box on page 56 for more information.]

The point is that immigrants have never had it particularly easy in this society, nor have they always been welcomed with open arms, despite Emma Lazarus's words on the base of the Statue of Liberty. ["Give me your tired, your poor, / Your huddled masses yearning to breathe free.] Nonetheless, most of those who came here from other countries found the struggle worth the effort. And these groups did, by and large, succeed in America.

Today, Italians, Jews, Poles, Greeks, and others of southern and eastern European background are virtually indistinguish-

halcyon: pleasant, calm, trouble-free.

Origins of the Quota System for Immigration

Prior to 1890, most immigrants to the United States arrived from Great Britain, Ireland, Germany, and the Scandinavian countries of northern Europe. The established population was predominantly Protestant and of English descent, and some problems arose due to the language differences of Germans and Scandinavians and the religious differences of the Roman Catholic Irish.

From about 1890 to 1910 immigration to the United States greatly increased, with more than 70 percent of the new arrivals coming from southern and eastern Europe, primarily Austria, Hungary, Italy, and Russia. The American population expressed fears and prejudices toward immigrants whose backgrounds seemed foreign. These feelings grew stronger after World War I, when the number of immigrants rose once again. The United States then began to restrict the immigration of certain nationalities, particularly Asians.

In 1910 the Dillingham commission, which had been appointed by Congress, issued a report on immigration, including so-called "scientific" findings proving the inferiority of recent immigrants compared to the original settlers from northern and western Europe. The Immigration Act of 1917 was based on this report. It required newcomers to prove they could read and write (in any language) and to meet standards as to their mental, physical, moral, and economic state. Known political radicals were excluded from immigrating. The act also precluded immigration of laborers from the "Asiatic Barred Zone," which included India, Indochina, Afghanistan, Arabia, the East Indies, and other, smaller Asian countries. China and Japan were already restricted by previous measures.

In 1921, the Dillingham Bill (also known as the Emergency Quota Act), established a **quota** system to restrict immigration even further. It allowed only three percent of the people of any nationality that had lived in the United States in 1910 to enter the country each year.

In 1924, the Johnson-Reed Immigration Act tightened up the quota system even more, limiting the annual quota to two percent of the people of any nationality that had lived in the United States in 1890. This totally excluded all Japanese and reaffirmed Chinese exclusion, while making it easier for people from northern and western Europe to enter the country.

able from so-called native-stock Americans on measure of earnings, status, and education. Even Chinese- and Japanese-Americans, who were subject to much greater discrimination than southern and eastern Europeans, have done exceedingly well and outperform most other groups on all indicators of social and economic success. But it took three generations for most of these groups to achieve this status....

quota: numerical limit; the number of people from a particular country allowed to immigrate to another country.

Linda Chavez

Is it possible, then, simply to mimic what we did in the past in treating this generation of newcomers? No. Let me concede that we did a great deal of wrong in the past, and immigrants succeeded in spite of, not because of, our mistakes. It would be neither compassionate nor legal to return to a system in which we put non-English-speaking children into public-school classrooms in which the instruction was entirely in English and expect those children to "sink or swim." In 1974 this approach was declared by the United States Supreme Court to violate our civil rights laws. Nor should we harken back to the "good old days" when Anglo conformity was the sole acceptable cultural model.

But in trying to right past wrongs, we should be careful not to reverse ourselves 180 degrees by attempting to educate

New immigrants to the United States eat lunch at Ellis Island, New York, in the 1910s, when the gateway to the United States was at its busiest

New U.S. citizens pledge allegiance to the flag at a reopening ceremony at Ellis Island, New York, 1990

inculcate: mold, shape.

eradicate: eliminate.

orthodoxy: set of beliefs or practices.

each group of immigrant children in their own native language and **inculcate** them in their own native culture.... If we insist on separate language instruction for all immigrant students—167 different languages are spoken in New York alone—we will close the door on integration, divide ourselves along cultural/linguistic lines, and thereby perpetuate inequalities rather than **eradicate** them.

It seems to me that too often those who propose multicultural education are so obsessed with the excesses of Anglo conformity that they fail to see the benefits of a shared, common culture—not entirely white, Anglo-Saxon, and Protestant—but common nonetheless. And they fail to see the dangers in substituting one **orthodoxy** with another, no less rigid.

The more diverse we become racially and ethnically, the more important it is that we learn to tolerate differences— and also to celebrate what we all have in common. Whether we came to the United States voluntarily or involuntarily, we all choose to live here now. And more people want to live here than anywhere else in the world. No other country accepts as many immigrants as we do. Surely, even those who criticize our so-called Eurocentric society must admit that it has something to offer or there would not be such long lines of those waiting to get in—very few of them European, by the way.

What is it we have that these Mexicans, Cambodians, Ethiopians, Filipinos, and others want? Two things primarily: economic opportunity and political freedom. The two, by the way, go hand in hand, and it is our legal and political institutions that protect both.

Now it so happens that those political institutions did not, in fact, develop in Asia or Latin America or Africa or even throughout most of Europe. It happens that the framework for our political institutions comes from England. The basis for American **jurisprudence** comes from English common law—not from Spanish adaptations of Roman law that governed most of Latin America, or from the legendary rulers of China or from the Hsia Dynasty or from Confucianism, or from [Africa's] Ghanian Empire, the Kush state in Nubia, or from Mali.

That is not to say that these others are not important civilizations deserving recognition in their own right, but it is to acknowledge the special importance to our particular political/legal system of the **Magna Carta, habeas corpus,** and trial by jury, all of which were handed down directly from England....

In our **zeal** to tell the stories of other civilizations, to include the history of those whose ancestors came from places other than England, we should not attempt to rewrite the history of our own founding and our political **antecedents.** Nor should we blush at the thought that this political/institutional history now belongs to children who come here from Mexico, Vietnam, or Ghana or whose parents came from those countries. These children are now

jurisprudence: law.

Magna Carta: the charter of political and civil freedoms that English noblemen forced King John to agree to in 1215.

habeas corpus: a type of legal document ordering someone to appear before a judge or a court.

zeal: eagerness.

antecedents: the events and characteristics from earlier times in one's existence.

American children, and this is their political inheritance as much as it is the inheritance of the child of Italian or Greek or Russian roots, certainly every bit as much as it is the child of English roots.

I believe that in our zeal to promote diversity we are forgetting that what makes this country virtually unique in the world is that we have forged an identity as a people even though most of us share very little in common in terms of our own personal histories. There is nothing wrong with holding onto personal history, but—given the incredible diversity of the country as a whole—it becomes increasingly difficult to expect the state to try to pass on that sense of personal history to each and every group. The most that can be expected, I think, is that we make sure that we recognize the contributions each group—once here—has made to the common history of this nation.

Is it possible to study the individual culture of the ancestors of each group represented in America? That depends on how superficial we're willing to be. I suppose it's possible to develop a dictionary of cultural literacy of every major group and teach children to memorize a few facts and dates about each. Given our current success with children's learning to locate Arkansas on a map of the United States or China on a map of the world, or to tell in what half a century the Civil War was fought, or to name more than four past presidents of the United States, I don't know what hope there is that such a project would have any lasting benefit....

So if we cannot—and perhaps should not—try to teach each group its own individual history through multiple ethnocentric curricula, how do we try to deal with this increasingly diverse student population?

First, black, Hispanic, Asian, and American Indian children need the same basic skills that we take for granted that white children need. This is an obvious point, but one that seems sometimes to be forgotten when the subject of multicultural education is raised. All children in American public schools need to be taught to read, write, and speak standard English well. Their ability to master these skills will affect their life chances more than virtually anything else they learn—or fail to learn—in school.

Second, they need to be taught the basic math and science that will enable them to function in an increasingly complex technological society.

Third, they need a broad understanding of our form of government and its institutions. We live in a country in which we enjoy great freedom, but we also live in a country in which people are highly **apathetic.** If we hope to preserve

apathetic: uninterested, uninvolved.

democracy, our young people must develop a better appreciation for our heritage and be committed to preserving it. Somewhere along the way we have become **reticent** about instilling in our young an appreciation for democracy. If we expect to preserve our democratic way of life, we had better begin to develop that appreciation once again. And that means emphasizing the duties and responsibilities that go along with good citizenship.

Fourth, we need to teach our children the history of this nation. Here, we sometimes failed in the past to include the contributions made by all the groups that made up this nation. I said earlier that we shouldn't shy away from teaching the essentially English antecedents of our political and legal institutions. But neither should we forget that many who built this nation were neither English, nor white, nor male. There are many excellent histories to consult....

Fifth, all American children need a better understanding of the world in which we live, an understanding that includes something of the history of other nations....

These recommendations are not exhaustive. Nor are they geared only to the child who comes from a nonwhite, non-European background. These recommendations are suited to all of our children.

The American public school was created on the **premise** that it would be a common school, one for all children. It has not always lived up to that ideal—certainly not before 1954—but that does not mean we should abandon the ideal. The face of America is changing, but we should not give up on the idea that we are one people, one nation. Our efforts should be dedicated to making that ideal a reality.

Is there no place, then, for the preservation of language and culture for those among new immigrants—or any others in this society—who wish to retain aspects of their former traditions? Of course there is. Some would have us believe that assimilation means that every group will be stripped of what makes it unique and that the American character will be forged into a colorless **alloy** in an indifferent melting pot. But, of course, that is not what has happened in this country. As a trip into the heart of any American city will tell you, ethnic communities are alive and well, even as their inhabi-

reticent: shy, hesitant.

premise: assumption; something taken for granted.

alloy: mixture, combination.

tants enjoy the fruits of social, political, and economic integration.

The question is not whether any ethnic group has the right to maintain its language, culture, and traditions, but whose responsibility it is to do so: Is it the individual's or the group's responsibility? Or should it be the responsibility of government to ensure that each group's separate traditions be maintained? This, of course, is the heart of the debate now raging in many circles—a debate in which I come down solidly on the side of personal responsibility. If Hispanics, Asians, Jews, Greeks, or the members of any other group wish to maintain their individual and unique cultures, languages, or traditions, it must be up to them to do so....

Those Hispanics who wish to maintain their native language and culture—and polls show that a majority of Hispanic immigrants do—should follow the example of their fellow ethnic Americans by establishing their own cultural societies by which to do so. Frankly, given the tremendous diversity within the Hispanic community, the only successful way for each group to ensure that its members know its history and traditions is to undertake that education itself. If government is entrusted with the responsibility, it is likely to **amalgamate** and **homogenize** in ways that make the original culture virtually **indecipherable.**

The government, after all, is capable of lumping all twenty-two million Hispanics in this nation into one category—a category that includes Cakchikel Indians from Guatemala, **mestizos** from Mexico, the descendants of Italian immigrants from Argentina, Japanese immigrants from Peru, Spaniards from Europe, and the descendants of colonists who settled the Southwest nearly four hundred years ago. Wouldn't it be better to entrust each of these very different groups with the responsibility of maintaining its own traditions without the interference—or assistance—of the government?

Some critics warn that the United States is in danger of fragmenting into competing racial and ethnic groups. Historian Arthur Schlesinger, Jr., has called it the "disuniting of America." No doubt, our task is more complicated today than at any time in the recent past. Nonetheless, I remain optimistic that we can—if we commit ourselves—successfully

amalgamate: combine.

homogenize: mix different elements into a uniform mixture.

indecipherable: incapable of being understood or recognized.

mestizos: people of mixed European and American Indian ancestry.

integrate the more than seventy million blacks, Hispanics, Asians, and American Indians into our society. That we can create a new *unum* out of the many already here and the many more who are to come.

But to do so will require the cooperation of us all—those who have been here for generations as well as those who are coming each day. It will require that each of us recognizes the **covenant** that exists between the old and the new: that we respect the rights of individuals to maintain what is unique in their ancestral heritages, but that we understand that our future is in forging a common identity of shared values and beliefs essential to the democratic ideal.

99

Sources

Books

Chavez, Linda, *Out of the Barrio: Toward a New Politics of Hispanic Assimilation,* Basic Books, 1991.

Periodicals

Commentary, "Hispanics Versus Their Leaders," October 1991, pp. 47–49; "What to Do About Immigration," March 1995, pp. 29–35.

Forbes, "The Fracturing of America," March 30, 1992, pp. 74–75.

Hispanic, "Making People Mad," August 1992, pp. 11–16.

Historic Preservation Forum, "Fostering Appreciation for Cultural Diversity," January/February 1993, pp. 12–19.

National Review, "Demystifying Multiculturalism," February 21, 1994, pp. 26–32.

New Republic, "Quitters," February 24, 1986, pp. 8–10; "Just Say Latino," March 22, 1993, pp. 18–19.

People, "Barbara Mikulski and Linda Chavez Stage a Gloves-Off Battle in a Women-Only U.S. Senate Race," November 3, 1986, pp. 115–16.

Washington Monthly, "Linda Chavez and the Exploitation of Ethnic Identity," June 1985, pp. 34–39.

unum: one, a reference to the phrase on the great seal of the United States, *E pluribus unum* ("from many, one").

covenant: agreement, understanding.

Henry G. Cisneros

1947–

Mexican American politician and businessman

During the early 1980s, a new face appeared on the national political scene—that of Mayor Henry G. Cisneros of San Antonio, Texas. Charming, intelligent, and energetic, he was regarded as one of the brightest stars of the Democratic party. Many praised his creative and forward-thinking approach to tackling urban problems such as unemployment, crumbling downtowns, and strained relations between whites and minorities. In 1993, he set out to take his formula for success nationwide as U.S. Secretary of Housing and Urban Development (HUD) in the administration of President Bill Clinton. At HUD, Cisneros worked to transform an agency known for its failures and inefficiency into a true friend of the urban poor.

Early Life

A native of San Antonio, Cisneros grew up in an atmosphere where both education and self-discipline were highly prized. His mother's father, for example, was a Mexican

"THE FEDERAL GOVERNMENT, AND CERTAINLY THE FIVE THOUSAND PEOPLE WHO WORK IN THE HEADQUARTERS OF HUD IN WASHINGTON, NEVER BUILD ONE SINGLE BUILDING, ONE SINGLE HOUSE, WITH THEIR HANDS. WE MUST RELY ON PEOPLE IN COMMUNITIES...."

journalist who was forced to flee his native country in 1926 for political reasons. He then settled in San Antonio and became active in the community. Cisneros's own father traced his ancestry back to early Spanish settlers in the American Southwest. He spent his childhood as a migrant worker in Colorado and then joined the U.S. Army during World War II. Afterwards, the elder Cisneros became a civilian administrator for the army and rose to the rank of colonel in the army reserve.

Spanish was the language of choice in the Cisneros household and in the middle-class neighborhood where the family lived. As a result, young Henry could not speak English when he first entered school. But he was a quick learner and a good student who even then had a great deal of personal charm, as his teachers later recalled.

After graduating from high school, Cisneros enrolled at Texas A&M University. His intention was to follow in his father's footsteps and become a military officer. Instead, he found himself drawn to the relatively new field of urban planning, which focuses on how cities develop and what can be done to shape that development. Cisneros earned his bachelor's degree in the subject in 1968. He then worked for several federal and city urban revitalization programs in and around his hometown while studying for his master's degree, which he received in 1970. By then, according to family members, Cisneros had already made up his mind that someday he was going to be mayor of San Antonio.

The young man's next stop, however, was Washington, D.C., where he began studying for his doctorate in urban administration at George Washington University. Meanwhile, he obtained a job as administrative assistant to the executive vice president of the National League of Cities. In 1971, Cisneros landed a prestigious White House fellowship, which is granted to young people who are interested in a career in politics. It enabled him to work in the administration of President Richard Nixon as an assistant to Elliot Richardson, who was the U.S. Secretary of Health, Education, and Welfare.

In 1972, Cisneros headed to Boston, Massachusetts. He spent the next two years there working on a master's degree in public administration at Harvard University's John F. Kennedy School of Government. During this period he also completed doctoral studies at the Massachusetts Institute of Technology (MIT) and served as a teaching assistant. Turning down an offer to join the MIT faculty, Cisneros returned to San Antonio in 1974 and became an assistant professor at the city's branch of the University of Texas. Soon afterward, he finished work on another doctorate—this one from George Washington University—and officially received his degree in 1975.

Launches Political Career in His Hometown

*Cisneros's return to San Antonio also marked the beginning of his political career. For more than twenty years, an organization of **Anglo** businessmen known as the Good Government League (GGL) had had tremendous influence over the city's political affairs. By the 1970s, however, the GGL had begun to lose some of its clout. More and more Hispanic American voters were turning instead to new community-based organizations they felt were more committed to Latino interests. So, in 1975, the GGL started looking for a Hispanic American candidate it could support in upcoming city council elections. Cisneros fit the bill, and the GGL added his name to their ticket. After running a fiercely independent campaign, Cisneros was elected to the city council on his own merits. At the age of only twenty-seven, he became the youngest city councilman in San Antonio history.*

From the start, Cisneros devoted himself to building bridges between the conservative Anglo establishment and the growing Hispanic American community. There were many years of hard feelings to overcome. Hispanic Americans had effectively been shut out of power in San Antonio; for years Anglos controlled the city, although Hispanics were the majority population. For the young city councilman, overcoming the resentment and suspicion between the two groups was a time-consuming and often frustrating process. At any given time leaders from one side or the other were angry with him for taking a stand they opposed.

Anglo: short for the Spanish word *angloamericano*, meaning a white, non-Hispanic U.S. inhabitant.

But his approach was popular with voters. He won reelection to the city council in 1977 and again in 1979.

First Hispanic American Mayor of a Large U.S. City

In 1980, Cisneros felt it was time to try for the mayor's office. During his campaign, he emphasized overcoming ethnic divisions in order to work together to encourage economic growth that would benefit all of San Antonio. It was a message people liked, and Cisneros captured the support of a majority of Anglo and Hispanic American voters in the 1981 election. His victory at the polls made him the first Hispanic American mayor of a major U.S. city.

Once in office, Cisneros launched an all-out effort to achieve his goals. The steps he took reflected his belief that economic growth is the key to solving social problems. After identifying the need for more variety in the local economy, he attracted many new businesses to San Anotnio, mostly in light manufacturing, high technology, medical services, and biosciences research. He also convinced local schools and colleges to develop programs that would teach students the skills needed to work in those new businesses. In addition, Cisneros boosted tourism by recruiting conventions and renovating the downtown area. Before long, he had attracted national recognition as a bold new political leader who was in touch with emerging economic trends.

Cisneros was elected to a second term as mayor in 1983. As he had promised voters, he then focused more of his considerable energies on quality-of-life issues such as improving city services and building an arts center and sports stadium.

Meanwhile, Cisneros's political visibility was increasing outside San Antonio. In 1983, President Ronald Reagan appointed him to the National Bipartisan Commission on Central America. The following year, he was second on the list of Democratic presidential candidate Walter Mondale's choices for vice president. And in 1985, Cisneros became president of the National League of Cities, another high-profile position. Yet this popular politician insisted that he did

The U.S. Department of Housing and Urban Development (HUD)

Created by Congress in 1965, the Department of Housing and Urban Development oversees a wide variety of programs that involve the nation's housing needs as well as the overall development of urban areas. A cabinet-level department, it is run by a secretary who is appointed by the president and then approved by the Senate.

In the area of housing, HUD has traditionally planned and financed many different kinds of construction projects, including the building of new homes, the renovation of older homes, and the development of apartment complexes. The department has also used loans and grants to encourage the private sector to build housing with low-income families in mind. HUD funds have helped low-income people buy their own homes; many others have benefited from HUD rent supplements. Special programs also exist to aid the elderly, the disabled, single women, and members of minority groups to buy or rent suitable housing. In addition, HUD is responsible for making sure that fair housing policies are followed so that those seeking public housing or applying for loans do not face discrimination.

At the community level, HUD has worked to clear slums and renovate entire neighborhoods. It has also funded improvements in public services and energy conservation efforts. To help stimulate private investment and economic development in especially hard-hit areas, the department awards grants and offers other assistance.

Almost from its beginnings, however, HUD has come under fire for being poorly managed, corrupt, and too far removed from the problems of the people it is supposed to help. Periodic scandals and controversies have rocked the department, giving opponents even more reasons to demand that it be abolished.

In 1989, for example, Samuel Pierce, President Ronald Reagan's HUD secretary since 1981, left office under a cloud of suspicion. A five-year investigation turned up evidence of massive fraud and mismanagement during his term as head of the department. By early 1995, sixteen of his top assistants had been convicted of various crimes and fined more than $2 million. Most of them had used HUD funds under their control in a way that benefited their friends, their families, or themselves. They often accomplished this by awarding money to favored developers or politically influential people and then taking kickbacks in return.

not wish to make the leap to higher office. He easily won reelection to the mayor's post in 1985 and again in 1987.

Withdraws from the Political Scene

In 1989, Cisneros surprised and disappointed his supporters when he declined to run for governor and instead announced he was quitting politics. (At the time, he was considered the front-runner in the race.) His major reasons for leaving public life were family-related. In 1987, his wife had given birth to a son with severe health problems. The baby's medical needs, plus the prospect of having to pay for the college educations of two older daughters, made Cisneros realize that he had to work at something that paid more money. (In San Antonio, the office of mayor is largely a ceremonial post that pays only $50 plus expenses per council meeting. A city manager actually oversees daily operations. Nevertheless, Cisneros had always put in full-time hours as mayor while earning some additional money by teaching and speaking before various groups.) So he went into business as founder and chair of the Cisneros Asset Management Company, a financial consulting firm.

Reenters Politics at the National Level

In 1992, Cisneros again felt the pull of politics when his friend and mentor Ann Richards was elected governor of Texas and Bill Clinton became president of the United States. Both had plans for the former mayor. Richards wanted him to run for the U.S. Senate seat that had been left vacant when Lloyd Bentsen of Texas joined the Clinton cabinet as Secretary of the Treasury. Clinton wanted him in the cabinet as Secretary of Housing and Urban Development (HUD). Cisneros decided to take the job he felt he had been training for all his life—running HUD. His hope was that serving as housing secretary would enable him to make a real difference in the lives of the poor and the homeless of the nation's cities.

On April 13, 1993, just a couple of months after he had taken over the reins at HUD, Cisneros addressed the National Press Club in Washington, D.C. In his speech, he talked about the many problems facing America's urban areas and offered his views on what HUD needed to do to begin solving those problems. HUD's Office of Public Affairs provided a copy of his speech, from which the following excerpt was reprinted.

❝

I feel that I'm one of the luckiest people around—able to work on the things I believe in, serve our country and serve a president who believes in communities, has worked in communities and is intent on making a difference in our country, in partnership with communities....

Like the president, all of us, you care about our country and its communities, about both their promise and their peril. We are inspired by the locally-inspired turnarounds, by the national promise of, say, Pittsburgh [Pennsylvania] or Baltimore [Maryland] in the east, of Indianapolis [Indiana] and Omaha [Nebraska] in the heartland, of Seattle [Washington] and Salt Lake [City, Utah] in the west. But we've also seen the peril of heightened crime, of the plague of drugs, of fear on the faces of the elderly, of neighborhoods that have lost their life force, with churches closed, ball fields empty, downtown stores with empty windows, factories with weeds that have overgrown their parking lots in communities of all sizes, in all regions, made up of people of all incomes and ages and races.

For every example of civic cooperation such as the promise of Minneapolis-St. Paul [Minnesota], there is another, the peril, where leaders glare across at each other across a **chasm** of misunderstanding, even hatred, refusing to cooperate.

For every Portland, Oregon, the promise, striving to literally redesign its future, there is a community in peril that has surrendered to the larger forces of the global economy.

For every city such as Fort Worth [Texas], the promise of sustaining attractive, graceful, and life-enhancing neighborhoods, there's a community in peril where the elderly are afraid to walk to the corner store with their Social Security checks, where children peek out of windows to see if the drug pushers are still at the pay phone across the street.

For every city such as Tampa [Florida], meeting its promise by building homes, ... there is the peril of a city where the homeless look for a wind-free alcove, a sheltered stairwell, a steam exhaust pipe to sleep through the frozen night.

chasm: wide gap.

Firefighters battle a blaze in south central Los Angeles during the turmoil on April 30, 1992

And for every community of promise, like Rockford, Illinois, where people have come together across traditional lines, there are those communities in peril where the slow burn of anger **smolders,** occasionally to flare into terrible intensity as in Los Angeles [California] last spring.

The morning after the civil disturbances began in Los Angeles, I called Mayor [Tom] Bradley and several members of the city council there and, in consultation with them, concluded that because it was not clear how extensive the civil disturbances might become in the Latino community of Los Angeles, that people like myself who might have a chance to do something should go, and so I did....

What I saw and smelled and felt makes it possible for me to speak to you today with greater clarity and certainty than

smolders: burns slowly and quietly without a flame or much smoke.

Henry G. Cisneros

ever. On a Los Angeles street that Thursday night the smoke was everywhere; it smelled of burning wire and plastic. The smoke was so thick that it obscured the lights of a helicopter circling directly overhead. Sirens screamed every few seconds as strike teams of fire engines, escorted by California highway patrol, convoys, literally convoys, of thirty vehicles with police, designed to protect the firemen as they would try to do their jobs at the next fire.

Pick-up trucks were pulled up next to electronics stores with the glass fronts bashed in, as men hurriedly loaded VCRs and television sets. One man told me he had just walked by a teenager around the corner. The young man had been shot in the head, lying arms wide, sprawled out on the city sidewalk, eyes open, staring straight up, dead.

Looters in south central Los Angeles, April 30, 1992

It was the urban **apocalypse** in smoky smelly orange, an assault on all the senses, people wide-eyed, all-out fear just one more loud bang away.

Well, that was Los Angeles that Thursday night, but it could be another city in America some other night. No, you say, no way, Los Angeles is different. Well, Los Angeles is different—it's bigger, it's more diverse, it's rapper street-smart, its edges are sharper, cooler, tougher, maybe readier to take offense. No, you say, it couldn't happen in my city.... Well, maybe yes, maybe no, maybe not the same form, maybe not the same intensity, maybe not the same flashpoint.

But the white-hot intensity of Los Angeles was the combustion of smoldering embers waiting to ignite. Like piles of dry wood with red coals underneath, other American cities can ignite, or maybe we'll call ourselves lucky and they'll just smolder away taking a human toll at a slower rate. Just smolder away.

Why are our cities smoldering? Well, perhaps it's a matter of isolation. Our cities and our neighborhoods have become more geographically segregated by race, class, and ethnicity. Fifty cities of more than 100,000 persons of population each now have populations that are better than majority African American, Hispanic and Asian. Among those cities with sixty percent of their population African American, Hispanic and Asian are Atlanta [Georgia], Baltimore, Washington, D.C., Chicago [Illinois], Detroit [Michigan]—Detroit is eighty percent minority; it's the most segregated city in the United States. White populations leave, some seeking the advantages of the suburbs, some fleeing the deteriorated crime-ridden city, and others escaping people, the minority populations themselves.

The result is desperation, distrust and poor populations left behind to fend for themselves in racial **enclaves.** And we ask—why are our cities smoldering?

Well, perhaps it's a loss of economic function amidst larger economic trends. Cities no longer play the same role that they did in the past, urban economies have been completely transformed from the manufacturing goods-producing engines of jobs that they once were, when thirty percent of the jobs in a community were in manufacturing, to the

apocalypse: huge and violent confrontation (from the biblical description of the end-of-the-world battle between good and evil).

enclaves: small territories that exist within a larger territory and maintain separate racial, cultural, and/or ethnic identities.

South Central Los Angeles Riots, 1992

On March 3, 1991, Rodney King, an African American motorist, was severely beaten by police officers after being stopped for a speeding violation. The beating was videotaped by a witness from his nearby apartment balcony. The eighty-one-second videotape revealed that officers continued beating King with nightsticks even after they had put him in restraints and he appeared unable to fight back. Police officers on the scene said that King had led them on a high-speed chase and that he had resisted arrest. Four police officers were charged in the beating, but on April 29, 1992, a California jury acquitted them.

Within hours of the acquittal, violent rioting broke out in predominantly black south central Los Angeles, lasting for three days. Youths brutally beat white motorists who drove through the area, and rioters burned and looted stores and businesses. Korean merchants in the area were particularly hard hit due to tensions that had been brewing between blacks and Koreans for some time.

By May 2, the 20,000 federal troops sent into Los Angeles brought order back to the area, but black, white, and Asian residents all said the police came too late and their response was insufficient. The property destruction from the rioting was estimated at more than $550 billion. Fifty-three people died in the violence, making this the deadliest riot in U.S. history. Two thousand people were injured, 3,800 buildings were destroyed, and 10,000 other structures were burned, vandalized, or looted.

Other major U.S. cities broke into riots while Los Angeles burned. Atlanta, Georgia, Seattle, Washington, and New York City all experienced violent disturbances. San Francisco, where more than 100 downtown businesses were damaged and 1,500 people were arrested, suffered more damage than any place outside of Los Angeles.

reality today of cities that offer finance and services jobs [that are] ill-matched to the populations who live [there].

And we ask, why are our cities smoldering?

Perhaps it has to do with the new face of poverty. Geographically isolated, economically depressed, racially segregated, cities have become warehouses of the poor. We now have more than two million families who are poor despite having an adult member in the household working a full-time week. One out of every five children in America is born in poverty; one out of every three Latino children in the United States is born into poverty; and one out of every two African American children in the United States—fifty percent, flip a coin—is born in poverty. And we ask, why are our cities smoldering?

Perhaps it has to do with the isolation of neighborhoods and the way people are forced to live. The economic crisis of cities is **exacerbated** in poor neighborhoods so that low-income families don't have access to the necessities the rest of us take for granted.

When they want to cash a check, they're forced to go to check-cashing outlets which often charge **gouging** rates; when they want to shop for groceries, they may have to travel miles to a major supermarket; when their children go to school, they often go to **dilapidated** schools that are outright dangerous; when they go to health clinics, they sometimes have no substitute but the **trauma center** of the public hospital.

When urban experts review this **litany** of realities, they reserve their harshest criticism for the role of the federal government reinforcing and exacerbating these terrible trends. Perhaps the clearest observation that I can bring you after the first two months on the job is that the federal government itself must change its way of doing business.

Large public housing developments have concentrated the poorest of the poor in housing that is overly dense, poorly designed, badly built and located in isolated, segregated neighborhoods. The preference rules for tenants assure that those with the worst-case needs are concentrated in such public housing. And our income-targeting rules enable only very low-income families to be eligible for federal housing assistance, **impeding** any economic mixing, the kind of mixing that makes possible role models and working families mixed with our very poor.

Cost **containment** and other rules of the past decade have assured that when we do build **subsidized** housing, it looks like subsidized housing, making the location and the siting of affordable housing a near-impossible task because people don't want it in their neighborhoods.

Fair housing laws have been enforced with little vigor or commitment despite **pervasive** evidence of discrimination in both the rental and the mortgage markets.

exacerbated: made worse.

gouging: excessive; extremely overcharging.

dilapidated: run-down.

trauma center: emergency room.

litany: list.

impeding: making difficult.

containment: the act of keeping under control or within certain limits.

subsidized: government-funded.

pervasive: widespread.

Regulations governing the affordable housing activities of Fannie Mae and Freddie Mac ... have been virtually ignored. ["Fannie Mae" and "Freddie Mac" are nicknames for two government-supported loan programs, the Federal National Mortgage Association, or FNMA, and the Federal Home Loan Mortgage Corporation, or FHLMC, that help people who are interested in buying a house.] And there's a total lack of coordination between HUD and other federal organizations. Within HUD itself a crazy-quilt of **disparate** programs have emerged, each supported by separate **constituencies** with little relation or connectedness.

So where do we go from here? Well, the **magnitude** of our urban problems and of our federal failures has helped paralyze the federal government and stifle **innovative** thinking. Yet the cost of doing nothing or doing something that responds to the wrong problem is vast, almost **incalculable.**

Los Angeles, in almost biblical terms, is a signpost, a guide post, a warning that America has to deal with its cities or its cities ultimately will seek vengeance. Over the past two months we've been engaged in an effort at HUD to set a framework for addressing the ills of urban America. It's not an urban policy, but a work in progress. And I regard today as a kind of progress report.

Our task has been to redefine our mission, ask what should HUD be doing in the 1990s, in the environment of urban America as we know it today? What are our priorities? What are our goals?

This has been an effort that we have attempted to make inclusive, bringing people together from across the department and from outside the department. And what has emerged after weeks of dialogue and interaction and listening and reflection is the beginnings of what I hope is a change in how we think about our cities and ourselves.

We've identified three themes, or values, which pull together what we stand for at HUD. They are, first, a commitment to the spirit of community; secondly, a commitment to economic lift and creating a ladder of opportunity; and, thirdly, a commitment to confront the behaviors that **ravage** our society—racism and the self-destructive patterns of life,

disparate: different.

constituencies: groups of supporters.

magnitude: size.

innovative: creative.

incalculable: incapable of being figured out or determined.

ravage: destroy.

behaviors which go to the heart of America's social contract of rights and responsibilities.

First, community. We hear that word "community" used in many ways. To some it means a physical place, to others it means a spirit of common bonds, to the new communitarians it means a specific **consensus** on how individual rights are balanced against the larger good.

But what does it mean for our nation's cities in modern terms, and their relationship with a large Washington bureaucracy? Well, we know what community is not. It's not streets darkened by the shadows of vacant shells of buildings, a street where no one goes without fear of sudden and vicious attack, and where no one will help. It's not public housing where children die in the crossfire of rival gangs, and where security guards crouch around staircases to avoid surprising the drug sentries with Uzis, posted at the end of the halls. It's not neighborhoods where everyone, young and old, 3-year-olds and 73-year-olds, are on their own. It's not decision-making where someone else—planners, architects, city officials, federal bureaucrats, housing authority managers—calls the tune.

What is community? It's a place where housing has been built with poor people that is as functional, as sturdy, as dignified, as attractive as in a nice suburb—in a central city neighborhood.... It's a place where activists have gained the respect of the city government and turned the city's attentions to their priorities—children.... It's a place where church parishes have served as the focal point for ... housing....

The common themes? Neighborhood organizing, strong institutions, local planning, and experts in partnership. And a government that respects community, that is organized to help communities, that **facilitates** the efforts of communities, that is not afraid to say that it will cost something, but not as much as we will pay for neglect, and that uses its resources where they matter the most.

It's important in a department like ours to recognize that the federal government, and certainly the five thousand people who work in the headquarters of HUD in Washington, never build one single building, one single house, with their hands. We must rely on people in communities—nonprofit

consensus: agreement.
facilitates: encourages, promotes.

organizations, community development corporations. The thrust of our efforts must be to create a department that enables communities to be masters of their own destinies, places where people can talk to each other and conduct a civic dialogue....

Secondly, we must **infuse** in our programs a sense of upward lift. It's not good enough to concentrate on **static** policies that maintain people. We must infuse into everything we do ... a sense of lift. Our business is not just to create housing but to make of housing a platform from which we create opportunities for people, opportunities to go from homelessness to rental housing, from public housing to homeownership, opportunities to go from a public housing experience without a job, without training, without education, to self-sufficiency....

I had a sad experience the week before last in Atlanta.... I was walking through a housing project and across the street noticed a man, his wife and three little children.... I walked across the street to visit with them....

And I talked to the man. He described his occupation. He's a roofer who works on commercial roofing projects. And then he said something that made me pause. He said, "I come by every afternoon to visit my family." He and his family are not separated ..., yet he explained to me he came by every afternoon after work, every afternoon, to visit his children ... because the rules of public housing make it impossible for him to live in the unit with his family because their income would rise so quickly that they wouldn't be able to stay in that unit.

Now, that's the kind of circumstance, repeated too many times in our cities, where we've created **Catch-22 rules and regulations** that crush the lifting opportunities for people to make something of their lives. I've described one instance from public housing. You know of similar dysfunctions in other parts of our system of support and service that we must change....

Third, and finally, let me say we at HUD must do an honest and truthful job of speaking to the most devastating division in American life, and that is race. Both sides of the racial divide must speak to each other truthfully across the chasm.

infuse: introduce throughout.

static: unchanging, rigid.

Catch-22 rules and regulations: policies that, if followed as intended, bring about unintended results that are the reverse of or counteract the policies' intentions.

Cisneros at work: "Los Angeles, in almost biblical terms, is a signpost, a guide post, a warning that America has to deal with its cities or its cities ultimately will seek vengeance."

engage: involve.

subordination: being placed in an inferior or less important rank or position.

We must speak about race and what it continues to do to American life. Denying people opportunity on the basis of nothing other than skin color—access to rental housing or to homeownership or to bank loans or insurance or the other essentials of being able to make it in American life—is wrong....

These are the circumstances of race in America. They're real. They exist. We don't like to acknowledge them. They create the circumstances that are impossible to overcome with governmental programs unless we **engage** the American people in broader discussion.

There are also other realities on the other side of the racial divide, another set of behaviors, those which have been bred by chronic **subordination**, those who have been bred by the isolation of ghetto life, those patterns of behavior that result in crime, result in dissolved families, that result in the reality of the wrongs **perpetrated** on children, the shortened childhoods that result in chronic and measurable depression and trauma in the lives of little children.

What we must do is work to change our own policies so that we can encourage people to see both sides of the contract that is rights and responsibilities—the right to an education but the responsibility to study, the right to decent and safe housing but the responsibility to maintain and improve it, the right to live in secure and safe communities but the responsibility to take a part in citizenship and improving them.

What can a federal department do? Well, it can identify and eliminate the structural and institutional barriers to equality of opportunity; it can fight crime and drugs and gangs and antisocial behavior, discourage teen pregnancy, create safe schools. But in order to do this a government must reinvent itself so that all of its arms and branches are working together, so that they make sense as they come together in a local community.... It's what we will continue to work on....

In the final analysis, we're all in this together, all Americans in all our communities, from Boston [Massachusetts] in the East to Santa Monica in Los Angeles in the west where the golden rays of the sun set, from the canyons of Manhattan [New York City] to communities on the edge of the canyons of Arizona—all races, all incomes, this **amalgam** that is peoples and traditions and heritage.

Let me close my remarks by recalling the words of the American poet, Archibald MacLeish, who in his poem "A Letter to the American People" wrote this—and I will close with his thought. He said:

> This, this is our land, this is our people,
> This that is neither a land nor a race. We must reap
> The wind here in the grass for our souls' harvest;
> Here we must eat our salt or our bones starve.
> Here we must live or live only as shadows.
> This is our race, we that have none, that have had
> Neither the old walls nor the voices around us,
> This is our land, this is our ancient ground—
> The raw earth, the mixed bloods and the strangers,

perpetrated: committed.
amalgam: combination, blend.

The different eyes, the wind, and the heart's change.
These we will not leave though the old call us.
This is our country-earth, our blood, our kind.
[Here we will live our years till the earth blind us—.]

We're all in this together—and we have a lot of work to do....

99

Cisneros won high praise for his efforts as HUD secretary. To reform the agency, he trimmed the staff, suggested program mergers or cuts, and stimulated creative ways of thinking. By giving the department a new sense of purpose and direction, he boosted morale among employees. Cisneros accomplished this while dealing with huge budget cuts aimed at drastically reducing HUD's size and the scope of its activities.

During his time in office, Cisneros helped the urban poor across the nation. He addressed the problem of crime in public housing projects by looking into legal ways to ban guns from all HUD buildings. He also ordered the demolition of rundown or abandoned public housing complexes in more than twenty cities so that they don't serve as hangouts for criminals. In addition, he tackled racial discrimination complaints involving HUD properties and projects. And he struggled to eliminate the practice of concentrating low-income people in inner-city projects. As part of a program he called "Moving to Opportunity," Cisneros laid the groundwork for programs that make public housing available in all kinds of neighborhoods, including middle-class and upper-middle-class suburban areas.

In 1995, the American Planning Association officially recognized Cisneros's attempts to reform HUD and refocus its mission by presenting him with its distinguished leadership award in honor of his dedication to the field of planning and his commitment to principles of fair housing.

Optimism Despite Frustration

Cisneros was very honest about how frustrating his job could be, particularly because there was little freedom to make major changes. He explained to a reporter for Time magazine, "You can't move this massive machinery or relate it to massive machinery in other departments real easily. You move with concrete blocks tied to your arms and legs. I can't believe how **gridlocked** the system is, how it runs counter to common sense sometimes, how **irrelevant** it is to things that are happening out in the country."

Racial issues were the foremost concern of Cisneros's career as public official in San Antonio and as the head of HUD. "I truly believe in my heart the country is in trouble on this agenda," he said in 1994. "Race. Class. Poverty. Cities. It is so clear when you try to understand the dynamics of what's happening in a city that people are making decisions of all kinds—housing patterns, school choice— based on race. I really think it's the great unresolved question of American life. And we can't fix our cities without addressing this question."

Personal matters led to difficulties for Cisneros. In July 1994, a former girlfriend filed suit against him, claiming that he had gone back on a promise to pay her $4,000 a month in support money. The affair itself was not news. Cisneros had publicly admitted to it in 1988 and acknowledged the problems it had caused in his marriage. (It was a factor in his 1989 decision to leave politics.) Neither was it a secret that he had agreed to help support the woman. At issue was the amount of money he reportedly gave her.

In late 1994, FBI agents who conducted background interviews with Cisneros after he was nominated to be HUD secretary indicated he had misled them about the payments, leading to a Justice Department investigation. Responding to news of this decision in March 1995, Cisneros predicted that he would eventually be cleared of all wrongdoing and vowed to remain in his job "and fight for this department." Meanwhile, he reached an out-of-court settlement with his former girlfriend in May 1995.

On November 21, 1996, on the heels of Bill Clinton's reelection as president, Cisneros announced that he was resigning his position at HUD. He told a New York Times interviewer that it was strictly a matter of "personal financial calculation."

gridlocked: stalled, jammed up.

irrelevant: not applicable; having no bearing on.

Sources

Books

Cisneros, Henry G., *The Entrepreneurial City,* Ballinger, 1986.

Contemporary Newsmakers: 1987 Cumulation, Gale, 1988.

Interwoven Destinies: The Cities and the Nation, edited by Henry G. Cisneros, Norton, 1993.

Gillies, John, *Señor Alcalde: A Biography of Henry Cisneros,* Dillon Press, 1988.

Henry, Christopher E., *Henry Cisneros,* Chelsea House, 1995.

Representative American Speeches: 1982–1983, edited by Owen Peterson, Wilson, 1983.

Representative American Speeches: 1985–1986, edited by Owen Peterson, Wilson, 1986.

Periodicals

Detroit Free Press, "HUD Secretary Builds Hope," August 3, 1994; "Independent Counsel to Probe Housing Secretary," March 15, 1995; "Vow to Stay Put Doesn't Surprise Cisneros' Friends," March 16, 1995; "Cisneros Gave GOP a Head Start on Cutting HUD, Hurting Poor" (column), March 19, 1995, p. 6F; "Cisneros Fights to Save Housing Agency as Many in Congress Reach for the Plug," April 7, 1995; "HUD Boss Cisneros Settles With Ex-Mistress," May 20, 1995, p. 2A.

Detroit News, "HUD Chief Proposes Major Cuts," December 15, 1994, p. 15A; "Cisneros Busily Reinvents HUD's Public Housing Policy" (syndicated column by William Raspberry), January 9, 1995, p. 7A; "Cisneros Won't Quit Despite Probe," March 15, 1995, p. 5A.

Grand Rapids Press (Grand Rapids, MI), "Red Tape Stifling HUD, Cisneros Says," May 3, 1994, p. A5.

Mother Jones, "Cisneros' Cross," March/April 1993, pp. 11–12.

Nation's Cities Weekly, "Cisneros Warns of Big Changes in HUD Programs," December 19, 1994; "Cisneros Says a New, Improved HUD Will Better Serve Families," March 20, 1995, p. 6.

Newsweek, "San Antonio: Putting Family First," September 14, 1987, p. 8; "'I Am Not Perfect,'" October 24, 1988, p. 25; "An Affair to Forget," September 26, 1994, p. 45.

New York Times, "Secretary Proposes Reshaping HUD to Save It," March 21, 1995, p. A19; "Housing Secretary Resigns, Citing Financial Pressures," November 22, 1996, p. A12.

Time, "'They Said I'd Get Used to It,'" December 6, 1993, p. 31.

U.S. News and World Report, "Fixing Disasters and Doing Penance," February 21, 1994, pp. 30–31; "A New City-Suburbs Hookup," July 18, 1994.

Additional information for this profile was taken from the following Knight-Ridder/Tribune News Service releases: "Cisneros Wants to Move the Poor Out of the Ghetto and In with the Rest of Us," July 12, 1994; "Henry Cisneros Story Is an American Tragedy," March 16, 1995.

Joseph A. Fernandez

1935–

Puerto Rican educator and organization executive

In January 1990, Joseph A. Fernandez accepted what many consider to be the toughest assignment in U.S. public education—that of heading the New York City school system. It is a job that involves overseeing the education of nearly a million students in an often troubled urban environment. But the energetic and strong-willed Fernandez looked forward to the challenge. The no-nonsense reformer led people to believe that if anyone could bring necessary changes to the school system, he could.

Early Life

Fernandez, the son of Puerto Rican immigrants, is a native New Yorker born and raised in the East Harlem district of the city. During his own youth, he wasn't the least bit interested in education. He was expelled from parochial school after the tenth grade for missing too many days of class, and he soon dropped out of the public school to which he had transferred. He then spent his days hanging around with a gang of neighborhood toughs for whom drugs, petty crimes, and street brawls were commonplace.

It wasn't long before Fernandez realized that he had to find a way out of East Harlem or risk going to jail—or worse. So he joined the U.S. Air Force at the age of seventeen. He spent the next four years in Japan and Korea and studied for his high school equivalency diploma in his spare time. After being discharged from the service in 1956, Fernandez married his childhood sweetheart and continued his education at New York's Columbia University, where he majored in mathematics. But when his infant son developed respiratory problems in the late 1950s and doctors suggested a change in climate, he moved his family to Miami, Florida. There Fernandez worked his way through the University of Miami, obtaining his bachelor's degree in 1963.

A Public Educator in Florida

Fernandez's first teaching job was as a math instructor at a suburban Miami, Florida, high school. Within just a year, he was chair of the math department. His ultimate goal was to move into administration, however, so he began studying for his master's degree at Florida Atlantic University and taking on extra assignments whenever he could. It was not long before Fernandez's efforts paid off. In 1971, he became a high school assistant principal, and in 1975, he was named principal of Miami Central Senior High, a predominantly black school located in a slum area.

Fernandez quickly made a name for himself at Miami Central. First of all, he introduced a strong new sense of order and discipline in hallways and classrooms where students had always felt free to smoke cigarettes and play loud music on their radios. He made attempts to broaden the faculty's racial base by hiring black teachers and administrators. He also established contact with parents and other members of the community in order to boost their involvement in the school. He even had trees planted around the building.

In 1977, Fernandez was named director of community services for Florida's Dade County schools. (Miami is located in Dade County.) He continued to move up the ranks, becoming an assistant superintendent in 1985 (the same year he earned his doctoral degree in education) and chief deputy to the superintendent the following year. Finally, in May 1987, the former dropout realized his dream when he was offered the Dade County superintendent's job. The promotion put him in charge of the nation's fourth-largest public school system.

Reforming the Dade County Public School System

Over the next two years, Fernandez made huge strides to improve public education in Dade County. He removed or transferred nearly fifty principals he felt were not performing up to his standards. He launched special Saturday classes in computers and music. He set up special "magnet schools" in the arts, computers, broadcasting, and other professional fields. He repaired broken equipment and fixed up buildings inside and out. And, making use of the space he had persuaded several companies to donate, Fernandez created satellite schools near major Miami employers so that children could attend classes not far from where their parents worked.

Above all, Fernandez fought for what is called "school-based management." Instead of concentrating all the schools' decision-making powers at the main office for the entire district, the idea of this program is to give committees of teachers, principals, and parents at each school the right to figure out what is best for their particular needs. These individual committees may determine who will work at their school, what subjects will be taught and how they will be taught, and how the money in their budget will be spent.

Fernandez and his ambitious Dade County experiment soon attracted national attention. In mid-1989, New York City public school officials approached him about the head job there. He hesitated at first but finally accepted their offer in late September.

Shaking Up the New York City Public School System

Even though he was not officially scheduled to take office until January 1990, Fernandez plunged right into his new assignment. Beginning in October, he held one meeting after another with state and local leaders not only from the field of education but also from business, politics, labor, and other areas. Fernandez also read stacks of reports to familiarize himself with the New York City system. Now and then, he released public statements to keep residents updated on his findings.

By the start of the new year, Fernandez had come up with a plan for reforming the district. And New Yorkers had a new hero—a blunt, tough-talking guy who really seemed capable of delivering on a promise to shake things up. As Fernandez himself remarked to a reporter for New York magazine, "I'm very impatient with people ... who say things can't be done because we've never tried them that way before. To move a large bureaucracy, sometimes you've got to kick people in the ass."

In his first year or so on the job, Fernandez did just that. He trimmed and reorganized the office staff at Board of Education headquarters. He got rid of the practice of "building tenure," which had made it impossible to transfer a principal to another school without his or her consent. He dismantled the Board of Examiners, a teacher certification agency that had long been regarded as incompetent and inefficient. He challenged the independence of the city's notoriously corrupt local school boards by threatening to take them over if they did not cooperate with him. He tackled the huge backlog in building maintenance projects. He campaigned to reduce the power of the custodians' union, whose labor contract strictly limited the off-hours use of school buildings. In addition, Fernandez was able to establish his school-based management program in about ten percent of the city's schools.

At the classroom level, too, Fernandez made waves. For example, he set up a panel to recommend changes in the subjects teachers covered and how they taught them. He had another group look into ways of dealing with overcrowding. He also took steps to have schools play a bigger role in combating drugs, violence, racial tension, and other social problems. He even managed to win approval for a condom distribution plan he hoped would help decrease

Fernandez speaking: "There is no American education—now or in the future—without its Great City Schools."

the teenage pregnancy rate and slow down the spread of AIDS and other sexually-transmitted diseases.

The "Rainbow Curriculum"

By 1992, however, Fernandez's power struggles with school-board officials over these and other issues had turned into an all-out war that threatened to overshadow his considerable achievements. Tensions finally came to a head over his proposed "Rainbow Curriculum." This special teacher's guide for elementary grades emphasized multiculturalism and encouraged tolerance of gays and lesbians. Thirty-one of the city's thirty-two local school boards eventually accepted Fernandez's plan without too much controversy. But a group of angry parents from the Queens district—backed by the Roman Catholic Church—charged that the Rainbow Curriculum was not education but "propaganda." They specifically condemned the section on homosexuality as an unacceptable violation of their religious and moral values.

Fernandez fought back, but in February 1993, he ran out of time. At the end of a day-long public hearing, during which dozens of people stood up to defend him, he watched as the central board voted not to renew his contract as head of the New York City public school system. Afterward, Fernandez told reporters, "Yes, I have made mistakes. But I have fought for children. I will always put their welfare ahead of political or special interests."

In July 1993, Fernandez assumed the presidency of the Council of the Great City Schools, or CGCS. The CGCS is a Washington, D.C.-based coalition of the nation's largest urban public school systems. Its goal is to improve inner-city education in the United States. Later that year, on September 7, Fernandez shared his views on the state of American public education and discussed the CGCS's goals in a speech before the National Press Club in Washington, D.C.

" "

I have been asked to speak to you today about the state of American education and what it will take to pull our nation's schools up to a point at which we are justifiably proud—a point at which you have no choice but to write glowing reports about our conduct and our results.

I cannot come at this topic of American education by any other direction than through the cities. There is no American education—now or in the future—without its Great City Schools.

Nowhere does the national **resolve** to strengthen our children's education face a tougher test than in our inner cities. Every problem is more **pronounced** there, every solution harder to **implement**. The **litany** is now familiar to you: poverty, drug abuse, family instability or no families at all, aging buildings and facilities, dropouts, teen pregnancy, poor health care, violence, racism and bigotry, AIDS, limited-English language **proficiency**, disabilities and malnutrition. And efforts to address these must be conducted in an atmosphere of enormous political, **demographic**, economic, cultural, social and religious complexity and diversity—usually with precious few dollars or backing.

It is often asked, however, why anyone should care. Why should the larger community want to help solve problems that are so **daunting**, so complex, remote, costly, **entrenched** and **divisive?** The reasons are actually uncomplicated.

First, it is in America's best self-interest to care. Urban children take up too large a portion of America's total children to expect that the country can survive without them. Of the nation's 15,000 school districts, our largest 50 city school systems educate about 38 percent of the nation's limited-English proficient children, 25 percent of the nation's poor children and 14 percent of its disabled children. About 40 percent of our nation's African American, Latino and Asian American children are educated each day in our major city schools. Our total enrollment ... would qualify us as the 80th largest of the 160 countries in the United Nations....

Second, unless action is taken to meet the challenges of urban education, our problems will soon enough become

resolve: determination.

pronounced: strongly marked or noticeable.

implement: put into effect.

litany: list.

proficiency: skill.

demographic: relating to the statistical characteristics of the human population.

daunting: challenging, difficult.

entrenched: established.

divisive: inclined to create disunity or disagreement.

prevalent in all but the most **elite** of the nation's schools. Finally, the country has a moral **imperative**, grounded in our own Constitution, to strive for individual justice and equality for its citizens, and education is the soundest way of endowing those rights.

The nation cannot afford to play a game of containment with us, hoping that our problems will stay inside the city limits. It is already too late for that and besides, we are too large a portion of the country and its future for such a strategy to work. And for our part, we cannot continue to pretend that we can do the job alone. The problems we face in our schools are so immense and so entangled with the problems of our nation and its cities, that we cannot hope to meet them ourselves. Nor can the nation realistically hope to meet its own goals and stay economically competitive without us.

It is how I come at the state of American education and what must be done to save it—through the cities.

Let me take a minute to describe where we are in urban education, let you draw your own conclusions about where American schools must be given what I have just described, then talk about what I think should be done and what we are doing specifically. It is a good news/bad news story. Let me give it to you in equal measure, goal by goal....

Fernandez then quoted statistics on topics such as preschool education and readiness for school, dropout rates, test scores, teachers and the teaching profession, school and employment opportunities for students after they graduate, safety, drug abuse, and the condition of school buildings and equipment. He described these statistics as "frightening" and "troubling" because they showed that urban schools usually lag far behind the nation's schools as a whole. As he pointed out, however, at least some of the differences could be blamed on social forces (poverty, teen pregnancy, drug abuse, inadequate health care, and so on) that were beyond the urban schools' control.

Fernandez was also quick to note that not all of the news from the urban schools was bad. He explained that many were experiencing positive developments in some areas, including declining dropout rates. This, he said, indicated "we are doing something right." He then continued his speech.

prevalent: widespread.

elite: the most choice part; superior, privileged.

imperative: duty; obligation.

Joseph A. Fernandez

But the promising signs cannot mask a serious problem, not just for urban schools but for the American society. I think we need to keep squarely in mind that these are not problems of kids—these are problems of adults. It is adults who manufacture and distribute the guns, who produce and show the violence on television, and who abuse and beat our children—kids don't do this, adults do.

What does all this add up to? What should we be doing to save our schools? My hunch is that we as a nation are doing better with our public school system than most people realize and what most critics suggest. But even if the critics are entirely wrong, there is no reason to think that our schools nationally shouldn't be substantially improved. Our economic global competitiveness certainly rests on it, as does our domestic **tranquility.**

And here is where I am brought back to urban schools and their centrality to our national purpose and our desire to lead the world educationally.

Let me start at home base with urban schools themselves and what they could be doing better.... Some of them actually cost surprisingly little money. Here is my "Top Ten List" for improving urban schools and improving the nation:

1. *Urban schools not only need to be more open to educational reform but actually lead it.* There are many cases where they have.... In fact, much of the reform movement that has now been somewhat **co-opted** by the states grew out of **initiatives** and experiments in city schools. Yet, urban education is often viewed as entrenched, immovable, self-protective and sluggish with bureaucracy. In too many instances this is the case, but the reformers among us can easily serve as models to the rest. It is, in fact, good for us to reform and it is better yet for us to reform ourselves—urban schools are in the best position to do that—and we do want to.

2. *Urban schools need to increase their **collaborative** arrangements with the community at large.* I said earlier that I thought that closer collaboration with other public and community agencies was necessary to deliver comprehensive services to our children. I will expand that here to include the churches, business, the media, the suburbs, the mayors and others. It also means keeping our facilities open to the community and designing our programs around the schedules and needs of

tranquility: peace.
co-opted: taken over.
initiatives: introductory steps.
collaborative: cooperative.

"Goals 2000:" Politics and American Education

In 1983, the U.S. government released a study of the country's public schools entitled "A Nation at Risk." It painted a disturbing portrait of students who were unprepared to meet the needs of their own society and unable to compete with their peers in Japan and Europe. The findings shocked most Americans and sparked efforts to reform the education system and hold schools and teachers responsible for improving student performance.

Six years later, President George Bush initiated an effort to formulate a set of national goals for American schools. In September 1989, he brought together the governors of all fifty states for this purpose. Since he targeted the year 2000 as the deadline for meeting these goals, his program came to be known as "Goals 2000."

Bush and the nation's governors later announced that they had reached agreement on six specific education goals they wanted to achieve by the end of the decade. First of all, they pledged to work with schools to make sure all children start kindergarten ready to learn. They also declared that students leaving grades 4, 8, and 12 should prove a thorough knowledge for their level of certain basic subjects (English, math, science, foreign languages, civics, the arts, history, and geography) and that U.S. students in general should lead the world in science and math. In addition, they aimed to boost the high school graduation rate to at least 90 percent (up from a 1990 rate of about 83 percent) and stated that every adult should know how to read. Finally, they vowed to make all schools free of drugs and violence.

Congress formally adopted these goals as part of U.S. policy in 1993. The new president, Bill Clinton, signed the Goals 2000 program into law in 1994 after adding two more goals: more professional

the community, not our own. As far as I am concerned, urban education cannot solve the problems faced by society alone. That does not mean that we shouldn't be involving ourselves in issues no one else will touch; it does mean that we are asking for help from all quarters now that we have accepted the challenge.

3. *Urban schools need to stop treating parents as the enemy.* Urban education has amazingly few friends. Not only can it not afford to **alienate** anyone, it must develop better strategies to reach out to parents on whatever terms or grounds they find themselves. We should not only be treating them as our number-one customer but also our number-one ally....

4. *Urban school leaders need to stop chewing themselves up on political agendas.* I am not sure how to do this but there are examples galore in every city where the fractured and desper-

alienate: create an unfriendly distance between people (or groups of people).

Joseph A. Fernandez

development programs for teachers and increased parental involvement in schools.

While the goals themselves have generated little controversy, putting them into effect has been a problem from the very beginning. For example, there is an ongoing conflict between the federal government and the states over who should set the standards for national educational excellence, what those standards should be, and who should pay for putting them into effect.

Heated battles have also erupted over what students should actually be taught. Perhaps the most notable example involves the U.S. and world history standards recommended by a panel of advisors from the University of California in Los Angeles. A number of people object to what they call a liberal bias among the panelists. For example they object to the portrayal of the United States as the aggressor in international events such as World War II. These same critics have also accused the panelists of playing up the contributions of women and minorities while ignoring those of white men.

Many have questioned whether poor urban districts can be expected to do as well as their richer suburban neighbors in light of the differences in their budgets. The issue becomes a stumbling block when others point out that letting some schools "off the hook" when it comes to meeting the national standards makes the act of setting goals virtually meaningless.

Given these and other challenges, the Goals 2000 program has come to be seen by many as a noble but impossible experiment. But the future of the Goals 2000 program is far from settled. Republican budget-cutters in Congress very nearly eliminated its federal funding in the 1997 spending plan. In the end, however, almost $500 million was set aside to continue the program until 1998.

ate nature of the community is leading educational leadership into **gridlock** that makes Washington seem pale in comparison. Part of what is going on can be traced to the extreme poverty and needs of the urban community badly wanting a quality education and a future, but the desperation has begun to turn inward [and destroy efforts for administrative progress].

5. *Urban schools need to do everything they can to stop sorting and tracking kids, and to raise the standards and expectations for their children.* Too much of schooling, not just in the cities but everywhere, is caught up in the **unwitting** sorting and tracking of students by ability or perceived ability. Too often the results lead only to sorting by race, sex and income and have nothing to do with the abilities or efforts of our children.

6. *Urban school boards, administrators and teachers should think more positively of their work.* People working in urban

gridlock: an unmovable jam.
unwitting: unintended.

schools have listened so long to people bashing them and their work that I think they have started to believe and act on it. It has led to a defensiveness about what we do and a corresponding reflex instinct when we are criticized. In fact, most of the people I know in urban education are some of the most talented, dynamic and intelligent people working anywhere.

7. *Urban schools need to downsize anything that touches children....* I think it is important that we reduce the size of our urban schools, particularly the high schools—even if they are only schools-within-schools. Children need warmth and individual attention to thrive and it is too hard to give it to them with schools the size of factories.

8. *Urban schools need to help break down the artificial barriers between managers and teachers.* Outside of students and parents, teachers should be our best friends in education but often they are not and we sometimes ensure it by how we act. Business has developed some very interesting models for how to establish more collaborative work settings and there is no reason why we shouldn't be looking at testing those in our settings. Education is, after all, a human endeavor where the merits of all our people need to be respected.

9. *Urban schools need to devote more time and effort to professional development, research and strategic planning.* So much of our work in urban education is crisis-oriented that we devote precious little time to planning for anything more than the next board meeting. Because education is a long-term endeavor, we need to plan and think long-term.

10. *Urban schools need to increase, not shy away from, their commitment to and emphasis on multiculturalism.* Urban schools often take a lot of heat for their efforts to celebrate and enhance the diversity of their students and teachers. But urban schools, in fact, are well ahead of a nation that will need to do the same thing very shortly. The nation could take a lesson from us here.

There are also things that I think that the states and the federal government could do to help us. Some of it has to do with money. While I don't think money cures all, I am a firm believer that money matters in schools like it does everywhere else.... Part of that belief rests on the fact that urban schools just don't have the resources of other school systems....

The long and short of it is that America is getting what it's paying for in urban education. I repeat: There is no future for America that fails to include its Great City Schools.

The **disparity** in funding between rich and poor schools is a national disgrace. To date the states have been slow to move to correct the situation without court intervention. But besides pressing to correct these **inequities**, I would urge the states and the governors to urge Congress to help on this front.... The governors should be pressing Congress for a major new education spending initiative or trust fund to help equalize the disparities and to deliver on the opportunity standards that many in Congress are calling for....

Ladies and gentlemen, America's schools have traditionally been at the heart of the communities they serve. As one of our fundamental institutions, public schools have been one of the few places where rich meet poor, the advantaged mingled with the disadvantaged, and where ideally, political, religious, and ethnic boundaries would not exist. As a nation, America has literally entrusted its future to our public schools.

This investment is doubly important in our urban schools, for they form one of the **crucibles** of American democracy. They are, in fact, one of the last frontiers of our democratic ideal. The nation cannot afford to survey our urban landscape—with its difficult terrain—and conclude that conquering our troubles is a lost cause. The year 2000 looms large and near. We—as a nation—cannot arrive there intact without its city kids. The alternatives are too bleak to imagine....

Fernandez left his post with the Council of the Great City Schools in the spring of 1995. Based once again in Florida, he now serves as an independent consultant on education.

Sources

Books

Fernandez, Joseph A., with John Underwood, *Tales Out of School: Joseph Fernandez's Crusade to Rescue American Education*, Little, Brown, 1993.

disparity: contrast, inequality.

inequities: inequalities.

crucibles: places, times, or situations in which many different forces come together and interact to produce change.

Periodicals

Chicago Tribune, "Bush, Governors OK School Goals," February 27, 1990; "New Standards for American Schools," October 25, 1993; "Clinton Signs Major Education Reform Bill," April 1, 1994; "Education Standards Debate Pits U.S., States," March 23, 1995.

Detroit Free Press, "NYC Schools Chief Ousted Over Sex Education Policy," February 11, 1993, p. 3A; "For School Systems in Big Cities, the Top Job Is a Revolving Door," March 7, 1993, p. 6F.

Detroit News, "Angry New York Parents Protest First Grade Class on Gay Lifestyle," December 8, 1992.

Grand Rapids Press, "NYC Won't Renew School Chief's Contract," February 11, 1993, p. A5; "Goals 2000 Is Under the Republicans' Ax," September 20, 1996, p. A8.

Hispanic, "King of the Blackboard Jungle," August 1990.

Nation, "Over the Rainbow," May 10, 1993, pp. 631–36.

Newsweek, "If He Could Make It Here...," December 21, 1992, p. 57; "Who Would Want This Job?" February 22, 1993, pp. 54–56.

New York, "The Report Card on Joe Fernandez," January 22, 1990, pp. 40–46.

New Yorker, "The End of the Rainbow," April 12, 1993, pp. 43–54.

New York Times Magazine, "Fernandez Takes Charge," June 17, 1990.

Reader's Digest, "Can a Former Dropout Save New York's Schools?" October 1990, pp. 78–82.

Time, "Bracing for Perestroika," January 8, 1990, p. 68.

U.S. News and World Report, "Rebel Without a Pause," October 1, 1990, pp. 76–78.

Henry B. Gonzalez

1916–

Mexican American member of the U.S. House of Representatives

Throughout his long and colorful political career, U.S. Representative Henry B. Gonzalez has enjoyed tremendous popularity among voters in his Texas district. Feisty, independent, and unpredictable, this liberal Democrat has always stood up for victims of injustice. He has also been outspokenly critical of underhanded behavior and abuses of power on the part of the federal government. And he is one of only a handful of politicians who consistently steers clear of any ties to special interest groups. In fact, writer Christopher Hitchens once remarked in Harper's magazine that Gonzalez is "one of the few just men to have spent any time at all on the Hill [in Congress]."

Early Life

Gonzalez was born in 1916 in San Antonio, Texas, to parents who had immigrated to the United States from Mexico five years earlier to escape the violent revolution going on there. His father had been a successful politician

"IT IS TIME TO LOOK FORWARD TO THE DAY WHEN THE FARMWORKER CAN SHARE IN THE FRUITS OF HIS LABORS. TODAY, FOR THE SWEAT OFF HIS BROW THAT HE LEAVES IN THE RICH AND ABUNDANT FIELDS AND ORCHARDS WHICH HE HARVESTS HE RECEIVES FOR HIS PART A PITTANCE, A PAT ON THE BACK, AND A PASSPORT TO NOWHERE."

and businessman in his home state of Durango. Once he settled in America, however, the elder Gonzalez became a journalist. He eventually served as the editor of what was then the only Spanish-language newspaper in the country, La Prensa.

Young Henry grew up in a household rich in exciting ideas and discussions but not in material wealth. As a result, he had to work part-time throughout his entire childhood to help support his five brothers and sisters. (He spent whatever spare time he had reading at the local public library.) Gonzalez became familiar with racial prejudice at an early age. His Mexican heritage made him the target of slurs and insults. And, he remembers being barred from "whites only" facilities such as restaurants and swimming pools.

After graduating from high school, Gonzalez attended San Antonio Junior College and then the University of Texas at Austin. His studies in engineering were interrupted, however, when he could not find a job to help pay his expenses. Returning home, he completed his education at St. Mary's University in San Antonio, earning his bachelor's degree and then a law degree in 1943.

During the rest of the 1940s, Gonzalez worked at a variety of jobs. He ran his father's Spanish-English translation service for a while and also acted as a public relations advisor for an insurance firm. He later became the chief probation officer for the county juvenile court system, but resigned after being denied permission to add a black person to his staff. In 1950, Gonzalez was appointed deputy family relocation director for the city of San Antonio's housing authority. In that position, he helped find new homes for families whose slum neighborhoods were scheduled to be torn down.

Enters Politics

In 1950, Gonzalez ran for a seat in the Texas House of Representatives and lost, but he fared better in 1953, when he was elected to the San Antonio City Council. One of his most notable accomplishments as city councilor was sponsoring a law that eliminated segregation in the city's recreational facilities. Three years later, Gonzalez won a seat in the Texas Senate; he was the first Mexican American to serve in that body in more than one hundred years. There he quickly became a very vocal opponent of a series of bills intended to preserve racial segregation.

In 1958, Gonzalez ran an unsuccessful campaign for governor of Texas. He again met with defeat in 1961 when he aimed for the U.S. Senate. But later that year, he won a special election to fill a vacant seat in the U.S. House of Representatives. His victory made him the first Mexican American from Texas ever to serve in that national legislative body.

Gonzalez has represented San Antonio and the surrounding area ever since then, easily winning reelection each time. In fact, over the course of sixteen campaigns, he has never faced an opponent in the Democratic primary. And only six times has he faced an opponent from another party in the general election.

Gonzalez is well known for downplaying his ethnic heritage. He points out that he has attracted support from all voters, not just Hispanics, and therefore has a responsibility to act on the needs and wishes of everyone he represents. This has frequently led to tensions between Gonzalez and some Mexican Americans who would prefer that he take a stronger stand on their behalf.

A Fierce Opponent of the Bracero Bill

During his early years in the U.S. House, Gonzalez was known as a fiery supporter of minority interests. He sponsored legislation on a variety of subjects, including civil rights, adult education and job training, the minimum wage, Puerto Rican rights, and an end to the poll tax (a fee paid to qualify for voting rights). But some of his most vigorous efforts were waged in the battle against extending Public Law 78, a controversial piece of farm labor legislation better known as the Bracero Bill.

Ever since the early 1940s, U.S. law had allowed thousands of Mexican day laborers known as braceros to cross the border for work. (See box on page 102 for more information.) Large vegetable and fruit growers who made use of this source of cheap contract labor to pick their crops strongly supported extending Public Law 78 every time it came up for renewal.

The *Bracero* Program

In 1942, during World War II, the governments of Mexico and the United States reached an agreement on a special program intended to help ease the labor shortage in the United States. Under the terms of this agreement—which became known as Public Law 45 once Congress officially approved it in 1943—unskilled Mexican contract workers known as *braceros* were brought into the country to work on farms and the railroads. The assumption behind the program was that the need for these day laborers was only temporary. Once the war ended, supporters reasoned, the labor shortage would end and so, too, would the *bracero* program and Public Law 45.

But the *braceros* quickly became a vital part of the agricultural economy in the Southwest and the West. Growers repeatedly persuaded Congress to extend the life of the program past World War II (which ended in 1945) by claiming that they still faced problems finding people able and willing to work. The outbreak of the Korean War in 1950 added to the need, and in 1951 Congress passed Public Law 78, which renewed and expanded the *bracero* program.

Growers were able to convince Congress to keep renewing Public Law 78 throughout the 1950s. By the end of the decade, more than 400,000 *braceros* entered the United States every year at harvest time to work in the fields.

In 1963, the question of renewing the Bracero Bill once again came up in Congress. In previous years, legislators had approved such renewals with little debate. But this time around, it ran into fierce opposition from Mexican Americans, organized labor, and members of various religious and civic groups. They insisted that because braceros were unprotected under most federal and state laws overseeing wages, working conditions, and other employment-related matters, they were often underpaid and otherwise mistreated by growers and labor contractors.

Leading the charge in Congress against extending Public Law 78 was Gonzalez. Time and time again, he took to the floor to condemn it as a "slave labor" bill. Farm workers, he declared, already toiled under conditions "somewhere between civilization and medievalism," and the Bracero Bill made it easy to keep on taking advantage of them.

These impassioned words helped defeat the measure in Congress in early 1964. But as Gonzalez and others well knew, the end of Public Law 78 did not mean the end of

*injustice for America's migrant workers. In fact, the years that followed saw a tremendous increase in unionization efforts among farm workers to fight ongoing abuses. (See entries on **César Chávez** and **Dolores Huerta** for more information.)*

Gonzalez therefore continued to bring the issue before his colleagues in Congress. He demanded improvements in how workers were recruited for jobs, how much they were paid, and under what kinds of conditions they had to work. On April 5, 1965, Gonzalez angrily responded to attempts by growers to bring back the bracero *program via new legislation. His remarks are reprinted here from the* Congressional Record, *89th Congress, 1st Session, Volume 111, Part 5, U.S. Government Printing Office, 1965.*

Mexican farm workers enter the United States under the bracero program, 1948

"

Any reasonable and literate person ought to be able at this late date to read the congressional handwriting on the wall. The 88th Congress, in its wisdom, decided that time had run out on the "temporary" *bracero* program, and that it should expire at the end of 1964. The president [Lyndon B. Johnson], in his wisdom, signed into law that decision and thereby obligated himself and his administration to carry it out. The 89th Congress, in its wisdom, is not going to buckle under the pressures that have been generated to revive the discredited *bracero* program. The president is not going to buckle under those pressures, and the secretary of labor is not going to buckle under those pressures.

The *bracero* program is as dead as the dodo bird. It is time for the leadership in the farm industry to stop looking for cheap, captive sources of labor. It is time for the leadership in the farm industry to exert itself in a positive and constructive and progressive manner in order to help solve the farm labor problem. It is time to look forward to the day when the farmworker can share in the fruits of his labors. Today, for the sweat off his brow that he leaves in the rich and abundant fields and orchards which he harvests he receives for his part a **pittance**, a pat on the back, and a passport to nowhere. Justice, decency, and humanity demand that progress not pass him over for yet another generation.

Farmworkers under state and federal labor laws are **relegated to** a second-class citizenship. Millions of Americans are protected by minimum wage, maximum hours, and child-labor laws. Millions of Americans are protected by workmen's compensation and unemployment compensation. Millions of Americans are assured decent housing for their families, good schools for their children, health and medical facilities. Not so the farmworker.

Historically, labor laws were designed to regulate and set a floor under the working conditions of employees in industry and trade. At first these laws were limited to specific types or places of employment or to certain industries. Some of these laws have been extended to cover employment generally, but

pittance: a very small amount of money.

relegated to: assigned.

usually agricultural employment is expressly excluded. Even where no specific exclusion exists and the laws could cover farmworkers, they often are not applied.

Gonzalez with John F. Kennedy and Lyndon B. Johnson

For example, in only eight states and Puerto Rico are there laws or regulations which specifically regulate farm labor contractors and crew leaders. Only a few states ... have laws setting safety standards for vehicles used in the transportation of farmworkers, and for the operation of such vehicles. Farm labor camps are regulated as to housing, location, and construction of the camp in thirty states. But in twenty states there is no such regulation. And even in the states where there are laws on this subject, the standards are very limited in most.

Only eleven states, Puerto Rico, and the District of Columbia provide a minimum age for employment of children on farms. This age is fourteen in Connecticut, Alaska, Hawaii, Missouri, Texas, the District of Columbia, and Puerto Rico. In four states the minimum age is twelve. In one state, Utah, the minimum age is ten. **Compulsory** school attendance requires children to attend school, usually to age sixteen, in most states. But in many states the laws permit children under sixteen or even under fourteen to be excused from school in order to work on farms.

In only four states and Puerto Rico do workmen's compensation laws cover all farm employment. Only seventeen states have any specific coverage for farmworkers at all. Only Hawaii and Puerto Rico provide any minimum wage coverage for all farmworkers. Hawaii requires a minimum of $1.25 an hour. Six states have wage payment laws and wage collection laws for farmworkers. Only Hawaii and Puerto Rico specifically cover farmworkers in their unemployment insurance laws. In one state, California, farmworkers are covered by a temporary disability law.

Federal laws **supplement** these deficiencies somewhat. The 88th Congress enacted more laws for the protection of farmworkers than perhaps any other Congress. The Economic Opportunity Act contains provisions for the assistance of migrant farmworkers and for low-income rural families. The Housing Act of 1964 provides for grants to states [and] private nonprofit organizations ... to assist in providing housing and related facilities for domestic farm labor.

Have these laws been utilized for the benefit of farmworkers? What are we doing now to implement them and to pass additional legislation in the area of minimum wages and workmen's compensation? These are the fruitful areas of work and inquiry where the time and energy of the people and the Congress could be well spent.

The farmworker is the forgotten man in the industrial revolution that has benefited almost every other class of worker. Part of the evil inherent in the *bracero* program was that it served to keep the farm industry in a constant state of

compulsory: mandatory, required.

supplement: make up for.

Henry B. Gonzalez

A Mexican man shows his permit to cross the border and work in the fields of South Texas under the bracero program

depression, as far as the workers were concerned. *Braceros* were a cheap source and a captive source of labor. They stifled competition and formed a crutch on which farmers and growers became accustomed to lean. That crutch is gone. It is now time for the farmer and the grower to walk without it, to seek his labor needs in the competitive market, and to give decent wages and working conditions to their employees.

"

Since the 1970s, Gonzalez has turned his attention to other matters. He has, for example, generated some headlines for examining various conspiracy theories in the assassinations of President John F. Kennedy and Martin Luther

King, Jr. During the 1980s, he fought the administration of President Ronald Reagan for more low-cost housing.

Gonzalez returned to the forefront of American politics from 1988 until 1995, when he served as chair of the powerful House Banking, Finance, and Urban Affairs Committee. In this role, he led the widely-publicized investigation into the collapse of hundreds of savings and loan institutions during the late 1980s. His persistent questioning during the hearings revealed the flawed procedures and deceptive deals that resulted in the loss of billions of dollars.

Afterwards, Gonzalez played a key role in drafting a special savings and loan "bailout bill." It tightened government regulations regarding savings and loan institutions and provided money to prosecute the people suspected of wrongdoing in the scandal. Gonzalez's findings ultimately inspired him to take a closer look at the banking industry, too. His goal there was to avoid a similar crisis by putting reforms into effect before any banks were forced to go out of business.

From time to time, Gonzalez has taken stands that some people found controversial. For example, he twice introduced resolutions calling for the impeachment of President Reagan. The first time was in 1983 over the U.S. invasion of the Caribbean island of Grenada. The second time Gonzalez called for Reagan's impeachment was in 1987 for his suspected role in the Iran-Contra scandal. (The president apparently was involved in a secret government deal that took the profits from secret arms sales to Iran to help fund anticommunist rebels in Nicaragua.)

In 1991, Gonzalez used the same tactic against President George Bush. He condemned Bush for going to war against Iraq without congressional approval, and for badly misjudging Iraqi leader Saddam Hussein in the months and even years prior to the invasion. Gonzalez was especially critical of the decision to make advanced weapons technology and materials available to Iraq.

In 1993, Gonzalez received the Philip Hart Public Service Award from the Consumer Federation of America for his "willingness to stand up for the American consumer regard-

less of the odds." In particular, the award mentioned his efforts to reform the banking and savings and loan industries and to improve enforcement of laws against the practice of redlining, or denying mortgages to buyers seeking housing in neighborhoods that are considered poor economic risks. And in 1994, Gonzalez was granted the John F. Kennedy Profile in Courage Award for the many times in his career he has chosen to take an unpopular position and hold firm despite criticism or ridicule.

Sources

Books

Congressional Record, 89th Congress, 1st Session, Volume 111, Part 5, U.S. Government Printing Office, 1965, pp. 6908–9.

Periodicals

Harper's, "No Fool on the Hill," October 1992, pp. 84–96.

Hispanic, "The Paradox of Henry B.: A Look at a Man Who Pulls No Punches, Yet Surprises People Who've Known Him for Years," October 1989.

Mother Jones, "Give 'em Hell, Henry," July/August 1991, pp. 12–13.

Nation, "Beltway Bandits," June 1, 1992, pp. 740–41.

New Republic, "Disregarding Henry," April 11, 1994, pp. 14–17.

Texas Monthly, "The Eternal Challenger," October 1992.

Time, "'A Bunch of Delinquents,'" January 21, 1991, p. 57.

Antonia Hernández

1948–

Mexican American civil rights attorney

"I KNOW ALL TOO WELL THAT IT IS EASIER TO 'CRACK DOWN' ON THE UNDOCUMENTED WORKER, EASIER TO PUNISH THE CHILDREN OF UNDOCUMENTED IMMIGRANTS, EASIER TO ASSUME THAT AGGRESSIVE POSTURE THAN TO DEAL WITH THE ROOT ECONOMIC CAUSES OF THE MIGRATION NORTH."

As president and general counsel (legal advisor) of the Mexican American Legal Defense and Educational Fund (MALDEF), Antonia Hernández is one of the country's most prominent activists. MALDEF is a national civil rights organization based in Los Angeles, California, with regional offices in Washington, D.C.; Chicago, Illinois; San Francisco, California; and San Antonio, Texas. It monitors the ways in which laws and public policy affect Latinos and then works through the court system to fight instances of injustice and inequality. This mission has been of the utmost importance to Hernández ever since she became head of MALDEF in 1985. Of particular interest to her are immigration issues, perhaps because she herself is a native of Mexico and is therefore very familiar with the problems many newcomers face after settling in the United States.

Early Life

Hernández was born in the town of Torreón in the state of Coahuila, located in the north central part of Mexico. She moved to the United States with her family when she was eight years old. They settled in mostly Hispanic East Los Angeles. There she and her five brothers and sisters grew up poor but secure in the love of their parents. All of the children were encouraged to seek higher education and find ways to make their lives meaningful in service to others.

With that goal in mind, young Antonia headed off to the University of California at Los Angeles (UCLA) after high school. There she earned her bachelor's degree in 1970 and a teaching certificate in 1971. Hernández was teaching English as a second language to ghetto youngsters when she came to the realization that she might be able to do more to help her community if she switched professions. So she enrolled in UCLA's law school, her sights set on becoming an attorney and working through the courts for changes that would help Hispanic Americans.

Launches Legal Career

Following her graduation from law school in 1974, Hernández hired on as a staff attorney with the Los Angeles Center for Law and Justice. Her duties there included handling civil as well as criminal cases. Three years later, she became directing attorney of a Los Angeles-area office of the Legal Aid Foundation, which provides legal services to people who don't have enough money to hire a lawyer. In addition to working once again on civil and criminal cases, she worked on behalf of various bills up for consideration in the state legislature.

In 1979, Hernández left her position with Legal Aid for a job in Washington, D.C., as staff counsel to the U.S. Senate Committee on the Judiciary. In this new role, she was responsible for keeping committee members informed about issues involving human rights and immigration. She also gained valuable experience in drafting legislation.

Hernández lost her job in the wake of the 1980 elections, when Republicans gained a majority in the Senate and therefore took charge of the Committee on the Judiciary. But it wasn't long before MALDEF approached her about becoming a staff attorney in the group's Washington office. Hernández then worked her way up through the ranks, *returning to Los Angeles in 1983 to direct the organization's lawsuits on employment issues. In 1985, she was offered the top spot at MALDEF, which she accepted.*

Assumes Control of MALDEF

*At MALDEF, Hernández supervised all pending court cases and advocacy programs and planned the organization's long-range goals and objectives. She has played a key role in a number of MALDEF's major undertakings, including defeating a bill in Congress that would have required Latinos to carry identification cards and challenging questionable school and voting district boundaries. She has also been involved in MALDEF's ongoing efforts to promote **affirmative action** in both the public and the private employment sector.*

Hernández is often called upon by professional, civic, and religious groups to discuss MALDEF's view on issues of particular importance to Latinos. She has delivered talks on subjects such as discrimination, bilingual education, voting rights, and even U.S. Census Bureau policies and statistics. But perhaps the hottest topic she has addressed in recent years is immigration.

In elections held during the fall of 1994, Californians were asked to vote on a bill known as Proposition 187. This controversial measure sought to ban illegal immigrants from benefitting from a wide variety of public services, including public education, welfare, and nonemergency health care. Also under the terms of Proposition 187, doctors, teachers, and others coming into contact with people they thought might be illegal immigrants were required to report their suspicions to the authorities.

While Proposition 187 sparked intense nationwide debate about immigration, it created an even bigger stir in California, especially as election time drew near. On several occasions that fall, Hernández was asked to appear before groups of interested voters and explain Proposition 187 and its possible impact. One such instance was on October 5, 1994, when she spoke at Temple Isaiah, a Jewish synagogue in Los Angeles. An excerpt from her remarks that evening is reprinted here from a copy of her speech provided by MALDEF.

affirmative action: programs and policies designed to improve employment and educational opportunities for minorities and women.

"

Immigration—legal and illegal—is an inherently difficult and complex issue that defies simplistic and **reactionary** solutions like 187.

On the one hand, I know all too well that it is easier to "crack down" on the **undocumented** worker, easier to punish the children of undocumented immigrants, easier to assume that aggressive posture than to deal with the root economic causes of the migration north.

There is no question that the **influx** has changed the dynamics of cities like Los Angeles, and its impact has been felt in Washington as surely as Sacramento.

We cannot ignore that fact.

Yet, despite all the **rhetoric** about undocumented immigrants living off the system, the fact is that they come to work and build a better life for themselves and their children, not to take advantage of our educational, medical, and public services. They come to share in our great American work ethic.

We know that many immigrants come from the lowest socioeconomic **strata** of Mexico and Central America. We know that the immigrant is no longer a male looking to work seasonally and then return to his native country. Entire families are migrating north and settling permanently.

It is therefore critical that we approach undocumented immigration with the facts.

•In 1993, only 1.5 percent of immigrants received Social Security.

•In 1992 the INS [Immigration and Naturalization Service, a part of the U.S. government] reported that 0.5 percent of undocumented immigrants received food stamps or AFDC [Aid to Families with Dependent Children] and about half had private health insurance while only 21 percent used any government health services.

•According to the Urban Institute, when all levels of government are considered together, immigrants contribute more in taxes paid than in services received.

reactionary: politically ultraconservative, inclined to be extremely moderate, cautious, and traditional.

undocumented: lacking the proper legal papers (such as a passport, work permit, etc.).

influx: the coming in of something.

rhetoric: discussion; discourse.

strata: levels.

Yet in the past few years, public **discourse** over immigration policy, shaped by misinformation, has shifted dangerously toward extremism. The by-product of that movement has created a rise in **xenophobia** and the **scapegoating** of immigrants.

Indeed, in the past several months, we have seen the federal government approve such proposals as banning emergency aid to undocumented immigrants who were victims of the earthquake in Los Angeles, funding the unemployment benefits extension program by cutting off benefits to legal permanent residents, and consider cutting off educational benefits to undocumented children in the public schools.

So taken by the effort to deny aid to undocumented immigrants who had been victimized by the earthquake, Secretary of Housing and Urban Development **Henry Cisneros** [see entry] was compelled to say: "It is sad that the circumstances of a disaster would result in making these kinds of distinctions about human suffering."

In California, the Department of Motor Vehicles on March 1 began requiring proof of citizenship or legal status in order to obtain a driver's license or identification card. And now, California faces an extremist immigration policy under Proposition 187, one that could cost California taxpayers $15 billion and do nothing to address any immigration concerns.

All of these efforts are extreme and **retrograde** and speak to the **virulence** of the anti-immigrant sentiment that has gripped the state and nation.

I will tell you that I have always been **averse** to extremism and no less so when it comes to immigration policy.

For me, the answer lies in compassion, moderation and—above all—reason.

While we all have legitimate concerns about illegal immigration, the truth is that Proposition 187 is intended to save money and solve problems but will only make the situation worse and create a host of new problems—expensive ones.

Proposition 187 does nothing to enforce the laws we already have, nor does it beef up enforcement at the borders.

discourse: discussion.

xenophobia: excessive and irrational fear of foreigners.

scapegoating: unfairly blaming or hating.

retrograde: going back to conditions that are worse than the present.

virulence: extreme bitterness or desire to do harm.

averse: opposed.

Student demonstrators protest the passage of Proposition 187 in San Francisco, California, 1994

Recklessly drafted, 187 violates federal laws that control federal funding to our schools and hospitals.... Passage of the proposition could cost [them] $15 billion in lost federal funds.

Let's put that staggering amount in a context that every Californian can understand. Replacing that money would necessitate a $1,600 annual tax increase for the average California family.

Proponents of the proposition claim that the state will save hundreds of millions of dollars by denying "nonemergency" medical care to the undocumented. First of all, the estimated undocumented immigrant use of the medical services that 187 would prohibit is very low, just a fraction of one percent of California's budget.

proponents: supporters.

Antonia Hernández   115

Also, refusal to provide fundamental health care is a severe danger to public interest. If 187 is successful in denying these basic services, undocumented persons will not be treated even if their medical problems are serious, even if they have **communicable** diseases, even if a low-cost dose of preventive medicine or an immunization could keep them from ending up in county emergency rooms with far more serious ailments that will cost the state even more to treat.... As a society, we are best protected by treating the disease, not by turning away the individual in need of care.

By imposing yet another bureaucratic procedure in providing services, the provision will increase **escalating** costs of publicly-funded health services. Moreover, requiring verification and denying benefits or services on the basis of suspicion could cause unnecessary, and potentially life-endangering, delays and denials of care to citizens and legal residents who are otherwise entitled to medical assistance....

When you get beyond all the misinformation, you realize that undocumented immigrants are already ineligible for the vast majority of public social services such as state welfare or food stamps. One-eighty-seven's provision to deny such services to the undocumented merely creates a costly, enormous and unnecessary bureaucratic burden....

One-eighty-seven is opposed by the California PTA and the entire education community because it will cost our schools more than it could ever save them. Even the U.S. Secretary of Education has informed state officials that 187 would violate federal laws and will force a cutoff of federal funds to California schools. At a time when California is working to improve educational quality, Proposition 187 would reduce the educational opportunities for all California children.

The provision to deny an education to undocumented children violates the United States Constitution under *Plyler v. Doe,* a 1982 United States Supreme Court case which recognized the right of all children to public education. [In *Plyler v. Doe,* the Supreme Court ruled that the state of Texas could not bar the children of illegal immigrants from attending public schools. The court ruled the Texas law unconstitutional and in violation of the equal protection clause because no

communicable: contagious.
escalating: rising.

state is allowed to deny any person the equal protection of the laws.] It would also violate the state constitution's right to education....

Moreover, this provision would officially establish our public schools as agencies of family investigation and arms of government law enforcement. School officials, teachers, and other school employees would become immigration officials, responding to rumors and suspicions instead of educating our children. Fear of being reported to the INS may also cause undocumented parents to withdraw their United States citizen children from school—creating an underclass of uneducated United States citizens....

One-eighty-seven will mean more crime, not less, because it will kick an estimated three hundred thousand kids out of school and onto our streets, with no supervision....

Additionally, 187s law enforcement provisions duplicate current law which encourages, and in some cases requires, local law enforcement to notify the INS of certain arrestees' immigration status. In fact, through a computerized booking system, police in several counties—including Los Angeles County—effectively report all suspected undocumented arrestees to the INS....

Aside from duplicating already-existing practices, these provisions of the proposition would severely endanger the public safety. An increased distrust of the police would develop in many communities, leading to reduced cooperation with law enforcement agencies, increased criminal behavior because many witnesses and victims would not report crime for fear of being reported to the INS, and the undermining of

A poster for National Migration Week, issued by the U.S. Catholic Conference

eugenics: a science that deals with the improvement of the human race's hereditary qualities by controlling who is allowed to mate.

efforts to implement community policing and other models of police-community cooperation.

There are additional disturbing questions about 187.... The people behind 187 are bankrolled by the Pioneer Fund, which is a secretive group that funds white supremacy research.

Alan Nelson, coauthor of 187, wrote the proposition while he was a paid lobbyist for the Federation for American Immigration Reform (FAIR). FAIR has received one million dollars from the Pioneer Fund, one of the longest and most consistent financial supporters of Nelson's FAIR. FAIR has also been the recipient of some of the Pioneer Fund's largest contributions in recent years. The Internal Revenue Service reports a long-standing financial relationship between the two groups....

Incorporated in 1937 by strict immigration, **eugenics** and sterilization advocates who saw selective breeding as a means of improving the quality of race, the Pioneer Fund remains an active, but secretive organization based in New York. In addition to FAIR, the Pioneer Fund supports a number of controversial research projects and organizational efforts. Among them are the much-criticized works of Dr. William Shockley, who called for the sterilization of individuals with lower than average IQs; the well-known Minnesota Twins Study; researchers claiming to prove the inferiority of blacks ...; organizations promoting the notion that the "purity" of the white race is endangered by "inferior genetic stock"; and the editor of the neo-Nazi "mouthpiece" *Mankind Quarterly,* with its close ties to the mentor of Josef Mengele of Auschwitz. [Nazi physician Josef Mengele was the chief medical officer of the Auschwitz concentration camp during World War II. He was notorious for performing gruesome experiments on prisoners.]

The ties of Nelson to these white supremacist supporters raise some very serious and fundamental concerns about 187 and sheds a whole new light on the "SUSPECT" reporting requirements of the proposition. I urge voters to read the 187 provisions which require that authorities report to the INS and the attorney general ANYONE they MERELY "SUSPECT" to be here illegally—in other words, anyone with "foreign" features, an accent or ethnic last name.

And 187 provides no protections for citizens or legal residents, particularly those with such **attributes**, against false accusations. Unlike current law, the proposition eliminates the required due process by not requiring an arrest to be lawful or that "suspicion" of undocumented status be "reasonable." The absence of "reasonableness" means there is little to protect immigrant witnesses and victims of crime from being falsely arrested and turned over to the INS. In effect, the provision turns police officers into INS agents, with all of the attendant fear that such status generates in immigrants, both legal residents and undocumented persons.

In summary:

- One-eighty-seven punishes innocent children by denying them health care and education.

- According to the state legislative analyst's offices, 187 will cost California taxpayers in excess of $15 billion in lost federal funds and in the development and administration of elaborate verification and notifications systems, and training of all state and local agencies.

- One-eighty-seven will severely endanger the public safety by kicking three hundred thousand unsupervised kids out of school.

- One-eighty-seven jeopardizes the privacy of Californians— forcing government employees, teachers, doctors, and other health care providers to act as INS agents, responding to rumors and suspicions instead of doing their jobs.

- The people behind 187 have close ties to a white supremacist group. By requiring all "suspects" to be reported to the authorities 187 would create a police-state mentality.

- One-eighty-seven is unconstitutional, blatantly violating a clear ruling of the United States Supreme Court, and will force a cut in federal funds for our schools.

- Finally, 187 does nothing to curb unlawful immigration into the state.

attributes: characteristics.

As a nation, we have been too apt to forget the benefits immigrants bring. We have also been given the opportunity to heed the lessons of our immigration history, and to this day we have **squandered** that opportunity. Instead, we have found ourselves in a **desultory** discourse that appeals to our worst nature as Americans, that plays to our darkest fears of "the foreigner."

Perhaps the saddest part of it all is that in so doing we have victimized not only voiceless immigrants but ourselves. For as I look upon this room and all the many faces, I am reminded again of this nation's great good fortune—that blessing—to be inheritor of such wealth, a true common wealth.

[Author] William Saroyan once wrote: "This is America, and the only foreigners here are those who forget it is America."

There has been all too much forgetting and not enough acknowledgment of our own immigrant stories, and the debate over immigration policy must be **refracted** through such a multicolored prism.

For if we are unable to bring some reason and decency to this debate, what is at stake is nothing less than who we are as a people, and how we define ourselves as a nation.

In the end, however, I remain optimistic that we will find our way to dealing compassionately and thoughtfully with immigrants. We will begin to move beyond the rhetoric and misinformation and **posit** the solutions to an issue that defies simplistic and reactionary approaches. I am optimistic because it is not our nature as Americans to turn our backs on those in need in the wake of a disaster—undocumented immigrants or not. It is not our nature to punish children and blame the ills of a nation on a small sector of our society. It is not our nature to turn away from issues that must be dealt with.

We will find our way to a reasoned and dignified policy by **adhering** to the sense of humanity that has made this country great, and acknowledges the role of the government controlling our borders. I know that we are a good and decent people—that is our nature and our **franchise** as Americans....

"

squandered: wasted.

desultory: marked by lack of a definite plan or purpose.

refracted: subjected to being bent or deflected and therefore viewed in a different way.

posit: suggest, propose.

adhering: sticking with, following.

franchise: right, privilege.

Antonia Hernández

Proposition 187 went on to gain the approval of California voters in November 1994. But immediately after the election, opponents launched various court challenges that continue to prevent it from going into effect. Meanwhile, some Americans still appear ready to deal with the problem of illegal immigrants in ways that might be considered excessively harsh. Hernández noted in a speech she gave on November 18, 1994, just a couple of weeks after the passage of Proposition 187:

"

While we [at MALDEF] are saddened by this tragic decision, we are not necessarily surprised. As civil rights advocates, we are all too aware of the realities faced by the immigrant community.... We know that the battle fought in California does not just belong to California. It is the nation's battle. And the organizations that are **instigating** it ... are not going to stop with their Prop 187 victory. They'll continue across the country, trying wherever they can to turn people's fears and frustrations into **regressive** policy dictated by poorly written and unfair laws.

"

Student Michelle Tellez watches rally against Proposition 187 on the UCLA campus, 1994

Sources

Books

Notable Hispanic American Women, Gale, 1993.

Periodicals

Hispanic, "Antonia Hernández: MALDEF's Legal Eagle," December 1990.

NEA Today, "Meet: Antonia Hernández," November 1990, p. 9.

Parents, "Law in the Family," March 1985.

instigating: provoking.

regressive: going back to conditions that are worse than the present.

Dolores Huerta

1930–

Mexican American labor leader and activist

*As cofounder with the late **César Chávez** (see entry) of the United Farm Workers (UFW), Dolores Huerta has been at the forefront of the American labor movement for well over thirty years. Her goal has always been to obtain fair wages and decent living and working conditions for those who pick the grapes, vegetables, and citrus fruits in American fields. Huerta's tireless efforts on their behalf have made her a hero to Hispanic Americans and a near-legendary figure among migrant farm workers.*

Early Life

Huerta was born in New Mexico to parents whose families originally came from Mexico, but she grew up in Stockton, California. Her mother and father divorced when she was very young, so she and her brother and sister were raised mostly by their mother and maternal grandfather in a loving and happy household. Huerta only occasionally saw her father, who earned a living as a miner and migrant worker. Yet his political and labor activism later proved inspirational to his daughter.

As was the case with many Americans, the Depression years of the 1930s were a struggle for Huerta's family. But the 1940s brought a new prosperity that made it possible for them to enjoy a more comfortable lifestyle. Young Dolores went to Stockton College after graduating from high school. She interrupted her studies to marry and raise two daughters, but the marriage soon ended in divorce. Huerta then returned to school and earned her associate's degree. Dissatisfied with the kinds of jobs available to her, she resumed her education once more and obtained a teaching certificate. Once in the classroom, however, Huerta quickly grew frustrated by how little she could really do for those students who didn't have proper clothing or enough to eat.

A Community Activist

Huerta's frustration eventually found an outlet in a Mexican American self-help group known as the Community Service Organization (CSO). The CSO first formed in Los Angeles after World War II and then spread across mostly urban areas of California and the Southwest. Huerta joined up during the mid-1950s. She became very active in the CSO's many civic and educational programs, including registering voters, setting up citizenship classes, and lobbying local government officials for neighborhood improvements. (Lobbyists try to influence public officials to support certain legislation—in this case, legislation that would benefit city neighborhoods.) Huerta was especially successful at lobbying, so it wasn't long before the CSO hired her to lobby for the group at the state capital in Sacramento.

During the late 1950s, Huerta found herself particularly disturbed by the plight of Mexican American farm workers, so she joined a northern California-based community interest group called the Agricultural Workers Association. It later merged with a similar union-affiliated group known as the Agricultural Workers Organizing Committee, for which Huerta worked as secretary-treasurer.

Joins Forces with Chávez to Organize Farm Workers

It was around this time that Huerta first met César Chávez, a fellow member of the CSO who had also taken

Dolores Huerta leads rally in San Francisco as part of the national boycott of grapes protesting the use of dangerous pesticides, 1988. With her are Howard Wallace, president of the San Francisco chapter of the UFW and Maria Elena Chávez, daughter of César Chávez.

an interest in migrant laborers. Together, they tried to persuade other members of the CSO to expand the group's focus to address the concerns of farm workers. When these efforts failed, they left the CSO and began their own organizing efforts among this overlooked segment of society. September 1962 marked the birth of the National Farm Workers Association, or NFWA (later known as the United Farm Workers, or UFW).

The task Chávez, Huerta, and the others who joined them set out to accomplish was especially difficult given the nature of the migrant worker. Most could not read or write. They were easily bullied by the growers, who warned these already desperately poor people that they were risking their jobs if they tried to unionize. And because their work kept them constantly on the move, they were not easy to keep track of and organize into a group. But with Chávez as president and Huerta as vice president, the NFWA slowly managed to attract people to their evening meetings across the agricultural heart of California. At those meetings, they talked of an aggressive but nonviolent "revolution" that would achieve justice for farm workers.

Throughout the 1960s and 1970s, the NFWA, and then the UFW—as it came to be called—staged a series of successful strikes, marches, and boycotts that focused national attention on the low wages and terrible living and working conditions migrant laborers endured. While Chávez became identified with fasting (going without food) as a method of protest, Huerta led countless picket lines and served as the union's chief contract negotiator. She firmly held her own against hostile Anglo growers who resented the fact that any Mexican American—and a woman, no less—would dare challenge them and the way they chose to do business.

Huerta was a forceful speaker. In September 1965, the up-and-coming farm workers' union (which by then claimed about two thousand members) voted to join Filipino grape pickers in their strike against growers in California's San Joaquin Valley. To reinforce the impact of the strike, César Chávez also called for a national boycott of table grapes. It was a move that quickly made headlines across the country, bringing national attention to the struggle that popularly came to be known as La Causa.

A few months later, in the spring of 1966, the NFWA organized a march of nearly three hundred miles from the California town of Delano to Sacramento. The purpose of the march was to dramatize the farm workers' determination to continue the strike and keep media attention focused on their efforts. On April 10, as demonstrators rallied to mark the end of the march, Huerta addressed the crowd. An excerpt from her speech is reprinted here from the April 28, 1966 edition of the Delano Record.

> “

This is the first time in [the] history of the United States that farm workers have walked three hundred miles to their state capitol; and the governor of this state [Edmund G. Brown, Sr.] is not here to greet them.

But this is not surprising. This is in keeping with the general attitude that the governor and the people have had toward farm workers. I can assure you that had doctors, lawyers, auto workers or any other organized labor group marched three hundred miles, the governor would be here to meet them....

The governor's **indifference** to our pilgrimage ... demonstrate[s] that we should not be taken for granted by any political party. As of this moment we wish to inform the Democratic party of this state that we will be counted as your supporters, only when we can count you among ours. The Democratic party does not have us in its hip pocket.

The leaders of this association do not want to meet with the governor in a closed-door session. We have met with the governor and his secretaries before in a closed-door session. We are no longer interested in listening to the excuses the governor has to give in defense of the growers, to his apologies for them not paying us decent wages or why the growers can not dignify the workers as individuals with the right to place the price on their own labor through **collective bargaining.**

The governor maintains that the growers are in a competitive situation. Well, the farm workers are also. We must also compete—with the standard of living to give our families their daily bread.

In 1959, the CSO and organized labor tried the first legislative efforts to give the farm workers minimal social legislation needed to **ameliorate** their terrible **oppression.** At that time the farm workers were not aware these attempts were being made and were therefore not there to testify and lobby in their own behalf, except for a delegation that César Chávez brought up from Oxnard [California].

In 1961 and 1963 through efforts of the CSO, National Farm Workers Association and the **herculean** efforts of then

indifference: lack of interest or concern.

collective bargaining: negotiations that take place between an employer and representatives of a labor union.

ameliorate: relieve.

oppression: unjust or cruel use of power and authority.

herculean: extraordinarily intense and powerful.

NFWA Grape Strike, 1966

Assemblyman—now Congressman—Phil Burton, we were able to obtain welfare legislation that would ameliorate some of the terrible suffering of the farm workers in the off-season.

And the growers are still complaining and fighting adequate administration of that law. Gus Hawkins also passed disability insurance for farm workers. That was eight years ago and we still have yet to see the needed legislation for a minimum wage enacted in this state.

But this is 1966.

Farm workers have not been driven down to a small closed-door session to see what the state can dole out to us in welfare legislation. The grape strikers of Delano [California] after seven months of extreme hardship and deprivation have walked step by step through the San Joaquin Valley—the valley that has been their "Valley of Tears" for them and their families. Not to beg, but to insist on what they think is needed for them.

The difference between 1959 and 1966 is highlighted by the **peregrination**, it is revolution—the farm workers have been organized....

César Chávez began ... [by] going through the San Joaquin Valley as a pilgrim inspiring the workers to organize; giving the confidence they needed through inspiration and hard work and educating them through the months to realize that no one was going to win their battle for them, that their condition could only be changed by one group—themselves.

He refused contributions and did not solicit money from any area. César felt that outside money was no good, and that the workers had to pay for their own organization and this was accomplished.

The National Farm Workers Association prior to the strike was supported entirely by its membership through the dues they paid. Furthermore, the members of the National Farm Workers Association put forth the programs that they felt were needed immediately, such as a credit union, a service program, a group life insurance plan—the credit union so they could save their money and borrow when necessary, a group life insurance plan for their families that would take care of emergencies that arise from sudden deaths, and the service program for their complaints of nonunion wages, injury and disability cases, etc., and other daily problems in which they are exposed and undefended.

Each worker that was helped by the association's program became an organizer and the movement has grown in this manner with each worker bringing in other members to make the union stronger. The foundation was built by César Chávez through his dedicated efforts and the successive sacrifices of his wife, Helen Chávez, and their eight children, and their relatives who assisted them during this crucial organizing period when financial aid was not forthcoming.

April 10, 1966, marks the fourth year of the organizing efforts of the National Farm Workers Association. And today our farm workers have come to the capitol of Sacramento.

peregrination: march, pilgrimage.

To the governor and the legislature of California we say: You cannot close your eyes and ears to our needs any longer, you cannot pretend that we do not exist, you cannot plead ignorance to our problem because we are here and we embody our needs for you....

The agricultural workers are not going to remain **static**. The towns that have been reached by the pilgrimage will never be the same. On behalf of the National Farm Workers Association, its officers and its members, on behalf of all the farm workers of this state, we unconditionally demand the governor of this state, Edmund G. Brown, to call a special session of the legislature to enact a collective bargaining law for the farm workers of the state of California.

We will be satisfied with nothing less. The governor cannot and the legislature cannot shrug off their responsibilities to the Congress. We are the citizens and residents of the state of California and we want to have rules set up to protect us in this state.

If the rules to settle our economic problems are not forthcoming, we will call a general strike to paralyze the state's agricultural economy, to let the legislators and the employers know we mean business. We will take economic pressures, strikes and boycotts to force recognition and obtain collective bargaining rights.

The social and economic revolution of the farm workers is well under way and will not be stopped until they receive equality.

As La Causa *became a national movement, Huerta headed east to direct the table grape boycott in the New York City area. Later, toward the end of the 1960s, she coordinated similar activities all along the East Coast at major distribution points for California produce. Under her leadership, the farm workers' drive to obtain decent wages and conditions expanded to involve activists of all kinds— religious, political, student, union, and consumer. Their efforts finally paid off in 1970, when the Delano growers agreed to contracts that ended the five-year-old strike.*

static: inactive.

Huerta spent much of the early 1970s back in New York overseeing UFW boycotts against other grape-growers as well as lettuce farmers. Again, the emphasis was on maintaining nationwide pressure to force changes in California. This required Huerta to travel extensively and share the UFW message anywhere she found an audience willing to listen, from college campuses to union halls.

In New Orleans, Louisiana, Huerta delivered the keynote address at the annual convention of the American Public Health Association. In her remarks, delivered October 21, 1974, Huerta focused on a topic she thought might be of particular interest to those in attendance—the unique health problems facing migrant workers and steps the union had taken to address them.

She also touched briefly on the problems the UFW was then having with another union, the Teamsters, which was trying to conduct its own organizing efforts among the farm workers. This bitter (and sometimes violent) battle was not resolved until 1977, when the two reached a settlement granting the UFW sole bargaining rights among farm workers. Huerta's speech is reprinted here in part from a copy in the archives of the Walter P. Reuther Library of Wayne State University in Detroit, Michigan.

I wish to bring you greetings and a hope for a very successful convention ... to all of you who have dedicated your lives to making life better for the world, for America. I think that your goals are very much like the goals of our union. We got into the business of organizing farm workers for mainly health reasons. It is no accident that farm workers have an average life span of forty-nine years of age. And those of you who have worked in rural communities I think know the reasons. Those of you that don't, I just want to give you a little picture of what health is like for a farm worker in a place where he does not have the United Farm Workers to represent him.

In Delano, California, I remember three specific instances. One, a worker who had his hand broken on the job ... was sent to his local doctor, who, by the way, is also a grape-grower. The doctor prescribed some ointment to put on his hand. The worker's hand started swelling. He came later to use our x-ray machine, which at that time was just a small trailer. We had this old x-ray machine from the year one, and we found out that his hand was broken. There was another farm worker [who was ill], Chala Savala, who another local grape-grower doctor said ..., "Why, you're pregnant." About six months later she found out she wasn't pregnant—she had tuberculosis. But by that time she had to have a lung removed. Farm workers who are poisoned with pesticides are told they have sunstroke. And it's always the same thing— you have no money, the doctor can't see you.

When we first won our contracts as a result of our first strike and our first grape boycott, we made some very fantastic changes. I'd just kinda like to ask, how many of you didn't eat grapes between 1965 and 1970? Raise your hands. Well, I'm glad to see that there were a lot of you. And I'm going to tell you some of the changes that you brought about in health for farm workers in Delano, California, this very same place that I'm talking about.

The first thing that we got when we got our contracts was a medical plan. And we named it the Robert F. Kennedy Medical Plan after our good friend [U.S. Senator and 1968 presidential candidate] Robert Kennedy. The plan was paid for by the growers. We made them pay ten cents an hour for every hour that the workers worked.... And the workers decided that they wanted doctor's visits paid for, they wanted maternity benefits, they wanted hospitalization benefits, they wanted x-ray [and] lab, they wanted prescriptions paid for under their medical plan.

And so we developed a really fantastic medical plan. Because every migrant worker, his wife, and all of his children are covered under our medical plan. If they only work fifty hours for the migrant medical plan they were covered for a nine-month period. Nine months, no matter where, they can make a medical claim and get paid for it. And the money goes directly to the worker. Our major medical plan is two hundred and fifty hours. Under this plan they get hospitalization, and surgical benefits, ambulance benefits, a minimum dental and eyeglass prescription care. Again, no matter where they are at.

See, the beautiful thing about our medical plan and the reason that we were able to do this fantastic medical plan for ten cents an hour is because we did not go through an insurance company. Now when we first tried to get this plan passed, many of the growers were very upset about it. They said you have to go through an insurance company. We are very lucky that César Chávez is a grammar-school dropout and he hasn't been educated to think that insurance is a way of life. He said he wasn't going to give any of his money to an insurance company, any of the workers' money.

So the way that our medical plan works is that the money comes in and it goes out directly to the workers. It's a nonprofit plan, and it's administered by the farm workers themselves....

But once we got the medical plan, we found that that really didn't stop the abuses, because the doctors were still not giving the workers good health care. So the next step was then to build a clinic. So the workers started to build their clinics....

I think our clinics are unique in that we call them people's clinics. The people built them, we raised the money for them. There is no government money at all in our clinics. And the kind of work that the clinic does is primarily, first of all, educational. And we don't have Mickey-Mouse clinics. Our clinics are really beautiful. I mean there is good medicine in our clinics. The workers are taught about nutrition, to combat diabetes, which is very common among farm workers. They are given prenatal instruction to have healthier babies and healthier mothers. They are taught about inoculations....

Our health workers go into the labor camps. They've done a vast service on tuberculosis and on other diseases that are contagious. And when we find a sick farm worker, someone that has tuberculosis, someone that has another disease that shouldn't be in the labor force, we take that farm worker out of the labor force. And he is put on some kind of disability compensation so that he doesn't have to work until he becomes well again. We do home visits. We have a team approach with the doctor, the health worker, the nurse, and we go right into the homes of the farm workers.

Needless to say, this kind of preventative medicine that we are now undertaking has saved so many lives that the statistics of Tulare County in California have changed. Last year I had my tenth baby in a hospital in Tulare County, and the doctor who was delivering my baby—who happened to be a specialist—along with our own doctor from our clinic told me that our health care was so good that we had actually changed the statistics of Tulare County. I think that's pretty fantastic, because our doctors are so dedicated, and because their medicine is so good.

Now, some of you might wonder how come I have ten children, right? One of the main reasons is because I want to have my own picket line. But all kidding aside, it's really nice to be able to go to a clinic when you are pregnant with your tenth baby and not have people look at you like you are kind of crazy, or like you don't know where they come from, or put pressure on you not to have any more children. Because after all, you know, Mexicans are kind of poor people, and you shouldn't have all that many kids. So that's another good thing about our clinics. Because unfortunately, that pressure not to have children translates itself in county hospitals and places where people have no power into dead babies because those babies aren't taken care of, and into very hard labor for mothers because they are trying to make it as hard on the mother as they can to have another one. And I guess I feel a little bit strongly about that because I've been in situations where I've seen children die, babies die, because somebody there thought they shouldn't have been born in the first place.

Now another great thing about our clinics is that we train farm workers as lab assistants, lab technicians, nurse's aides, we train farm workers to do the administration of the clinic.... So what we're doing is we're not only just giving good health care—fantastic health care—but we are training our own people to be able to do the health work and to administer the program.

The amazing reason that we have been able to build these clinics in such a short period of time is because our clinics are

Farm workers picking strawberries in Salinas, California, 1963

nonprofit. The doctors that come to work with us work the way that we do. We work for no wages. Our doctors get a little bit more for some of you out there that might be interested. But nevertheless it is a sacrifice. And that's important. Because you can't help poor people and be comfortable. You know, the two things are just not compatible. If you want to really give good health care to poor people you've got to be prepared to be a little uncomfortable and to put a little bit of sacrifice behind it.

Now there [are] other ways that the union has changed things in terms of health care. And I'm going to talk a little bit about the pesticides, because ... we raised the issue many years ago and a lot of people have been concerned about [it], but it was sort of a no-no. Nobody could talk about it openly. What we have in our union are ranch committees. Where we have a contract we elect a ranch committee. The workers elect their own committee. That committee is responsible [for making] sure that no pesticides that can be harmful to them or harmful to the consumers can be used in that ranch. They check out to see what kind of pesticides are going to be used, what the antidotes are, what the re-entry periods are, everything that there is possible to know about that pesticide.

Do you know that we were amazed to find out you can get all kinds of information about what's harmful to a pet, but you can't get any information about what's harmful to a farm worker? Because there has been very little research done in this area....

When we were negotiating contracts—I was in charge of the contract negotiations for the union—we called up a friend of ours who worked with the Los Angeles County Health [Department], and he gave us some information on one of the organic phosphates that we wanted to know. Well, one of the growers who was in on the negotiations tried to get him fired for giving us that information. And this man worked for the Los Angeles County Health Department. But this shows you—and I'm going to talk about that a little bit more—about the kind of repression that I know a lot of you are faced [with] when you do try to make real changes or when you try to get into those controversial areas where you have conflicts of power.

In our contracts, we banned DDT, Aldrin, Endrin, 2,4-D, 2,4-T, Tep and many of the other—Monitor 4—many of these other pesticides. We banned these pesticides in our contracts starting from 1970. It is interesting that just recently, the government has come out against Aldrin and Endrin. And the Farm Workers Union banned these pesticides many years ago. We find that the only way that you can be sure that the so-called laws are administered, that the so-called laws are carried out, is when you have somebody right there on the ranch, a steward, a ranch committee, somebody that can't get fired from the job, somebody that has the protection of a union contract to make sure that these things are carried out.

All of these great things that we were able to do—and all of you that didn't eat grapes helped us to accomplish—are being wiped out now. And they are being wiped out because last year, as many of you know, we lost our contracts. The growers brought in the Teamsters union, they signed back-door contracts with them, fourteen thousand farm workers went out on strike. Four thousand farm workers—this was not a war, this was a strike—four thousand farm workers were jailed for picketing, two hundred farm workers were beaten and injured by Teamsters and police, and two farm workers were killed. It is sad for us to report this, but the clock has been turned back and California agriculture, with the exception of a handful of contracts that we still hold, we now have the labor contractor, the crew leader system back again, we now have child labor back again.

There was a bus accident—to talk to you about health standards and safety standards—there was a bus accident in Blythe, California, on January 15. This was under a Teamster contract. Nineteen farm workers were drowned when their bus turned over into an irrigation ditch. This was a school bus. It had no business transporting people seventy miles to work. The seats of that bus were not fastened to the floor. The people got tangled in the bus. They couldn't get out of the bus. They were crushed to death and they were drowned. Among those that were drowned was a thirteen-year-old child and his fifteen-year-old brother. There were four women that were drowned. The labor contractor who owned that bus got a fifty-dollar fine for the deaths of nineteen farm workers. I'm sure that many of you didn't read about it in your local newspapers because this is common among farm workers, these kinds of accidents. Twenty-five farm workers have been killed because of [the] lack of safety precautions in the fields since the Teamsters took over the contracts.

We now have a return to pesticides—forty thousand acres of lettuce were poisoned with Monitor 4. This lettuce was shipped to the market. In California, it was sold as shredded

lettuce in Safeway stores. That's nice to have Monitor 4 with your shredded salad, huh?

Migrant workers doing "stoop labor," 1963

And we have a return back to the archaic system that we had, [a] primitive system that existed before and still exists, where we don't have United Farm Workers contracts. People working out there in those fields without a toilet, people working out there in those fields without any hand-washing facilities, without any cold drinking water, without any kind of first-aid or safety precautions. All of this has come back again.

The California Rural Legal Assistance just did a spot survey of about twenty ranches in the Salinas and the Delano area just a couple of months ago. And [in] every single instance they found either no toilet or a dirty toilet.... And this is something consumers don't understand—that that lettuce, those grapes are being picked right there in that field. If there's a dirty toilet, it's right next to the produce, and that produce is picked and packed in that field and shipped directly to your store. The way you see grapes in your market, the way you see the lettuce in that market, it comes directly from the field. It doesn't go through any cleansing process. It's direct.

I remember talking to the head of the Food and Drug Administration in San Francisco. You know, I found out that there was a law that says no produce can be shipped for interstate commerce if it has been picked or packed in a way that it might become contaminated. Well, if you've got a field where you've got several hundred people or a thousand people working, and there's no toilet, that produce can be contaminated. You know what he told me? He said, "I've got to enforce the Food and Drug Administration law in four states. I can't go out there and check every field to see if there is a toilet or not, or hand-washing facilities." You know, these are these little tiny things that are kind of overlooked. And they're so serious. But I'll bet that if any public health person brings this up, there are going to be repercussions because they bring it up.

The Teamsters have brought back illegal aliens. And now when I say this, I want to tell you what's happening to these people. Today, President [Gerald] Ford is meeting with [Mexican President Luis] Echeverría in Mexico. And they're going to talk about a *bracero* program, which is a slave program for workers, for Mexican workers. And Mexico needs this because they've got a fifty percent inflation rate in Mexico, and they've got a thirty or forty percent unemployment rate. So they want to get rid of the people. They want to get rid of the problem.

But what does it do to people over here? They want to bring in one million Mexicans from Mexico. We've already got close to a million people here illegally. And how are they being treated? They are paying three hundred dollars each to come over the border. They are being put in housing where you have thirty or forty people in a room without any kind of a sanitary facility. We have one report of an illegal alien who was picking peaches on a ladder; the ladder was shaky, [and] it broke. The ladder went right through his anus. And they didn't give him any medical attention. Luckily, one of our members found out about it and brought him to one of our clinics for treatment. We're having illegal aliens who are coming in, who are being blinded by pesticides, for treatment. This is slavery. And it's wrong. And we've got to see what way we can stop this.

We can't really wait for legislation. You know, there's a lot of things that we can do right away. I think that the one thing that we've learned in our union is that you don't wait. You just get out and you start doing things. And you do things in such a way that you really help people to lay the foundations that you need.

We don't have to talk about a charitable outlook. You know, people come in with a lot of money and they give people charity. We've got to talk about ways to make people self-sufficient in terms of their medical health. Because when they go in there with charity and then they pull out, then they leave the people worse off than they ever were before. We've got to use government money to help people. And I don't think that this is so radical. Lord knows that the growers are getting billions of dollars not to grow cotton, all kinds of supports and subsidies. Well, if any money is given for medical health, it should stay in that community. It shouldn't just come in there at the pleasure of the local politicians and be pulled out at the pleasure of the local politicians.

And I don't think that public health people should be repressed. It worries me when I see a clinic in a farm-worker community that is afraid to put out a Farm Worker flag or put up César's picture because they are afraid that they are going to get their money taken away from them. And yet this has happened. And this is wrong. But the only reason it happens is because we let it happen. We've got to take the side of the people that are being oppressed. And if we can't do that, then we're not doing our job, because the people in that minority community or in that community are not going to have any faith in the medical program that is in there if you can't take their side. They're going to suspect you. We've got to be able to stand up and fight for our rights. We can't any longer cooperate with any kind of fear, any kind of bigotry, any kind of racism, anything that is wrong. We've got to be able to stand up and say, "That is wrong." And it's going to

Huerta speaks about the work of UFW cofounder César Chávez (shown in portrait, top left) after his death in 1993

take that kind of courage, I think, the same kind of courage that César has taught the farm workers, to make the kind of changes that are needed.

Health, like food, has got to be to cure people, to make people well. It can't be for profit. Food should be sacred to feed people, not for profit. Health has got to be a right for every person and not a privilege. You would be sad to know that many farm workers—before we had our clinics—had never been to a doctor. And I'm sure like farm workers, there are many, many other people who have never been to a clinic or to a doctor. And many times that is even out of fear because they see the doctor or they see the medical person not as their friend but they see that person as their enemy.

Now I hope that what we have done, our experience, will serve some use to what you're interested in and what you're doing. I hope that you will help us get back what we have lost, which are our union contracts, so that we can continue this fantastic health program that we have that we started in California. And you can do this very easily just by not eating any grapes until we win, by not eating any lettuce until we win, and by not drinking any Gallo wine. And I'm saying that lightly. It's not light. It's a very serious situation.

Within the next year they are spending millions of dollars to destroy the United Farm Workers. They are spending millions of dollars to tell what a bad administrator César Chávez is. Have you seen these articles in the *New York Times* and *Time* magazine? They say César Chávez is a bad administrator. What they really mean is he is the wrong color.... Can you imagine five clinics, a medical plan, a credit union, a retirement center for farm workers, fantastic increases in wages, the removal of the labor contract system—all of this César did in a few short years. What would he do if he was a good administrator?

We have a booth here ... where we're giving out information about our clinic. I implore all of you, if you can give up a year of your life or two years of your life, drop out and come and help us. The only reason we haven't got more clinics is because we need doctors. In our Delano clinic right now, we only have one doctor working. Please come and join the people and help us build health care for everybody, and we will give you a little bit of money, not too much. But we all work for five dollars a week. None of us gets paid. Even César gets five dollars a week for his personal benefit. We get five dollars a week for food. We live off of donations. All of the money that we need to run our boycott and our strikes. We have a button table where we invite you to buy a button. And please wear our button. As I say, all the contributions that you can give will be greatly, greatly appreciated, because we do need money very desperately.

We're also going to be showing a film, the film of our strike, of the bloody strike that we had in California last summer.... I'd invite all of you to come and see the film. You'll never forget it. And you will really see—when we talk about the principle of nonviolence, you will see it in action. Because you will see farm workers getting beaten and killed, and you will see that the farm workers do not fight back with violence. We are using a nonviolent action of the boycott, so we really need your help in that.

Let's say a few *vivas* now, OK? You know what *viva* means? That's what you're all about—long life. Long life. And we always say that in the Spanish community, we say *viva,* which means "long life." So we're going to say a few *vivas,* and we're going to say some *abajos.* You know what *abajos* are? That means "down." And then we will say one other thing—*Si se puede.* Can we have this dream that we are talking about? Health for everyone, brotherhood, peace? "It can be done"—*si se puede.* And we'll all do the farm workers' handclap together to show that we're united in thought and action and in love. The farm workers' handclap starts out very slow, and then it goes very fast.

So let's try it. We're going to say first *"Viva la Causa,"* which is the cause of labor, peace, and health, *"Viva la justicia,"* which is justice, and then we will say *"Viva Chávez,"* for César, may God give him long life. And then we'll say "down with fear," *abajo,* and "down with lettuce and grapes," *abajo,* and "down with Gallo wine." Because Gallo is on the boycott, too. *Abajo....*

OK, let's try it now. All together! I'll say, *"Viva la Causa!"* and everybody yells *"Viva!"* really, really loud, OK? *Viva la Causa! Viva!* Ugh—that was very weak. This is very important. This is like kind of praying together in unison, so it's really important. Let's try it again: *Viva la Causa! Viva! Viva la justicia! Viva!* Now—so César can hear us in the hospital where he's at and the growers can hear us where they're at: *Viva Chávez! Viva!* OK, now we'll try *abajo.* Down with fear! *Abajo!* Down with lettuce and grapes! *Abajo!* Down with Gallo! *Abajo!* You know, this really works.... Can we live in a world of brotherhood and peace without disease and fear and oppression? *Si se peude,* right? OK, let's all do it together. *Si se puede.* [Clapping.] *Si se puede, si se puede....* [Clapping.]

Thank you very much.

> *9 9*

In 1975, Huerta played a key role in yet another UFW triumph when California passed the Agricultural Labor Relations Act. This was the first law to recognize the right of farm workers to take part in collective bargaining. During the last half of the decade, she turned her attention to running the union's political department, which once again called upon her talents as a legislative lobbyist.

More recently, however, the UFW has seen its influence decline due in part to changes in the economic and political climate at both the state and national levels. The death of César Chávez in 1993 also dealt a blow to the organization, which is struggling to keep his spirit alive as well as increase membership. But the UFW still has a fighter in Huerta, who remains active in the ongoing struggle to achieve justice for farm workers.

Sources

Books

Day, Mark, *Forty Acres: César Chávez and the Farm Workers,* Praeger, 1971.

Dunne, John Gregory, *Delano: The Story of the California Grape Strike,* Farrar, 1976.

Levy, Jacques, *César Chávez: Autobiography of La Causa,* Norton, 1975.

Matthiessen, Peter, *Sal Si Puedes: César Chávez and the New American Revolution,* Random House, 1969.

Notable Hispanic American Women, Gale, 1993.

Periodicals

Delano Record, "Text of Mrs. Huerta's Speech at Capitol Rally," April 28, 1966, p. 1.

Ms., "Dolores Huerta: La Pasionaria of the Farmworkers," November 1976, pp. 11–16.

Nation, "'You Find a Way': The Women of the Boycott," February 23, 1974, pp. 232–38.

Progressive, "Stopping Traffic: One Woman's Cause," September, 1975, pp. 38–40.

José Martí

1853–1895

Cuban American writer and revolutionary

Although one hundred years have passed since he waged his battle for Cuba's freedom, the name of José Martí is still celebrated as a symbol of sacrifice to the cause of resistance against foreign control in Latin America. In his short life, the young leader not only laid the groundwork for the revolution that finally liberated Cuba from Spain's colonial control, he was also a noted journalist, translator, novelist, and a highly acclaimed poet. Upon his death in battle at the age of forty-two—before he could see his dream of a free Cuba come true—Martí was hailed as a hero and a martyr in the cause of Latin American freedom.

Early Life

One of eight children, Martí was a native of Havana, Cuba. His parents, however, had been born in Spain. His father was a sergeant in the Spanish Royal Artillery at the time of José's birth. The elder Martí later worked as a guard, a police officer, and a low-level government employee.

"THE SCORN OF OUR FORMIDABLE NEIGHBOR [THE UNITED STATES] WHO DOES NOT KNOW US IS OUR AMERICA'S GREATEST DANGER.... ONCE IT DOES KNOW US, IT WILL REMOVE ITS HANDS OUT OF RESPECT."

Except for a period of about two years when the family moved back to Spain to live, Martí spent his childhood in Havana, where his father's earnings barely covered the family's basic necessities. Despite poverty, Martí was an excellent student. He was admitted to the respected Institute of Havana after primary school, where a teacher, Rafael María de Mendive, took a liking to him and made sure he was allowed to continue his education.

Mendive's influence went beyond the classroom. A strong Cuban nationalist, the teacher secretly worked for his country's independence from Spain. Cuba had been Spanish-controlled since the 1500s. In the 1860s, revolution was definitely in the air, especially after an uprising in late 1868 touched off **guerrilla warfare** *between Cuban rebels and the Spanish military. The warfare dragged on for a decade and became known as the Ten Years' War.*

Imprisoned and Deported for His Political Activism

Mendive was arrested during the early fighting in the Ten Years' War. In response to his teacher's arrest, Martí, only sixteen years old, helped write and publish the newspaper La Patria Libre (The Free Nation). *In October 1869, he was arrested and charged with treason. In January 1871, after six months of hard labor, he was deported to Spain, where Cuban authorities hoped he would be too far away to cause any trouble.*

Martí soon met up with other Cuban exiles in Spain and continued his struggles for the independence movement. He also resumed his education at Central University in Madrid and later transferred to the University of Zaragoza, from which he received both a law degree and a liberal arts degree in 1874.

After a brief visit to Paris, France, Martí left Europe for Mexico, where his parents had settled. Working out of the capital, Mexico City, he contributed articles and poems to a leading local newspaper, some under his own name and some under a pen name. He also wrote a play that was well received upon its first public performance in December 1875.

guerrilla warfare: a type of war characterized by small, independent groups of people carrying out acts of harassment and sabotage.

In 1877, Martí returned to Havana using a false name. Conditions there were so terrible, however, he soon moved to the Central American nation of Guatemala. With a friend's help, he was able to find a job as a high school teacher. But he had to leave there in mid-1878 after offending Guatemalan government officials with his criticisms. This time, Martí was able to return to Cuba openly, because the agreement that had just ended the Ten Years' War granted pardons to those who had been driven out of the country for political reasons. In Cuba, Martí clerked in a law office while unsuccessfully trying to obtain permission to practice law himself.

Nothing dimmed Martí's enthusiasm for the Cuban independence movement. His weapon of choice was the word—both written and spoken. Once again, he sought out others in his native land who shared his goal of freedom from the Spanish. In September 1879, his activism led colonial officials to charge him with conspiracy. They quickly deported him to Spain, where he remained only until December.

Leads the Movement from New York

By January 3, 1880, Martí had made his way to New York City, which remained his base of operations for the next fifteen years. The city housed a large community of fellow exiles, many of whom had left Cuba during the Ten Years' War. Martí immediately joined the Cuban Revolutionary Committee, a group that had been organized some two years earlier by a veteran of the war with Spain, General Calixto García.

Martí's years in New York City were not just devoted to the Cuban independence movement, however. It was a time of remarkable creative achievement for him as well. He actually earned his living as a writer, although he didn't make very much money at it. He contributed articles to some of the leading newspapers in Latin America and to top Spanish-language publications in the United States. His work also appeared in several English-language newspapers based in New York.

"BAGHDAD." Ankommer Til Havana.

Harbor of Havana, Cuba, Martí's birthplace

In his spare time, Martí wrote poetry, fiction, and children's stories. He also translated a variety of literary works. In addition, Martí wrote an exceptional number of essays, pamphlets, and reviews. The originality of expression that he brought to his essays and poetry helped inspire a new movement in Spanish literature known as Modernism.

Before long, Martí's extensive writings, political activism, and personal charm had combined to make him a major force in the Cuban independence movement and a respected figure throughout all of Latin America. He even served for a time as the official representative in New York of the governments of Uruguay, Argentina, and Paraguay. Then Spain's ambassador to the United States questioned how proper it was to have a Cuban revolutionary acting as a diplomat for other nations. Martí's response was to resign from his posts, supposedly to spend more time on his efforts to liberate Cuba.

Cultural Interpreter Between the Two Americas

During this period one of Martí's most frequent topics in his speeches and writings was the lack of understanding between Latin Americans and the people of the United

States. In fact, he often found himself acting as a kind of "interpreter" between the two cultures. He tried to explain each group to the other and resolve the differences that existed between them.

But the longer Martí lived in New York, the less impressed he was with the United States. He was very disturbed by the nation's treatment of its black and Native American minorities. And he was highly critical of the U.S. emphasis on becoming rich—a goal he considered shallow.

Martí was troubled by signs that the United States was seriously thinking about taking over Cuba. Gradually, he came to believe that the growing U.S. taste for acquiring overseas territories posed a dangerous threat to Latin America. In his view, an independent Cuba just might be able to stand in the way of any such plans.

Martí embraced the idea of a united Latin America, which he often referred to as "Our America" (Nuestra America) or simply "America." He saw this new creation rising from the shared historical, political, social, and economic experiences of Spain's former colonies. By joining together, he reasoned, Latin Americans would be in a much better position to oppose the overwhelming influence of the United States in the western hemisphere.

These beliefs were at the heart of the following speech, delivered in New York and later published in La revista ilustrada (The Illustrated Review) on January 10, 1891. An excerpt from it is reprinted here from a version that appears in The Hispanic-American Almanac, Gale, 1993.

In this famous address, Martí analyzes social and political conditions in Latin America. He criticizes those who lack the courage and the character to fight for freedom because they are too busy seeking wealth or pleasure. He condemns Latin Americans who are ashamed of the mixed European and Indian heritage of their countries. He scolds Latin American countries for ignoring the realities of the New World as they try to force old European traditions of government on their peoples. He also makes a strong case for Latin American unity in the face of U.S. interest in the region. Martí's observations firmly established for all time *the idea of two distinctly separate Americas in the western hemisphere—one consisting of the United States and Canada, and one consisting of the Latin American nations. Note that thoughout his speech, when Martí refers to the Americas, American nations, and Our America, he means the Latin American nations.*

The conceited villager believes the entire world to be his village. Provided that he can be mayor, or humiliate the rival who stole his sweetheart, or add to the savings in his **strongbox**, he considers the universal order good, unaware of those giants with seven-league boots who can crush him underfoot, or of the **strife** in the heavens between comets that streak through the drowsy air-devouring worlds. What remains of the village in America must rouse itself.... [This is the time for] weapons of the mind, which conquer all others. Barricades of ideas are worth more than barricades of stone.

There is no **prow** that can cut through a cloudbank of ideas. A powerful idea, waved before the world at the proper time, can stop a squadron of iron-clad ships.... Nations that do not know one another should quickly become acquainted, as men who are to fight a common enemy. Those who shake their fists, like jealous brothers **coveting** the same tract of land, or like the modest cottager who envies the **squire** his mansion, should clasp hands and become one....

We can no longer be a people of leaves living in the air, our foliage heavy with blooms and crackling or humming at the whim of the sun's caress, or buffeted and tossed by the storms. The trees must form ranks to keep the giant with seven-league boots from passing! It is the time of **mobilization**, of marching together, and we must go forward in close order, like silver in the veins of the Andes [Mountains].

Only those born prematurely are lacking in courage. Those without faith in their country are seven-month weaklings. Because they have no courage, they deny it to others. Their puny arms—arms with bracelets and hands with painted nails, arms of Paris or Madrid—can hardly reach the bottom

strongbox: a solidly-made chest for storing money or other valuables.

strife: conflict.

prow: the pointed front part of a ship.

coveting: desiring, craving.

squire: the major landowner of a particular district.

mobilization: coming together for action.

limb, and they claim the tall tree to be unclimbable. The ships should be loaded with those harmful insects that gnaw at the bone of the country that nourishes them. If they are Parisians or from Madrid, let them go to the Prado [museum in Madrid] under lamplight, or to Tortoni's for a sherbet.

Those carpenters' sons who are ashamed that their fathers are carpenters! Those born in America who are ashamed of the mother who reared them, because she wears an Indian apron, and who disown their sick mother, the scoundrels, abandoning her on her sickbed! Then who is a real man? He who stays with his mother and nurses her in her illness, or he who puts her to work out of sight, and lives at her expense on decadent lands, sporting fancy neckties, cursing the womb that carried him, displaying the sign of the traitor on the back of his paper frockcoat?

These sons of Our America, which will be saved by its Indians and is growing better; these deserters who take up arms in the armies of a North America that drowns its Indians in blood and is growing worse! These delicate creatures who are men but are unwilling to do men's work! The [George] Washington who made this land for them, did he not go to live with the English ... at a time when he saw them fighting against his own country? These **"iconoclasts"** of honor who drag that honor over foreign soil, like their counterparts in the French Revolution with their dancing, their **affectations**, their drawling speech!

For in what lands can men take more pride than in our long-suffering American republics, raised up from among the silent Indian masses by the bleeding arms of a hundred apostles, to the sounds of battle between the book and the processional candle? Never in history have such advanced and united nations been **forged** in so short a time from such disorganized elements.

The **presumptuous** man feels that the earth was made to serve as his pedestal because he happens to have a **facile** pen or colorful speech, and he accuses his native land of being worthless and beyond **redemption** because its virgin jungles fail to provide him with a constant means of traveling over the world, driving Persian ponies and lavishing champagne like a tycoon. The **incapacity** does not lie with the emerging

iconoclasts: people who attack or destroy established beliefs or institutions.

affectations: attitudes or behaviors that are faked or artificial, usually to impress other people.

forged: created, established.

presumptuous: arrogant, impolite.

facile: skillful.

redemption: rescue.

incapacity: inability.

country in quest of suitable forms and a **utilitarian** greatness; it lies rather with those who attempt to rule nations of a unique and violent character by means of laws inherited from four centuries of freedom in the United States and nineteen centuries of monarchy in France....

To govern well, one must see things as they are. And the able governor in America is not the one who knows how to govern the Germans or the French; he must know the elements that compose his own country, and how to bring them together, using methods and institutions originating within the country, to reach that desirable state where each man can attain self-realization and all may enjoy the abundance that Nature has bestowed on everyone in the nation to enrich with their toil and defend with their lives. The government must originate in the country. The spirit of the government must be that of the country. Its structure must conform to rules appropriate to the country. Good government is nothing more than the balance of the country's natural elements.

That is why the imported book has been conquered in America by the natural man. Natural men have conquered learned and artificial men. The native halfbreed has conquered the exotic **Creole**. The struggle is not between civilization and **barbarity**, but between false **erudition** and Nature. The natural man is good, and he respects and rewards superior intelligence as long as his humility is not turned against him, or he is not offended by being disregarded—a thing the natural man never forgives, prepared as he is to forcibly regain the respect of whoever has wounded his pride or threatened his interests. It is by **conforming** with these **disdained** native elements that the **tyrants** of America have climbed to power, and have fallen as soon as they betrayed them. Republics have paid with **oppression** for their inability to recognize the true elements of their countries, to **derive** from them the right kind of government, and to govern accordingly....

In nations composed of both cultured and uncultured elements, the uncultured will govern because it is their habit to attack and resolve doubts with their fists in cases where the cultured have failed in the art of governing. The uncultured masses are lazy and timid in the realm of intelligence, and

utilitarian: useful, sensible, practical.

Creole: a person descended from the early Spanish and French settlers of the New World.

barbarity: backwardness.

erudition: learning, knowledge.

conforming: adjusting, following.

disdained: scorned, rejected.

tyrants: rulers with absolute power that they use harshly.

oppression: unjust or cruel use of power and authority.

derive: obtain from a source.

they want to be governed well. But if the government hurts them, they shake it off and govern themselves.

How can the universities produce governors if not a single university in America teaches the **rudiments** of the art of government, the analysis of elements **peculiar** to the peoples of America? The young go out into the world wearing Yankee or French spectacles, hoping to govern a people they do not know. In the political race entrance should be denied to those who are ignorant of the rudiments of politics.... Newspapers, universities, and schools should encourage the study of the country's **pertinent components.** To know them is sufficient, without mincing words; for whoever brushes aside even a part of the truth, whether through intention or oversight, is doomed to fall.... It is easier to resolve our problem knowing its components than to resolve it without knowing them....

Knowing is what counts. To know one's country and govern it with that knowledge is the only way to free it from **tyranny.** The European university must bow to the American university. The history of America, from the Incas to the present, must be taught in clear detail and to the letter....

The bookworm redeemers failed to realize that the revolution succeeded because it came from the soul of the nation; they had to govern with that soul and not without it or against it. America began to suffer, and still suffers, from the tiresome task of reconciling the hostile and **discordant** elements it inherited from a **despotic** and **perverse** colonizer, and the imported methods and ideas which have been **retarding** logical government because they are lacking in local realities....

"What are we?" is the mutual question, and little by little they furnish answers.... The frockcoats are still French, but thought begins to be American. The youth of America are rolling up their sleeves, digging their hands in the dough, and making it rise with the sweat of their brows. They realize that there is too much imitation, and that creation holds the key to salvation. "Create" is the password of this generation. The wine is made from **plantain**, but even if it turns sour, it is our own wine! That a country's form of government must be in keeping with its natural elements is a **foregone conclusion....** Freedom, to be **viable**, has to be sincere and complete. If a

rudiments: basics, foundation.

peculiar: unique.

pertinent: important, appropriate.

components: parts or elements of the whole.

tyranny: rigid and brutal control held by a single ruler who has all the power.

discordant: clashing, disagreeing.

despotic: characterized by an oppressive use of unlimited power.

perverse: corrupt, stubborn.

retarding: slowing down, hampering.

plantain: a banana-type fruit common in the tropics.

foregone conclusion: a certainty, something that doesn't need to be argued.

viable: capable of surviving and growing.

republic refuses to open its arms to all, and move ahead with all, it dies....

The new Americans are on their feet, saluting each other from nation to nation, the eyes of the laborers shining with joy. The natural statesman arises, schooled in the direct study of Nature. He reads to apply his knowledge, not to imitate. Economists study the problems at their point of origin. Speakers begin a policy of moderation. Playwrights bring native characters to the stage. Academies discuss practical subjects. Poetry shears off its romantic locks and hangs its red vest on the glorious tree. Selective and sparkling prose is filled with ideas. In the Indian republics, the governors are learning Indian....

But perhaps Our America is running another risk that does not come from itself but from the difference in origins, methods, and interests between the two halves of the continent, and the time is near at hand when an enterprising and vigorous people who scorn or ignore Our America will even so approach it and demand a close relationship....

The scorn of our **formidable** neighbor [the United States] who does not know us is Our America's greatest danger. And since the day of the visit is near, it is **imperative** that our neighbor know us, and soon, so that it will not scorn us. Through ignorance it might even come to lay hands on us. Once it does know us, it will remove its hands out of respect. One must have faith in the best in men and distrust the worst. One must allow the best to be shown so that it reveals and **prevails** over the worst. Nations should have a **pillory** for whoever stirs up useless hates, and another for whoever fails to tell them the truth in time.

There can be no racial **animosity**, because there are no races.... Man's universal identity springs forth from triumphant love and the turbulent hunger for life. The soul,

Student looks at the KKK (Ku Klux Klan) letters painted on a statue of José Martí in 1954. Martí spoke out often against racism in the Americas: "Whoever foments and spreads antagonism and hate between the races, sins against humanity."

formidable: forbidding, impressive.

imperative: absolutely necessary.

prevails: wins out, predominates.

pillory: a public means of punishing or ridiculing someone.

animosity: hatred.

The Spanish-American War

José Martí's most fervent wish was realized just three years after his death when Cuba gained its independence from Spain. At the same time, one of his deepest fears was also realized: the United States had established a foothold in his land and elsewhere throughout the world due in large part to the revolt he had organized.

After the uprising in 1895 that claimed Martí's life, the Spanish government in Cuba cracked down even harder on its colony, hoping to halt the guerrilla warfare. A system of concentration camps was put in place forcing rural Cubans to live in confinement in selected military towns. Thousands of people died in these camps from starvation and disease. Stories in the U.S. newspapers about the brutal conditions in Cuba moved the U.S. public to sympathize with the Cuban struggle.

At the same time, U.S. businesses had heavy investments in Cuba and were experiencing financial losses due to the warfare there. The United States was also quite interested in expanding its own powers and viewed Cuba as an essential base in its dealings with Central America.

Feelings against Spain were strong when, in 1898, the U.S. battleship *Maine* was sunk in the Havana harbor. Two hundred sixty men drowned. Although it was never proven that Spain sank the *Maine,* the United States blockaded Spanish ports and war broke out between Spain and the United States within two months.

The Spanish-American War was short, with consistent victories on the United States side. Within two weeks of declaring war, the United States sent a squadron to Manila, Philippine Islands, also ruled by Spain, which quickly defeated the Spanish forces there. Seventeen thousand U.S. troops entered Cuba, and heavy fighting with the Spanish occured during the month of July. The Spanish surrendered on July 17. U.S. troops had also occupied Puerto Rico.

In December 1898 the Treaty of Paris set the terms of peace. Spain had lost its empire. Cuba was freed, but remained under U.S. supervision. Guam, Puerto Rico, and the Philippines were all ceded to the United States. Cuba, freed from Spanish control, found itself temporarily subjected to a U.S. military government. In 1901, however, the United States acknowledged an independent Cuban government, although it demanded many limitations on the independence to be written into the new Cuban constitution.

equal and eternal, **emanates** from bodies of various shapes and colors. Whoever **foments** and spreads **antagonism** and hate between the races, sins against humanity.

But as nations take shape among other different nations, there is a condensation of vital and individual characteristics of thought and habit, expansion and conquest, vanity and

emanates: flows.

foments: encourages, promotes.

antagonism: conflict, hostility.

greed which could ... be turned into a serious threat for the weak and isolated neighboring countries, declared by the strong country to be inferior and perishable.... One must not attribute, through a **provincial antipathy**, a fatal and inborn wickedness to the continent's fairskinned nation simply because it does not speak our language, or see the world as we see it, or resemble us in its political defects, so different from ours, or favorably regard the excitable, dark-skinned people, or look charitably from its still uncertain **eminence** upon those less favored by history, who climb the road of **republicanism** by heroic stages.

The self-evident facts of the problem should not be obscured, because the problem can be resolved, for the peace of centuries to come, by appropriate study, and by **tacit** and immediate unity in the continental spirit. With a single voice the hymn is already being sung. The present generation is carrying industrious America along the road enriched by their sublime fathers; from the Rio Grande to the Straits of Magellan, the Great Sem, astride his condor, is sowing the seed of the new America throughout the Latin nations of the continent and the sorrowful islands of the sea!

By 1884, Martí had persuaded two heroes of the Ten Years' War—General Máximo Gómez and General Antonio Maceo—to join the independence movement. His relationship with them, however, was rocky from the very beginning. Martí favored a civilian government for Cuba and would not support any uprising that would result in a military dictatorship. Gómez and Maceo felt quite differently, and the three men went their separate ways for some time.

Meanwhile, in late 1891 and early 1892, Martí spent some time in Florida. There he worked with Cuban rebel groups in Tampa and Key West to produce a statement outlining the aims of the independence movement. In April 1892, all of the various exile groups came together to form the official Cuban Revolutionary Party. They elected Martí to serve as president. Around the same time, Martí also became publisher and editor of the newspaper Patria. *It*

provincial antipathy: hatred that springs from narrow-mindedness or lack of sophistication.

eminence: noble or prominent stature.

republicanism: supporting a representative form of government.

tacit: implied, understood.

was a New York-based weekly publication that served as the official voice of the party.

The sinking of the U.S.S. Maine in the Havana Harbor, 1898

Prepares for Revolution

Martí spent much of 1893 on the road between New York and Florida. His efforts were focused on making plans for the revolution, raising funds for supplies, and rallying fellow exiles behind the cause. By the end of 1894, everything was in place to launch an invasion of Cuba from three different sites in the Caribbean—Costa Rica, the Dominican Republic, and Key West. However, one of the conspirators tipped off U.S. authorities, who confiscated the rebels' ships and arms before they could make it to Cuba.

Martí was devastated by this turn of events. But with the

encouragement of his friends, he developed a new strategy. In the meantime, he passed along orders to his supporters within Cuba to launch the uprising there. When news came in late February 1895 that the revolution had indeed begun, Martí's invasion plans shifted into high gear.

General Gómez, as one of the operation's military commanders, urged Martí to return to New York and oversee events from there. But Martí insisted on accompanying the invasion force to Cuba. On April 12, 1895, he finally set foot on the island, accompanied by a group of five other men, including Gómez. Their intention was to meet up with General Maceo and his forces, which they did on May 5.

Falls in Battle

As the rebels moved slowly westward across the island, they came under attack by Spanish troops. Gómez ordered Martí to stay behind in their camp for his own safety. Martí ignored him and, as the story goes, he jumped on a white horse and rode into the thick of the battle. There he was recognized by one of the Spanish soldiers, who shot and killed him.

The revolution did not die with Martí, however. Gómez and Maceo continued the guerrilla war against the Spanish. After Maceo died in action in late 1896, Gómez carried on with the help of General Calixto García. They were still fighting when the United States entered the conflict in April 1898 on the side of the rebels. That involvement touched off the so-called Spanish-American War, which ended just a few months later in defeat for Spain. Under the terms of a peace treaty signed later that same year, Cuba finally achieved independence from its former colonial ruler.

A U.S. military government then ran the island until May 1902, at which time the Cuban republic was officially established. Yet, as Martí had feared, the United States more or less continued to dominate Cuban economic and social affairs for years afterward. It was not until communist dictator Fidel Castro seized power in 1959 that the U.S. presence in Cuba truly came to an end.

Sources

Books

Appel, Todd M., *José Martí,* Chelsea House, 1992.

Gray, Richard Butler, *José Martí, Cuban Patriot,* University of Florida Press, 1962.

The Hispanic-American Almanac, edited by Nicolás Kanellos, Gale, 1993.

José Martí, Revolutionary Democrat, edited by Christopher Abel and Nissa Torrents, Duke University Press, 1986.

Kirk, John M., *José Martí, Mentor of the Cuban Nation,* University Presses of Florida, 1983.

Mañach, Jorge, *Martí, Apostle of Freedom* (translated from the Spanish), Devin-Adair, 1950.

Martí, José, *Inside the Monster: Writings on the United States and American Imperialism,* edited by Philip S. Foner, Monthly Review Press, 1975.

Martí, José, *Our America: Writings on Latin America and the Struggle for Cuban Independence,* edited by Philip S. Foner, Monthly Review Press, 1977.

Periodicals

American History Illustrated, "Who Was José Martí?" July/August 1990.

Vilma S. Martinez

1943–

Mexican American civil rights attorney

"THE PROCESSES BY WHICH THIS COUNTRY CONDUCTS ITS ELECTIONS ARE RIDDLED WITH SUBTLE, AND NOT SO SUBTLE, DISCRIMINATORY DEVICES, WHICH HAVE THE EFFECT OF EXCLUDING MINORITIES."

In 1965, the civil rights movement in the United States won a major victory when the U.S. Congress passed the Voting Rights Act. This important bill outlawed various schemes that were intended to prevent African Americans from registering to vote. (See box on page 164 for more information.) Ten years later, in 1975, legislators tackled the matter of extending the Voting Rights Act and broadening its scope to include not only blacks but Hispanic Americans. The woman responsible for convincing Congress to take that historic step was Vilma S. Martinez, then the president and general counsel (attorney and legal advisor) of the Mexican American Legal Defense and Educational Fund (MALDEF). Ever since it was founded in 1969, MALDEF has been at the forefront of the civil rights struggle, monitoring the impact of laws and public policy on Hispanic Americans and challenging inequities in the courts.

Childhood Commitment to Civil Rights

Martinez is a native of San Antonio, Texas. She earned a bachelor's degree from the University of Texas in 1964 and then obtained a law degree from New York City's Columbia University in 1967. Because she was personally very familiar with the kind of prejudice that Mexican Americans often face, Martinez had made up her mind while she was still quite young that she would devote her life to fighting injustice and discriminatory practices. This strong commitment led her into civil rights work right after her graduation from law school.

Martinez's first job was as a staff attorney with the Legal Defense and Educational Fund of the National Association for the Advancement of Colored People (NAACP). In this role, she argued cases on behalf of minorities and poor people who were victims of illegal discrimination.

In 1970 Martinez left the NAACP for a position with the New York State Division of Human Rights. There she functioned as an expert on equal opportunity rights as new rules and procedures were created and put into effect. Martinez then spent two years, from 1971 until 1973, as a labor lawyer with a private New York law firm. During this period, she became one of the first two women invited to serve on the board of MALDEF.

Named Head of MALDEF

In 1973, Martinez was named president and general counsel of MALDEF. Typically, she divided her time between fund-raising activities, establishing links with other groups interested in civil rights, and handling various legal cases. Many of these cases involved issues that she felt violated the spirit of the 1965 Voting Rights Act, which technically applied only to blacks and Puerto Ricans.

MALDEF had noted numerous examples of Mexican Americans who were denied the right to vote in ways that were very similar to those used to stop African Americans from going to the polls. Sometimes, it was an outright threat of violence that scared away potential voters, or the requirement that they pay a special "poll tax." On other occasions, polling places might suddenly "run out" of bal-

lots whenever Mexican Americans arrived to vote. In addition, the failure to provide ballots printed in Spanish excluded all those would-be voters who could not speak or write English.

When the Voting Rights Act came up for extension in 1975, Martinez led MALDEF's efforts to make sure that the bill would specifically protect Hispanic Americans. Her stand on the issue received the support of other groups such as the Congressional Black Caucus, organized labor, and Japanese Americans. She then took the fight to the halls of Congress.

On March 24, 1975, Martinez faced members of a House subcommittee to deliver lengthy testimony on the abuses she had witnessed through her work with MALDEF. An excerpt from her opening statement is reprinted here from Hearings Before the Subcommittee on Civil and Constitutional Rights of the Committee on the Judiciary, House of Representatives, 94th Congress, 1st Session, on H.R. 939, H.R. 2148, H.R. 3247, and H.R. 3501, Extension of the Voting Rights Act, *Serial No. 1, Part 1, U.S. Government Printing Office, 1975.*

As you may know, the Mexican American Legal Defense and Educational Fund, MALDEF, is a nonprofit organization which works to **redress** the **grievances** and **vindicate** the legal and constitutional rights of over six million United States citizens of Mexican ancestry. Today our community constitutes the second largest minority in America. It is predicted that within the next decade and a half the Spanish-surnamed community—and we [Mexican Americans] are 65 percent of the Spanish-surnamed community—will become the largest minority in this country.

Its needs, gentlemen, are enormous. The barriers it faces are **legion.** The discrimination it has endured and continues to endure is **pervasive.** But I should like to believe that its hope and its ultimate faith in this country are **abiding** and deep-sprung. Today we are calling on this committee and this Congress to vindicate that hope and that faith.

redress: correct, make up for.

grievances: complaints.

vindicate: confirm, honor, defend.

legion: numerous, many.

pervasive: widespread.

abiding: enduring, constant.

I will not be reading my entire statement because you do have a copy of it. I would like to highlight certain of the aspects here. I know how boring it is to sit and listen to statistics, but I do want you to know that the statistics tell a lot here.

In terms of the poverty level you will see that in Texas over 35 percent of our people are at the poverty level. In terms of representation to elective office in California as well as Texas, you will see that in Texas Mexican Americans comprise 18 percent of the population and only 6.2 percent of the 4,070 elected offices are held by Chicanos. In California it is even worse....

In 1970, of 15,650 major elected and appointed positions at all levels of government, federal, state, and local, only 310, or 1.98 percent were held by Mexican Americans. This result is no mere coincidence. It is the result of **manifold** discriminatory practices which have the design and effect of excluding Mexican Americans from participation in their own government and maintaining the **status quo.**

I would like to share with this committee, at some length, two things: First, is ... what we have found through the work of the U.S. Commission on Civil Rights to be **extant** today in Uvalde County, Texas; and second, to share with you what the Mexican American Legal Defense Fund has had to **litigate** over the past seven years in the voting rights area.

What the Commission found in Uvalde exists all across the state of Texas. The pattern of abuses in Uvalde County is strikingly reminiscent of the Deep South of the early 1960s. The Civil Rights Commission's study documents that duly registered Chicano voters are not being placed on the voting lists; that election judges are selectively and deliberately **invalidating** ballots cast by minority voters; that election judges are refusing to aid minority voters who are illiterate in English; that the tax assessor-collector of Uvalde County, who is responsible for registering voters, refuses to name members of minority groups as deputy registrars; that the Uvalde County tax assessor repeatedly runs out of registration application cards when minority voter applicants ask for them; that the Uvalde County tax assessor-collector refuses to register voter applicants based on the technicality that the

manifold: numerous, various.

status quo: the existing state of affairs.

extant: existing.

litigate: take to court.

invalidating: nullifying; making something not count.

The Voting Rights Act

In 1965, the United States Congress responded to the pleas of civil rights activists and passed new legislation aimed at ending discrimination in the voter-registration process. Conditions were especially bad in the southern states of Alabama, Arkansas, Mississippi, Texas, and Virginia. Segregationists there had long used a variety of tactics to keep African Americans away from the voting booth. Sometimes, the threat of violence was enough. In other cases, white officials relied on literacy tests and poll taxes.

For example, a black voter could be disqualified if he or she didn't give the "right" answers to a complicated series of questions that supposedly proved whether a person was smart enough to vote. Another very popular strategy for denying the vote to certain people was the charging of a poll tax. Poor people of all colors who could not afford to pay this special tax were barred from voting.

The Voting Rights Act of 1965 expanded the powers of the federal government to eliminate such discrimination at the state level. It banned the use of literacy tests and poll taxes. It also authorized the U.S. attorney general to send in federal officials where necessary to register black voters.

Because the Voting Rights Act of 1965 was drafted to address the problems faced by African Americans, it did not really tackle the issue of discrimination faced by other minorities. For example, Puerto Ricans were the only Hispanic Americans specifically mentioned in the text of the bill. This was because of Puerto Rico's special commonwealth status, which voluntarily links it

application was filed on a printed card bearing a previous year's date.

Other abuses were uncovered by the study of the Civil Rights Commission in Uvalde County, and elsewhere in Texas: Widespread **gerrymandering** with the purpose of **diluting** minority voting strength; systematic drawing of at-large electoral districts with this same purpose and design; maintenance of polling places exclusively in areas **inaccessible** to minority voters; excessive filing fees to run for political office; numbered paper ballots which need to be signed by the voter, thus making it possible to discover for whom an individual cast his ballot.

The Civil Rights Commission field investigation in Uvalde also uncovered widespread economic threats and **coercion** directed at citizens who became involved with **insurgent** political forces. Again and again, interviewees express fear of

gerrymandering: dividing an area into political units in such a way that one group has advantages over another.

diluting: watering down, weakening.

inaccessible: not easy to reach; unavailable.

coercion: persuasion through intimidation.

insurgent: rebellious; opposed to established leaders.

to the United States while leaving it free to run its own affairs.

It was not until the Voting Rights Act of 1965 came up for renewal in 1975 that Congress considered the question of discrimination against non-English-speaking minorities. Of special concern were Spanish speakers in Texas. A strengthened version of the Voting Rights Act reinforced the national ban on literacy tests. It also forbid states from dividing up voting districts in ways that would decrease the power of the minority vote. And perhaps most significant of all, it made bilingual ballots a requirement in some areas of the country.

In 1982, the Voting Rights Act once again came up for renewal. It passed with an important amendment prohibiting *any* voting law or practice—intentional or not—that results in discrimination on the basis of race, color, or language. But the amendment has periodically faced challenges in court and in Congress, mostly by those who feel it grants too much power to the federal government when it comes to overseeing how states and smaller political units establish election laws and voting procedures. And ever since redistricting efforts got under way in the early 1990s, the government and the courts have battled over how voting districts are determined. The decisions resulting from those battles may well threaten the future of established minority districts.

Still, the provisions contained in the Voting Rights Act have paved the way for much greater minority participation in politics. As a result, increasing numbers of minority candidates regularly run and win elections at the local, state, and national level.

reprisals as one reason for low voter registration and turn out. As one woman put it bluntly, "Jobs are at stake." The Uvalde County school system fires teachers who attempt to run for office.

Local officials in Uvalde County have shown ingenuity and determination in depriving Mexican Americans of their right to vote. The city council of the town of Uvalde, for example, met and unilaterally decided in secret not to print on the ballot the name of a Chicano candidate for the council, even though he had duly qualified to stand for election....

To better acquaint you with Uvalde, Texas, I would like to point out that last December I argued before the fifth circuit [court] in New Orleans a school desegregation case coming out of Uvalde, Texas. In Texas, as many of you know, children were required to be educated in either the white or the colored school. Officials in Texas, and I have in mind Pecos

reprisals: retaliation, revenge.
ingenuity: cleverness, creativity.

County and Nueces County, which have large percentages of Mexican American people, could not decide whether Mexican Americans were white or colored, so we got no schools. In most other schools, as in Uvalde, we were in fact put into a third category of school, called the Mexican school.

In order to **prevail** in Texas, we have to argue what is now known as the northern *de jure* segregation cases. [The concepts of *de jure* and *de facto* segregation figured prominently in the civil rights struggle. *De jure* segregation refers to discriminatory practices that are ordered and supported by law. *De facto* segregation refers to discriminatory practices as they actually exist in everyday life, even if there are laws against them.] We **culled** through the school board minutes going back to 1919. We traced the development of their school construction policies, their school assignment policies. We noticed that even toys were provided on the basis of race; twice the amount was spent for children in the Anglo schools as for children in the Mexican school, even though there were double the number of children in the Mexican schools as in the Anglo schools.

This, then, is the situation in at least one of the 254 Texas counties. As the Civil Rights Commission found, the processes by which this country conducts its elections are riddled with **subtle**, and not so subtle, discriminatory devices, which have the effect of excluding minorities. The atmosphere in which those elections are conducted is heavy with the clouds of discrimination and coercive control.

Consider, if you will, the multitude of suits which would have to be filed by private parties to remedy each of these separate abuses which the Civil Rights Commission uncovered there. Consider the enormous pressure to which the suing party would be subjected. Consider the time which such litigation would consume. Consider the cost. And then consider that these problems by no means are found in Uvalde County alone. They exist all across the great **swath** of Texas where Chicanos are attempting to share in decisions affecting their county, their city, and their schools, decisions which are crucial to their daily lives. It is thus crucial that the constitutional rights of these citizens be enforced.

But it is simply not possible to guarantee to these people a

prevail: win.

culled: sorted, sifted.

subtle: hidden.

swath: a long, broad strip of something.

Vilma S. Martinez

meaningful right to vote with private litigation alone. There is an alternative remedy, an expansion as well as extension of the Voting Rights Act....

Most, if not all, of the types of abuses that I have outlined for you this morning would be routinely objectionable under ... the Voting Rights Act. These abuses ... demand legal resources which are simply too great for private **litigants** like MALDEF to bear....

In reading the Supreme Court's decision in *South Carolina v. Katzenbach,* upholding the constitutionality of the Voting Rights Act, I noted that at page 314 of the opinion of the Court, they said voting suits are unusually **onerous** to prepare, sometimes requiring as many as 6,000 man-hours. I am sure some of them were women-hours spent combing through registration records in preparation for trial.

At page 315, the House Committee on the Judiciary was quoted, and the Court noted the House Committee's concern that the voting rights litigation in Dallas County, Alabama, had taken four years to open the door to the exercise of constitutional rights **conferred** almost a century ago. This committee said, "Four years is too long; the burden is too heavy; the wrong to our citizens is too serious; the damage to our national conscience is too great not to adopt more effective measures than exist today."

My question to you today is: do you feel that way about Mexican Americans? Basically, this is a senseless waste of legal resources by both private attorneys and the courts; and it points up the need for a more rational approach to the problems we encounter, certainly in Texas, but also in many other parts of the Southwest, including California.

More importantly, a privately funded organization like MALDEF does not have the resources to litigate against discriminatory voting procedures in every county in Texas or even to identify exhaustively where discriminatory voting procedures are being employed. Only the Justice Department with its public resources, its expertise in this field gained over the past ten years, and with the aid of the presumptions set forth in the **statutory** language of [the Voting Rights Act] can effectively insure that minority voters' rights in the Southwest are secured....

litigants: people or groups involved in a lawsuit.

onerous: burdensome.

conferred: granted.

statutory: created and enacted by the legislative branch of government.

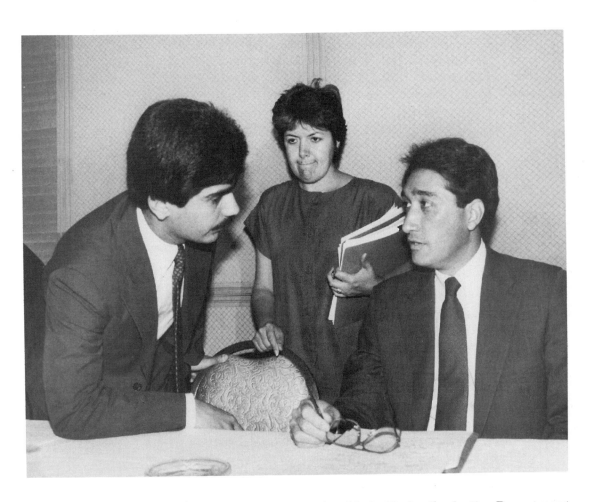

Vilma Martinez in 1984, as chair of the Hispanic Immigration Conference, talks about immigration reform with Henry Cisneros (see entry) and Arnold Torres, director of United Latin American Citizens

amending: changing; making right.

amendatory: corrective.

afford: grant, provide.

fervent: passionate.

This committee should clarify for the Justice Department its responsibilities under the Voting Rights Act of 1965. By **amending** the statutory definition of test or device [to include registration materials and ballots that are available only in English and thus cannot be read and understood by many Spanish-speaking Americans], the Congress will only write into law what we believe the Supreme Court has already held, but what the attorney general refuses to enforce.

The Congress should pass **amendatory** language which would **afford** Mexican Americans in Texas and elsewhere in the Southwest the powerful protections of ... the Voting Rights Act.

In all this there lies only the **fervent** desire to be heard, to participate in our own government, and to insure that electoral rules and procedures **foster,** not **foreclose,** our opportunity for self-expression at the polls. And ultimately, if this legislation is passed by the Congress and enforced by the Justice Department, it will mean better local government, it will mean better education for our children, it will mean better street lighting and police protection, and other vital services. It will mean the beginnings of a fair share for Mexican Americans. I sincerely hope this committee will help us make that new beginning here today....

99

The following month (April 1975), Martinez delivered a similar message to members of the U.S. Senate Subcommittee on Constitutional Rights of the Committee on the Judiciary. They were considering their own version of the Voting Rights Act extension. Once again, she tried to persuade the legislators that in order to eliminate the problem of voter discrimination in the United States, they needed to take her recommendations to heart. Finally, on July 28, 1975, Congress approved the extension of the Voting Rights Act, agreeing with Martinez that it should be broadened to include Spanish-speaking Americans and others the legislators defined as "language minorities."

Martinez went on to score victories in a number of other significant cases while with MALDEF. In 1982, for example, she successfully argued the case of Plyler v. Doe, *which challenged a Texas law denying free public school education to the children of illegal immigrants. The U.S. Supreme Court ruled the Texas law unconstitutional and in violation of the equal protection clause because no state is allowed to deny any person the equal protection of the laws.*

Later in 1982, feeling that it was time to move on both personally and professionally, Martinez left MALDEF for a partnership in the large Los Angeles law firm of Munger, Tolles & Olson. There she has specialized in handling commercial litigation as well as federal and state court civil litigation involving issues such as wrongful termination (being fired from a job) and employment discrimination. She has also been active on several corporate and institutional

foster: encourage.
foreclose: shut out.

boards (including MALDEF's) and served for fourteen years as a member of the University of California Board of Regents (a university governing board).

Sources

Books

Extension of the Voting Rights Act of 1965: Hearings Before the Subcommittee on Constitutional Rights of the Committee on the Judiciary, United States Senate, 94th Congress, 1st Session, on S. 407, S. 903, SD. 1297, S. 1409, and S. 1443, U.S. Government Printing Office, 1975.

Hearings Before the Subcommittee on Civil and Constitutional Rights of the Committee on the Judiciary, House of Representatives, 94th Congress, 1st Session, on H.R. 939, H.R. 2148, H.R. 3247, and H.R. 3501, Extension of the Voting Rights Act, Serial No. 1, Part 1, U.S. Government Printing Office, 1975.

Notable Hispanic American Women, Gale, 1993.

Jorge Mas Canosa

1939–

Cuban American businessman and activist

One of the most influential—and controversial—members of Miami, Florida's Cuban exile community is Jorge Mas Canosa. He is the longtime chair of a group known as the Cuban American National Foundation (CANF). Under his forceful leadership, CANF has organized itself to push for U.S. sanctions against Cuban president Fidel Castro. The organization is also prepared to assist in restoring capitalism and democracy to the the island nation if Castro and his communist regime should be removed from office. "Castro's days are numbered," declared Mas in a 1992 interview broadcast on the television news magazine 60 Minutes. "Castro is going to fall, and he's going to fall in the immediate future, and we must be prepared to bring freedom and democracy back to Cuba, but most important, prosperity."

Life in 1950s Cuba

The son of a Cuban army veterinarian, Mas was born in the port city of Santiago de Cuba. During the late 1950s,

"THE POLITICAL AND ECONOMIC ISOLATION OF FIDEL CASTRO MUST REMAIN THE CORNERSTONE OF U.S. POLICY AS LONG AS CASTRO CONTINUES TO REJECT ANY MEANINGFUL REFORM AND REFUSES TO SURRENDER POWER."

he became a student activist opposed to the brutal and corrupt government of military dictator Fulgencio Batista, who had seized power in 1952 with the help of the Cuban army. Mas's public condemnation of Batista got him into trouble with the authorities. Faced with the prospect of their son's arrest, his parents sent him to the United States. There he attended Presbyterian Junior College in Maxton, North Carolina.

Meanwhile, back in Cuba, a young lawyer-turned-revolutionary named Fidel Castro was emerging as the head of an underground, anti-Batista movement. He led a failed uprising against the dictator in 1953, but was arrested and imprisoned for two years for his part in the rebellion. After his release, Castro fled Cuba, but returned in 1956 to launch a new guerrilla mission against Batista. From its beginnings as a small group of men fighting from camps in the mountains, this mission picked up an impressive amount of popular support. Batista was finally forced to leave Cuba in January 1959, and Castro assumed control the following month.

Castro's revolution brought hope to many Cubans. For over fifty years, since Cuba gained independence from Spain in the Spanish-American War in 1898, Cuba had experienced U.S. domination in its economics and politics—particularly in its thriving sugar industry. Batista's dictatorship had welcomed American corporations and strongly favored the ruling classes in Cuba. Castro, once in power, worked to return Cuba to the working people. He prohibited foreign powers from operating plantations, effectively expelling U.S. corporations from his country. In the early years of Castro's rule, land reform and many other measures significantly improved the living conditions of the poorer classes of Cubans; the upper classes of Cubans, however, saw their status challenged and their property reduced. While many Cubans hailed Castro's socialist reforms, others were concerned that he had formed another dictatorship, allowing neither democracy nor opposition to his administration.

Although the U.S. government initially had little concern about Castro's takeover, among the new leader's land reforms was the expulsion of American businesses from Cuba. The United States, with this threat to its large investments in Cuba, actively began to work against Castro's newly formed government. Largely because of U.S. hostility, Castro allied his country with the Soviet Union, from whom he received financial and military support. Cuba was almost instantly thrown into **Cold War** politics.

A massive migration of Cubans to the United States took place in the years after the Cuban Revolution. Between 1959 and 1962 more than 155,000 people migrated and, in 1965, 257,000 more Cubans arrived in the United States. An overwhelming majority of these people were middle and upper class Cubans who felt betrayed by the revolution and were fiercely hostile to Castro. Mas, who had returned home a week after the overthrow of Batista to enroll in law school at the University of Oriente, soon became active in the anti-Castro movement. Once again he found himself facing arrest. Thus, in 1960, he fled to Miami.

The Bay of Pigs Invasion

In Miami's Little Havana neighborhood, Mas quickly made contacts with other Cuban exiles who had settled there. He also joined the famous 2506 Brigade, which participated in the disastrous Bay of Pigs invasion of Cuba in 1961. (See box on page 174 for more information.) Like the rest of the veterans of that unsuccessful U.S.-backed attempt to overthrow Castro, Mas was offered a commission as a lieutenant in the U.S. Army. He accepted the offer, believing that he and his fellow exiles would be called on to lead another invasion some day. But as soon as he realized that no such plans were under consideration, he resigned his commission and returned to Miami.

Mas then worked at a series of jobs—dishwasher, shoe salesman, milkman—to support himself and his growing family. He also became active in an organization of militant anti-Castro Cuban exiles with ties to the U.S. Central Intelligence Agency (CIA). Their goal was to get rid of Castro in any way possible, even if it meant resorting to terrorism and violence. During this period, Mas worked as a commentator on a CIA-backed radio station that broadcast anti-Castro messages to Cuba.

Cold War: a period of extreme political tension between the United States and the former Soviet Union that lasted from about 1945 until 1989.

The Bay of Pigs Invasion

When Fidel Castro seized power in Cuba in 1959, Americans as well as Cubans hoped that relations between the two countries would remain friendly. But it wasn't long before Castro made it clear how much he hated the United States and its domination of the Cuban economy and politics. The States had, in fact, often felt free to meddle in Cuban affairs in the past, and the U.S. business community in particular had been on good terms with the dictator Castro overthrew, Fulgencio Batista. By January 1961—just days before John F. Kennedy took office as president—conditions between Cuba and the United States had worsened to the point that President Dwight Eisenhower broke off all diplomatic relations with the island nation.

While Eisenhower was still president, however, plans were under way for an invasion of Cuba. Coordinating the effort was the Central Intelligence Agency (CIA), which had recruited and trained over a thousand anti-Castro Cuban exiles. President Kennedy gave the go-ahead for the invasion in the spring of 1961. On April 17, nearly two thousand men armed with U.S. weapons landed at the Bay of Pigs on Cuba's southern coast. They had counted on sparking a revolt among the Cuban people as they marched across the island toward Havana, but instead they met up with Cuban army troops. Two days of fighting left almost a hundred of the exiles dead and most of the rest captured. (Private groups in the United States later bought their freedom from Cuba.)

As news of the botched invasion became public, the Kennedy administration became the target of harsh criticism for its handling of the affair. Some people were angry because they felt the exiles had been doomed from the very start of the operation due to a lack of direct military support from the United States. (Members of the Cuban exile community in particular were left with feelings of bitterness and betrayal.) Others objected to the idea that such an invasion was even considered, let alone carried out, against a legitimate government.

The incident proved to be a major embarrassment for the new president. It also fueled Castro's suspicions of the United States and strengthened his ties to the former Soviet Union. Consequently, the United States has maintained a strict trade **embargo** on Cuba that has lasted into the late 1990s and has had severe consequences for Cuba's economy. It also instituted an open-door policy toward Cuban immigrants that lasted into the 1980s.

embargo: a prohibition against trading with.

Later in the 1960s, Mas entered the business world as a partner in a local contracting firm, Iglesias y Torres. It was a time of tremendous growth in the Greater Miami area, and Mas's company prospered doing construction work for utilities and other public service corporations throughout southern Florida. By the end of the decade, he had bought

Cuban president Fidel Castro, 1985

out his partners and changed the firm's name to Church & Tower, an English-language version of its Spanish name. (In 1994, it merged with another company; the combined firm now goes by the name MasTec.)

As a result of the tremendous success he continued to enjoy throughout the 1970s, Mas began to branch out into other businesses, including one that supplies light and heavy equipment to the construction industry. Before long, the once-impoverished immigrant was a multimillionaire.

Leader Among Miami's Cuban Exiles

While he was making his fortune in business, Mas became involved in politics. He forged especially close relationships with local and state government officials who *were sympathetic to the anti-Castro exiles. He encouraged them to adopt a tough, unbending approach toward Cuba.*

Following the election of staunch anticommunist Ronald Reagan to the presidency of the United States in 1980, Mas felt the time was right for Cuban Americans "to stop the commando raids and concentrate on influencing public opinion and governments." So he and fourteen other wealthy members of the Miami exile community who shared his views established the Cuban American National Foundation (CANF). Its purpose was to pass along information to the American public on conditions in Cuba and promote the idea of encouraging political change there.

*As CANF's chair, Mas immediately began developing contacts in Washington, D.C., to drum up support for the organization's first big undertaking—a private radio station that would broadcast news and other information to Cubans. Their objective was to break Castro's control over what the Cuban population heard about the rest of the world. The battle over Radio Martí, as it was known (in honor of Cuban patriot **José Martí** [see entry]), raged for a couple of years while Congress debated the need for it and the State Department warned of a possible backlash from Castro.*

Finally, in 1982, Radio Martí became a reality when Congress passed a bill making it part of the U.S. Information Agency. Its first broadcast was in 1985. TV Martí soon followed. Mas was named to head the advisory board that oversees both stations, putting him in a position to exercise considerable influence over news coverage and personnel decisions. But the very existence of Radio and TV Martí has long been a subject of debate in Washington and elsewhere. Cuban officials successfully jam their signals, so very few Cubans actually receive the broadcasts. Many people consider Radio and TV Martí a huge waste of taxpayer dollars.

The Transformation of CANF

Throughout the 1980s, Mas built CANF into one of the most powerful lobbying organizations in Washington. He managed to persuade important members of both political parties—including presidents Ronald Reagan and George Bush—that Fidel Castro represents a continuing threat to democracy in the Western Hemisphere. This idea in turn helped shape U.S. foreign policy during the 1980s, especially with respect to Central America and the Caribbean.

Mas made overtures to a couple of dozen world leaders as well. As always, he urged them to isolate Castro and Cuba. One of Mas's greatest triumphs came in 1993, when Russian President Boris Yeltsin ended all economic and military aid to Cuba. Castro had relied heavily on the support of the former Soviet Union for more than thirty years.

In the United States, CANF has backed measures aimed at making life difficult for Cubans and therefore for Castro. For instance, CANF fought to limit the amount of money Cuban exiles can send home to their families in Cuba. The organization also approved cutting off flight service from Miami to Cuba to make it harder for families to visit each other. In the 1990s, CANF supported the U.S. government's new and restrictive policy on illegal immigration from Cuba to the United States. Cubans who attempted to flee their homeland by boat were held at Guantánamo Bay, a U.S. military base on Cuba's southeastern shore. (That practice ended on January 31, 1996, when the last of the "boat people" were finally taken off the base.) On the other hand, Mas worked out a special arrangement with the U.S. Immigration and Naturalization Service allowing Cuban exiles living in other countries to enter the United States— but only with sponsorship from CANF.

Looking ahead to the future, Mas has established contacts with major multinational corporations, banks, brokerage firms, and wealthy individuals who are all eager to invest in Cuba after Castro is gone. CANF has even worked with lawyers to draft a new constitution for Cuba. And the group's version of the Peace Corps, Misión Martí, has trained volunteers who are ready to head to Cuba and guide it through the economic transition from communism to capitalism.

CANF Champions Harsher Trade Embargo on Cuba

In late 1991, Mas played a key role in drafting the Cuban Democracy Act (S. 2918) for consideration in the

U.S. Senate. This bill proposed strengthening the decades-old ban on trade with Cuba. Opponents of the measure argued that it was unfairly harsh and would only result in more suffering among the Cuban people. The United Nations and most major allies of the United States criticized the continuing trade embargo as a violation of international law. They also saw it as tired old Cold War strategy. CANF and its supporters, on the other hand, viewed the bill as a way to increase the Cuban people's frustrations with their living conditions, encouraging them to rise up against Castro.

When first introduced in February 1992, the bill attracted little support. The State Department condemned it as a "self-destructive" move guaranteed to anger our allies because it banned trade with Cuba by branches of U.S. companies located in Third World countries. Even Mas's close friend and ally, President George Bush, did not want to back a measure that was so unpopular both at home and abroad. But during a visit to Miami in April 1992, Democratic presidential candidate Bill Clinton announced his support of the Cuban Democracy Act. South Florida donors responded by contributing over a million dollars to his campaign. Bush soon reversed himself, and suddenly the future looked considerably brighter for S. 2918.

As he had done several times in the past for other pending legislation regarding Cuba, Mas personally appeared before members of the House and Senate to present the case in favor of the Cuban Democracy Act. His testimony before the Senate took place on August 5, 1992. The following excerpt from his remarks that day is taken from the official report entitled The Cuban Democracy Act of 1992, S. 2918: Hearing Before the Subcommittee on Western Hemisphere and Peace Corps Affairs of the Committee on Foreign Relations, United States Senate, *102nd Congress, 2nd Session, U.S. Government Printing Office, 1992.*

It is my honor to appear before ... the distinguished members of the Senate Foreign Relations Committee to talk about

Mas Canosa raising the arm of Argentine president Carlos Menem at a rally in Miami, 1994

U.S. policy toward Cuba. I sincerely hope that our discussion today will lead to decisions that in some way can bring an end to the suffering of the Cuban people, including the tragedy taking place in the Straits of Florida where thousands of Cubans are dying while trying to escape Fidel Castro's **tyranny** in unseaworthy rafts and boats....

Fidel Castro's trip to Spain two weeks ago for the Ibero-American summit served as a telling indicator of the current state of his regime. Everywhere he went, he was heckled and jeered, the Spanish press criticized him, and all Latin American heads of state in Madrid openly criticized him in public. It was such a setback for Castro that he cut his visit several days short, and even shorter still when mere rumors about troop movements on the island caused him to flee back to Cuba....

tyranny: oppressive power; dictatorship.

Jorge Mas Canosa   **179**

This growing global intolerance of Fidel Castro, evident in numerous meetings I have had with heads of state around the world, demonstrates that a policy of isolating Fidel Castro is not simply a United States position, but it is one that is gaining the increasing support of the world community.

If Castro is a **pariah**, it is the Cuban people who continue to bear the very heavy burden of his **arrogance** and **intransigence** in the face of the global march toward freedom and democracy. Press reports out of Cuba and personal testimonies describe an ever more depressing situation on the island; an economy grinding to a halt, **pervasive rationing**, a skyrocketing **underground economy**, widespread discontent and alienation, and widespread **repression** of human rights.

Just in case any Cuban citizen gets the idea that they may want to publicly disagree with the regime, rapid action brigades—thugs reminiscent of [Adolf] Hitler's brown shirts—have been organized to torment and physically abuse anyone considering such action. [During World War II in Germany, "brown shirts" were members of a private Nazi army of soldiers called storm troopers, who were known for their brutality.] These measures ... actually are desperate reactions to a growing phenomenon in Cuba today: increasing numbers of Cubans who will not accept socialism or death, who are moving decisively beyond **dissident** activity to outright open opposition to the regime.

This leads me into the topic of today's discussion—U.S.-Cuba relations and specifically, S. 2918, the Cuban Democracy Act of 1992.... I am grateful that we have moved beyond the sterile debate over whether to engage in dialogue with Fidel Castro to a more promising discussion on options for accelerating Castro's departure from power and building a foundation for a new and democratic Cuba....

We believe the current situation, both inside and outside Cuba, **mandates** a new approach to promoting a peaceful transition to democracy in Cuba. That is why we in the Cuban American [National] Foundation support the Cuban Democracy Act, which applies the stick to Castro by tightening U.S. **sanctions** against his regime, and extends a carrot to the Cuban people by **facilitating** humanitarian assistance and expanding lines of communication.

pariah: outcast, misfit.

arrogance: pride.

intransigence: stubbornness.

pervasive: widespread.

rationing: daily allowances for food or other goods, generally enforced in times when supplies are limited or economy is uncertain to ensure equal portions for everyone.

underground economy: a secret trading operation in which goods are bought and sold illegally.

repression: the act of putting down something or someone by force.

dissident: disagreeing with an opinion or a group of people.

mandates: requires.

sanctions: military or economic actions taken by a nation or group of nations against another nation to persuade it to stop violating a law.

facilitating: making easier.

I might add that a recent poll of Cuban Americans showed sixty-nine percent of the community also supports the bill. More importantly, so do numerous peaceful opposition groups on the island, including the Cuban Democratic Coalition, the largest opposition organization on the island, several groups of the Cuban Democratic Convergence, and twelve more independent opposition groups....

The Cuban Democracy Act is reminiscent of the U.S. approach toward South Africa, where a comprehensive policy of economic and political isolation made a very real contribution toward **fostering** change in that society. The political and economic isolation of Fidel Castro must remain the cornerstone of U.S. policy as long as Castro continues to reject any meaningful reform and refuses to surrender power. Why? Number one, it sends a message to those in leadership positions around Castro that he, Castro, is the obstacle to Cuba's **reintegration** into the family of nations....

When you provide resources to Cuba, all of those resources go in the hands of Fidel Castro, and him alone. He has used the roughly $100 billion in aid received from the Soviet Union, not to help the Cuban people, who have been issued rationing books since 1960, but to buy the loyalty of those around him to **sustain** himself in power. The embargo deprives Fidel Castro of those resources and will continue to shrink his inner circle.

Indeed, to see who would benefit from trade relations with Cuba ..., follow the money. The Cuban American National Foundation has obtained from sources inside Cuba a financial audit of a Cuban front company in Panama called CIMEX, one of many he uses to **circumvent** the U.S. embargo to get U.S. products into Cuba and to get Cuban products into the United States.... These financial records show ... that at a time of outrageous **austerity** measures being imposed on the Cuban people, Fidel Castro is hoarding $300 million in total assets in CIMEX, one of his personal piggy banks, including $100 million in cash, twice the amount of the total reported cash reserves held by the Castro regime.

These are the types of activities Fidel Castro continues to be engaged in, and it is why we want to make the U.S. embargo more effective. One measure in the Cuban Democ-

fostering: encouraging.

reintegration: the act of restoring unity.

sustain: support, prop up.

circumvent: avoid, get around.

austerity: enforced or extreme simplicity of living and efficient use of resources.

Cuban refugees prepare to board U.S. Navy warship

racy Act that does so is what is known as the Mack Amendment ..., a provision that would restore the embargo to its original language by closing the loophole opened in 1975 that allows foreign **subsidiaries** of U.S. companies to trade with Cuba.

It is truly distressing that at a time when Russia has radically reduced trade relations and eliminated **subsidies** to Castro, U.S. companies are extending a trade lifeline to Fidel Castro through their foreign subsidiaries. Even more so when subsidiary trade is not allowed with any other nation embargoed under the Trade with the Enemy Act.

Equally important to increasing economic pressure on the Castro regime is the idea of improving communications with the Cuban people. We support the elements of the Cuban

subsidiaries: branches.
subsidies: financial support.

Jorge Mas Canosa

Democracy Act that would **institute** careful and direct openings to the Cuban people quite apart from the regime, to contribute to the opening up of Cuban society. What can we communicate to the Cuban people? That there is life after Castro and that the international community is in **solidarity** with them.

In every available forum, the U.S. must **reiterate** that the Cuban people face no threat from the United States, that they should not fear a change in government, and that the United States is eager to restore traditional ties of economic and diplomatic cooperation with a free Cuba. We should not let Castro get away with the fear and hysteria over an American invasion that never seems to come.

We can also go a long way in **rebutting** the **ludicrous** charges made regularly in certain media circles that sinister Cuban exiles are plotting to return to Cuba and seize property and resources once Castro is gone from power. Indeed, if one were to believe this reporting, you would think that people on the island are **vehemently** anti-American, fearful of an invasion by Cuban exiles and foreign capitalists, and **repulsed** by the free-market system.

This cartoon **caricature** of the Cuban people could not be more inaccurate. Cubans on the island are painfully aware that communism does not work and that Cuban Americans enjoy tremendous opportunities that are denied [citizens of Cuba]. Let us not **delude** ourselves by automatically **equating** Cuban nationalism with anti-Americanism. It is not that simple. Let me also state for the record that Cuban exiles have no intention of going back to Cuba to buy the island, to conquer the island, to hold people in Cuba **accountable** for the actions in Cuba during the last thirty-three years.

We must reassure the Cuban citizens on the island that we, the Cuban people, are one nation divided by one man, this outdated dictator, Fidel Castro. The only one who fears the reunification of the Cuban people is Castro.

Finally ..., [we turn to] the last dimension of the Cuban Democracy Act, stating what the U.S. is prepared to do to help Cuba, once Castro is out of power and free and fair elections are held. This includes, among other measures, removing the U.S. embargo.

institute: establish.

solidarity: unity among a group of people based on its common interests and goals.

reiterate: repeat, restate.

rebutting: contradicting, exposing the untruthfulness of something.

ludicrous: ridiculous.

vehemently: strongly, intensely.

repulsed: disgusted, sickened.

caricature: an exaggeration that distorts characteristics of the person(s) or thing(s) being depicted.

delude: fool, trick.

equating: comparing, regarding as equal.

accountable: responsible.

I cannot overestimate the symbolic importance of this for the Cuban people. It says that this powerful nation [the United States] is waiting to help and will do what it can to **alleviate** the **inevitable** and tremendous difficulties of transforming a country **decimated** economically and spiritually by thirty-three years of **Marxist** dictatorship. It will also make a positive contribution to ensuring that those positions of power in Cuba ... support a peaceful, nonviolent transition.

Fidel Castro has attempted to crush the Cuban people's hopes for the future and the future of their children. I believe the Cuban Democracy Act will restore that hope. We must not let the Cuban people down. The Cuban people are going to decide for themselves their own destiny.

It is our responsibility to do what we can to **hasten** the **demise** of the Castro regime and the **advent** of a free democratic and prosperous Cuba. All that is needed is the vision and the will to seize this opportunity to help eliminate, once and for all, a bizarre political experiment that has plagued our era. Then, and only then, can the suffering of the Cuban people be replaced by a new golden age of national self-determination and economic revival....

99

By the fall of 1992, the Cuban Democracy Act no longer faced any significant opposition in Congress. It sailed through the House and the Senate and was signed into law by President Bush at an October ceremony in Miami. As predicted by some, it has led to a greatly reduced standard of living for the Cuban people, who, under Castro's reforms, once enjoyed plenty of food and a health-care system widely considered the best in the Third World. It has also triggered refugee crises from time to time as desperate Cubans climb aboard crudely made boats and rafts to escape across the Straits of Florida to the United States.

This hardline approach has produced a growing split in the Cuban American community. On the one hand are Mas and CANF, eager to push Cuba until it explodes in revolution. They feel that such a revolution will pave the way for democracy and capitalism. More moderate voices favor end-

alleviate: ease.

inevitable: unavoidable.

decimated: devastated.

Marxist: in the style of Marxism (the political philosophy of socialism developed by German thinker Karl Marx that aimed for the establishment of a classless society).

hasten: speed up.

demise: fall, collapse.

advent: birth, arrival.

ing the trade ban and opening discussions with Castro to put an end to the inhumane suffering of the Cuban people.

In addition, there are disagreements over the role the exile community should play in any transition period once Castro is gone. CANF sees itself playing a key role in bringing about a new Cuban government based on capitalist free-market principles. Others insist that such decisions should be made by the Cuban people themselves.

Meanwhile, Castro shows no sign of losing his grip on Cuba. More significantly, the anti-Castro Cuban exiles who arrived during the early 1960s—generally a well-educated and prosperous group—are middle-aged and older now. Few of them are interested in returning to live in the country they left more than thirty years ago. They have little in common with the younger generation of exiles who have arrived since the 1980s. Most of the newcomers have less education and are from a working-class background.

Mas, however, is a member of the older generation who still dreams of the day when he can once again live in the town where he was born and grew up. As he once told a reporter for the Los Angeles Times, as quoted in an Esquire article: "I am a Cuban first. I have never **assimilated**. I love America, and I would die for it. I'd never have been so successful in Cuba. But people like me need to be fed with more than success. I have all the money I'll ever need. I don't do this for the money. I do this because I feel like a tree without roots."

Sources

Books

The Cuban Democracy Act of 1992, S. 2918: Hearing Before the Subcommittee on Western Hemisphere and Peace Corps Affairs of the Committee on Foreign Relations, United States Senate, 102nd Congress, 2nd Session, U.S. Government Printing Office, 1992.

Periodicals

Christian Century, "U.S. Cuba Policy Is Obsolete," September 7–14, 1994, pp. 803–4.

Common Cause, "Mr. Mas Goes to Washington," January/February 1991, pp. 37–40.

assimilated: blended in, become a part of something larger.

Esquire, "Who Is Jorge Mas Canosa?" January 1993.

Nation, "Will Congress Kill TV Martí?" August 22–29, 1994, pp. 194–96; "Minority Report," December 26, 1994, p. 787.

New Leader, "Mas Canosa vs. Betancourt: Struggle Among the Cuban Exiles," March 19, 1990, pp. 9–11.

New Republic, "Our Man in Miami," October 3, 1994, pp. 20–25.

Newsweek, "How Can We Say No?" September 5, 1994, pp. 28–29.

Progressive, "The Cuban Obsession," July 1993, pp. 18–22.

Time, "The Man Who Would Oust Castro," October 26, 1992, pp. 56–57.

U.S. News and World Report, "Castro's New Revolution," June 24, 1991, pp. 38–41; "After Castro Moves Out," May 4, 1992, pp. 42–44.

Additional information for this profile was taken from a transcript of *60 Minutes* (television news program), Volume 26, Number 51, Burrelle's Information Services, September 4, 1994, and from a Knight-Ridder/Tribune News Service press release titled "White House May Replace Cuban Exile Leader on Advisory Panel That Oversees U.S. Broadcasts to Cuba," August 8, 1995.

Luis Muñoz-Marín

1898–1980

Puerto Rican journalist and political leader

A reporter for the New York Times *once described Luis Muñoz-Marín as a man with "the mind of a politician and the soul of a poet." Muñoz-Marín played a key role in achieving commonwealth status for Puerto Rico. (A commonwealth is a political unit that runs its own affairs while choosing to be associated with another state or nation.) His strong and engaging leadership helped transform the island colony once known as "the poorhouse of the Caribbean" into a Latin American success story. Muñoz-Marín is thus credited with helping to establish among Puerto Ricans a sense of self-respect and an appreciation for democratic traditions.*

Muñoz-Marín may well have inherited the skills that made him such an effective leader from his father, journalist and politician Luis Muñoz-Rivera, who was revered for his efforts to obtain his homeland's independence, first from Spain and then from the United States. In 1897, he successfully pressured Spain into granting Puerto Rico (then

"IT IS OF THE UTMOST IMPORTANCE TO DEMOCRACY THAT THE UNITED STATES SHALL NOT CEASE TO BE THE CHAMPION OF DEMOCRATIC RIGHTS IN THE MINDS OF MEN AND WOMEN EVERYWHERE."

one of its colonies) limited self-government. A year later, when the island came under U.S. control after Spain's defeat in the Spanish-American War, Muñoz-Rivera's commitment to independence remained firm. (See box on page 155 for more information on the Spanish-American War.) In 1910, he became Puerto Rico's resident commissioner in Washington, D.C. There he held a nonvoting seat in the U.S. House of Representatives. Although he died in office in 1916, Muñoz-Rivera is recognized as having paved the way for Congress to extend U.S. citizenship to Puerto Ricans in 1917.

Early Life

Luis Muñoz-Marín was Muñoz-Rivera's only son. He was born in San Juan just a few months before American troops occupied Puerto Rico at the close of the Spanish-American War. Young Luis spent much of his youth with his father, first in New York City and later in Washington, D.C.

A less-than-enthusiastic student who bounced from school to school, Muñoz-Marín quit for good following his father's death and decided to establish himself as a writer. He spent most of the next fifteen years in New York City, contributing articles to various newspapers and magazines on topics ranging from U.S. foreign policy to the latest Broadway show. Muñoz-Marín also edited a magazine on Latin American culture and translated into Spanish the poetry of such noted American literary figures as Walt Whitman, Carl Sandburg, and Robert Frost.

Takes an Interest in Puerto Rican Politics

But Muñoz-Marín could not turn his back on his heritage. He returned to Puerto Rico several times during the years he lived in New York City, each time involving himself in politics a bit more. His philosophy was decidedly less conservative than his father's. For instance, Muñoz-Marín worked on behalf of Latin American labor and unity movements and was briefly a member of the Socialist party until joining Puerto Rico's newly-formed Liberal party in 1926. In the pages of La Democracia, the newspaper his late father had founded, Muñoz-Marín demanded complete independence *for his native land and increased attention to the needs of its poorest citizens, the landless peasants known as* jíbaros.

It was not until he settled permanently in Puerto Rico in 1931, however, that Muñoz-Marín was able to shake the image many had of him as someone who just "played" at politics now and then. The country he saw on that particular visit was still reeling from the devastating effects of two hurricanes. There was no sugar cane, coffee, or tobacco to harvest, so the jíbaros *had crowded into the island's few major cities. Poverty, disease, and illiteracy were widespread.*

In 1932, Muñoz-Marín ran for and won a seat in the Puerto Rican House of Representatives. He scored points almost immediately by obtaining some financial aid for the island from President Franklin Roosevelt. Muñoz-Marín's popularity soared to even greater heights among the people of Puerto Rico as a result of his role in two important events. In one instance, he helped get rid of an unpopular governor. (At that time, Puerto Rico's governor was appointed by the United States, not elected by the citizens.) He also pushed through legislation that broke up some of the larger sugar plantations and redistributed the land among the peasants.

A library on wheels brings books to children in rural Puerto Rico in the 1950s. Muñoz-Marín said of Puerto Rican people: "I sincerely and proudly believe that in their hinterland of the world they constitute the best rural school of democracy in America today."

Creates a New Political Party

By 1937, Muñoz-Marín had broken with the Liberal party because of disagreements regarding how best to help the peasants. He then established a new party of his own, the Popular Democrats. During this time, his political beliefs had changed. Muñoz-Marín no longer felt Puerto Rico was ready politically or economically to stand completely on its own as a state or a nation. So, under the slogan "Bread, Land, and Liberty," he traveled to countless towns and villages campaigning vigorously against independence and for continued support from the United States to help the island deal with its many problems.

In Puerto Rico's 1940 elections, the Popular Democrats did surprisingly well. They won control of the Senate and *fell just two votes short of controlling the House. Muñoz-Marín received more votes than any other candidate and was elected president of the Senate. Thanks to skillful politicking, he was able to form an alliance with other legislators that essentially gave him control over the House as well.*

Over the next few years, Muñoz-Marín launched some ambitious land reforms and industrial and farm development plans that counted heavily on government supervision and financial aid. These programs often were not very popular with the island's appointed governor and with the U.S. Congress, not to mention some of his fellow legislators. But Muñoz-Marín charged ahead anyway. The Puerto Rican people regarded him as their hero and gave him their overwhelming support.

On quite a few occasions, Muñoz-Marín took his case directly to the American people in an effort to win their backing for what he was trying to accomplish in his homeland. On May 26, 1945, for example, he addressed a national radio audience over the CBS network. The topic of his speech was the future of Puerto Rico and the role of the United States in that future. It was just a couple of weeks after World War II ended in Europe, and Muñoz-Marín's thoughts were on shaping the world in the coming years. Perhaps, he suggested, it was time to take a fresh look at the relationship between the United States and Puerto Rico. Complete independence might not be the answer, he said, but certainly increased freedom from direct U.S. control was something to consider. Muñoz-Marín's remarks are reprinted here from Vital Speeches of the Day, *August 1, 1945.*

The future peace of the world depends to an important degree on the solution or solutions that may be found to the colonial problem. It also depends, to a still greater degree, on the prestige of the United States among the peoples of the world—on the confidence that the common man everywhere shall continue to have in the human understanding and the democratic sincerity of the American people.

It is of the utmost importance to democracy that the United States shall not cease to be the champion of democratic rights in the minds of men and women everywhere. It is clear that our great ally Russia is making a bid for the confidence and that trust which have been the traditional heritage of the United States. Of course, Russia's attitude in this respect should not be unwelcome. There is no such thing as too much good will, as too much recognition of rights and liberties. The world certainly needs as much of that as it can get from all possible sources. But certainly Russia's attitude should not be allowed to displace and substitute the traditional American attitude, but only to complement it and support it. Russia's developing international liberalism would appear best in its proper place, that is, as a follower of the tradition that the United States has made its own these many years.

In the treatment of colonies and of otherwise dependent peoples, the United States has an **eminent** field for sustaining, strengthening, and developing its policy for a good, for a confidence inspiring, for a lasting peace under the principles that have reared the national greatness of the American people.

I am proud to say that in this respect my own country, Puerto Rico, which has contributed without **stint** to the war effort, is now making what is perhaps a still more important contribution to the peace effort. Puerto Rico is a Caribbean island country of two million people which came under the **jurisdiction** of the United States as a result of the Spanish-American War almost half a century ago. Puerto Rico is a colony of the United States. It is a colony, it is true, that has been administered in a mild, though not always **intelligible**, way, by the United States government. But it is a colony. It is what each of the original thirteen states were before 1776; basically its government does not **derive** its powers from the consent of the governed. That is, by the time-honored definition written by [Thomas] Jefferson, what colonialism means to the American mind; and by that definition, Puerto Rico is a colony of the United States.

Puerto Rico is also a very poor country in its economic geography. It has but 3,500 square miles of territory. Half of its land is not **arable**, much of the rest is not of very good quality; there is not much mineral wealth under that land,

eminent: distinguished, notable.

stint: limit, end.

jurisdiction: control, authority.

intelligible: understandable.

derive: obtain.

arable: fertile, productive.

and two million people, that is 560 persons per square mile, must make their living from the top of that land. In order for so many people to subsist on such a scarcity of resources, the bulk of production must be of intensive cash-crops that can be sold in extensive markets at reasonably good prices.

It is this same people of Puerto Rico, to whom nature has been so harsh, who have reached their political maturity, according to a message of the late President Roosevelt to the Congress. They have given proof of this maturity. Eighty-five percent of the registered voters vote on the basis of universal adult **suffrage.** Although political passions frequently run high, elections are absolutely peaceful and orderly. Defeated candidates recognize their defeat and the fairness of the electoral process. The buying of votes has been unheard of for quite some time. The people vote on the clear understanding that they are giving a **mandate** for certain laws to be enacted and certain policies to be carried out insofar as their elected legislators have the legal authority to do so, and they are **vigilant** as to whether their clear-cut democratic mandates are carried out or not. The Puerto Rican people, in fact, are more than just a politically mature people. I sincerely and proudly believe that in their **hinterland** of the world they constitute the best rural school of democracy in America today, and that there is profit in looking to its poverty-stricken electorate as an example of sound democratic practice.

It is these people, so politically sound and so economically harassed, that are now contributing to the peace effort, as they are contributing to the war effort. They are now proposing to the Congress and the government of the United States a plan for **self-determination.** This plan may well serve as a basis for dealing with the colonial problem in many other parts of the world as well as in Puerto Rico. It should also help the United States in clarifying, maintaining, strengthening, and developing that leadership of hard-pressed mankind everywhere which is of such decisive importance to world justice and world peace.

The legislature of Puerto Rico has unanimously proposed to the Congress of the United States a clear-cut, straightforward method of solving the colonial problem, on the basis of self-determination, in democratic terms, and in the fiber of American policy and tradition. The Puerto Rican proposal is as follows:

At the request, the unanimous request, of the legislature of Puerto Rico, all political parties **concurring**, a bill has been introduced in the Senate by United States Senator Millard E. Tydings, of Maryland, and in the United States House of Representatives by Resident Commissioner Pinero, of Puerto

suffrage: right to vote.

mandate: order, authorization.

vigilant: watchful, alert.

hinterland: a place far away from the major cities and centers of the world; a remote area.

self-determination: freedom to choose one's own political future.

concurring: agreeing.

Luis Muñoz-Marín

Rico. This bill contains four titles and offers three alternative forms of government to the people of Puerto Rico.

Title 1 provides that there shall be a **referendum** in which the people of Puerto Rico shall decide whether they want independence under certain economic conditions necessary for their survival, or statehood, or dominion status similar to that of Australia or Canada in the British Commonwealth of Nations. ["Dominion status" means that while both Australia and Canada are independent, self-governing nations, they recognize the British king or queen as the head of state.] Title 2 describes independence. Title 3 describes statehood. Title 4 describes dominion status.

If a majority of the people of Puerto Rico vote for independence, then Title 2 shall go into effect. If they vote for statehood, then Title 3 shall go into effect. If they vote for dominion status, then Title 4 shall go into effect. In this manner, if the bill is approved, the people of Puerto Rico themselves will choose their own future, on the basis of an offer by the American Congress, and in choosing it they will have before them the fullest possible picture of what they are voting about.

It is worthy of note that the proposal provides that the United States shall have **in perpetuity** all the military and naval bases and rights that they may need in Puerto Rico for the defense of the United States and the Western Hemisphere. This is of very great importance, as Puerto Rico constitutes one of the chief military protections of the Panama Canal, and has been called by military authorities "the Gibraltar of the Caribbean." [Gibraltar is a rocky peninsula located at the southern tip of Spain, just a short distance from the coast of North Africa. A British possession since 1704, it has long been of strategic importance because ships must pass through the Strait of Gibraltar to enter or leave the Mediterranean Sea at its western end.]

Parallel with these perpetual rights of the United States, under any form of government that the people of Puerto Rico may choose, certain minimum economic conditions are established, also under any form of government that the people of Puerto Rico may choose. These minimum economic conditions are considered necessary if the people are to survive in the face of the difficult economic circumstances that

referendum: vote.
in perpetuity: forever.

The Puerto Rican flag flies
alongside the U.S. flag in San
Juan following the celebration of
Constitution Day, 1952

confront them. I should call attention to the fact that these
minimum economic conditions do not represent any
increase in economic facilities. Therefore the granting of
them would not in any way increase the commitments of the
United States, but would rather decrease them. What is,
therefore, proposed is to wipe out political discontent without intolerably increasing economic suffering and discon-

tent. This is of importance, not only as a matter of justice and of American leadership in democracy but also as a means of surrounding important military defenses with the greatest possible democratic good will.

Let us look at what the colonial problem means in broad terms. Obviously, the United States will have need of military and naval establishments in many parts of the world. But just as obviously these establishments are a second line of defense. The need for military establishments is **predicated** upon the sensible provision that all good-will means of keeping the peace may fail. The first line of defense is the maintenance of peace, the creation of conditions that, so far as human understanding and good sense can make it so, will tend to keep the world at peace with itself. For that reason, the need for military establishments—the second line of defense—should not contradict the need for democratic procedure in the maintenance of world confidence in American leadership. Neither, of course, should the need to maintain this leadership weaken in any way America's maximum ability to defend itself if peace should fail. The Puerto Rican proposal is made in the clear recognition of these two **paramount** factors.

Military and naval establishments may be needed in two broadly different kinds of places. They may be needed in small places scantily populated, and they may be needed, as they are in Puerto Rico for instance, among large populations with a developed civilization, with a recognized political maturity, and an acute consciousness that the principles of freedom are applicable to them also. The United States is making this distinction clear at the San Francisco Conference. [Held in 1945, the San Francisco Conference was a gathering of fifty countries committed to developing a peace plan and a system of international cooperation. Their efforts led to the founding of the United Nations.] Military and naval bases and establishments, of course, must be where strategy says they must be, whether on small rocks of the sea where the problems of the population are at a minimum or in developed communities where the problems of the people are of great significance and importance with relation to the general democratic principles and policies at stake.

In offering its proposal for self-determination, Puerto Rico is bearing in mind these considerations. The United States, at

predicated: based.
paramount: supreme, major.

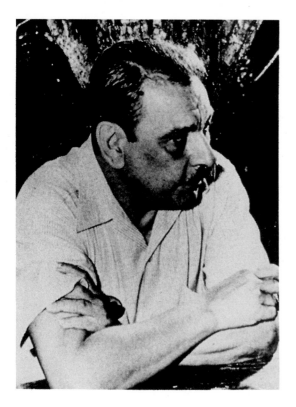

Muñoz-Marín, the architect of the commonwealth of Puerto Rico

San Francisco, are standing for self-government to colonies, which may include independence. The Puerto Rican proposal is a specific proposal for self-government on the basis of an alternative offer by Congress of different forms of self-government, which may include independence, and an acceptance by the people of Puerto Rico, in referendum, of one of the forms of self-government offered by Congress.

The proposal that the legislature of Puerto Rico has unanimously presented to the Congress of the United States is a self-determination proposal as embodied in Senate bill 1002 and in House bill 3237. We make this proposal both as a claim of justice for Puerto Rico and as a contribution to American leadership—a leadership so completely necessary for the prevention of future wars—in the minds and hearts of average men and women the world over. For both reasons we hope to receive for our proposal the support of the American people.

99

In 1947, the U.S. Congress voted to make the post of governor of Puerto Rico an elected position instead of an appointed one. In the 1948 elections, Muñoz-Marín was the runaway winner in the race for governor. Under his leadership, the "Operation Bootstrap" program began. With its emphasis on investment in light industry and manufacturing (mostly by U.S. firms attracted by generous tax breaks), Operation Bootstrap resulted in lower unemployment rates in Puerto Rico and improved housing, schools, and health care. It also encouraged the growth of a conservative Puerto Rican middle class that favored maintaining close ties with the United States.

While Operation Bootstrap was not entirely successful in getting rid of poverty, it did raise the overall standard of living in Puerto Rico, especially in comparison with many other Latin American countries. Nevertheless, thousands of the island's poorest citizens headed to the United States in search of jobs and higher wages. Most settled in New York City and other parts of the Northeast.

Commonwealth Status and a Constitution

In 1950, at the urging of Muñoz-Marín, the U.S. Congress tentatively granted Puerto Rico limited self-government when it approved commonwealth status for the island and urged Puerto Ricans to write their own constitution and put it to a popular vote. After months of work, the measure passed in Puerto Rico and also received the backing of Congress. The island officially became a commonwealth as of July 25, 1952. Under this new status, Puerto Ricans enjoyed the freedom to run their own affairs. They were also eligible to receive federal funds and were excused from paying federal taxes. However, they were not able to vote in mainland elections and were given only a nonvoting presence in the U.S. Congress.

Later in 1952, Muñoz-Marín won reelection to his second term as governor. He returned to office for two more four-year terms. In 1964, he bowed out of the race for a fifth term over the objections of his many supporters within the Popular Democratic party. Four years later, he was elected to the Senate.

Muñoz-Marín remained active in politics for the rest of his life. He kept a particularly close eye on the shifts in power between those who wanted to continue Puerto Rico's commonwealth status and those who favored statehood. (Members of a much smaller and more radical third group demand complete independence. They have occasionally tried to further their aim through violence and terrorism, including a 1950 assassination attempt on President Harry Truman). When the statehood movement picked up steam during the 1970s following the election of a pro-statehood governor, Muñoz-Marín—by then nearly eighty years old and in failing health—again traveled throughout the towns and villages of Puerto Rico to ask the people to side with the backers of commonwealth status. As before, he believed it was the best way to preserve the island's Hispanic culture while taking advantage of the security and economic aid offered by the United States.

Muñoz-Marín died in 1980, but the commonwealth versus statehood battle still rages in Puerto Rico. Most recently, in a special referendum held in November 1993, forty-eight percent of islanders approved a measure to retain commonwealth status, forty-six percent favored statehood, and four percent chose independence.

Sources

Periodicals

Grand Rapids Press, "Puerto Rico Votes to Stay U.S. Commonwealth," November 15, 1993, p. A3.

New York Times, "Luis Muñoz Marín Is Dead at 82; Began Puerto Rico's Fight on Poverty," May 1, 1980, p. D19; "Adios to a Democrat," May 2, 1980, p. 26.

Vital Speeches of the Day, "The Future of Puerto Rico," August 1, 1945, pp. 619–20; "The Substance of Freedom," November 1, 1956, pp. 40–42.

Antonia C. Novello

1944–

Puerto Rican physician and public official

In 1990, Antonia C. Novello made history as the first woman and the first Hispanic American to hold the post of United States surgeon general. (Appointed by the president, the surgeon general is the person in charge of the U.S. Public Health Service, the government agency responsible for protecting and improving the health of the nation's citizens.) In this role, Novello focused attention on what she identified as the special health-related needs of women, children, and minorities. Her goal, as she once said, was to speak up "for the people who are not able to speak for themselves."

Childhood Health Problems Motivate Medical Career

Novello was born in Fajardo, Puerto Rico. She was inspired to enter the medical profession as a result of her own childhood experiences with serious illness. Novello was born with a painful birth defect in her large intestine. She battled almost constant health problems until the defect was repaired surgically when she was in her early twenties.

> "I BELIEVE THAT OUR KIDS ARE SMART— PERHAPS SMARTER THAN WE WERE AT THEIR AGE— AND IF WE WILL GIVE THEM HONEST AND FACTUAL INFORMATION AND TREAT THEM WITH RESPECT, THEY WILL MAKE GOOD DECISIONS."

Novello never let anything stand in the way of achieving her goals. After graduating from high school, she went on to college at the University of Puerto Rico, earning her bachelor's degree in 1965 and her medical degree in 1970. She then completed her internship and residency in pediatrics at the University of Michigan Medical Center in Ann Arbor from 1970 until 1973. There, after rapidly earning a reputation as a caring and effective physician, she became the first woman to receive her department's "Intern of the Year" award.

Novello remained in Ann Arbor until 1974, doing advanced research in the university hospital's pediatric (children's) nephrology unit. (Nephrology is the branch of medicine that deals with the kidneys.) While caring for young patients waiting for kidney transplants, she was especially saddened by those who had "fallen through the cracks" at some point in their lives. Many were sick because they had not received proper treatment when they needed it, often because their families couldn't afford it or didn't know where to turn for help. Seeing these harsh struggles that could have been avoided made Novello think about entering the health service field at the government level. By doing so, she thought she might be able to find solutions to problems like inadequate health care and infection with AIDS that hit children particularly hard.

Joins the U.S. Public Health Service

In 1978, after spending two years in the pediatric nephrology unit at Georgetown University Hospital in Washington, D.C., and two years in private practice, Novello went to work for the National Institutes of Health, or NIH. (See box for more information.) Her first post with the NIH was as a project officer at the National Institute of Arthritis, Metabolism and Digestive Diseases. There she worked with the artificial kidney and chronic uremia (kidney disease) program.

Novello then served as a staff physician at the NIH before taking a job as executive secretary in the NIH's Division of Research and Grants beginning in 1981. During this period, she also earned her master's degree in public health

The National Institutes of Health (NIH)

Established in 1930, the NIH is a branch of the U.S. Public Health Service. It consists of thirteen separate institutes that each conduct research on the causes, cures, and prevention of various diseases and other health-related issues. Among the NIH's many research topics are cancer, heart disease, disorders of the lungs and blood, infectious diseases, environment-related problems, allergies, dental health, aging, and mental illness. The institute's studies are conducted by medical profes-sionals and scientists in NIH laboratories or by other NIH-backed researchers in univer-sities and private facilities across the coun-try. NIH also funds training programs in the health professions and the construction of new research centers.

At any given time, there may be thou-sands of NIH research projects in progress. The results of these studies are eventually passed along to doctors and other health-care providers in the hope that they will improve the overall health of the American people.

---

from Johns Hopkins University. In 1986, Novello moved to another part of the NIH, becoming deputy director of the National Institute on Child Health and Human Develop-ment. There she took a particular interest in pediatric AIDS as both a medical and a social problem.

In late 1989, U.S. surgeon general C. Everett Koop announced that he was retiring from his post. When offi-cials in the administration of President George Bush began their search for a replacement, Novello emerged as a favorite—an accomplished and dedicated physician whose views were in line with those of the president. The Senate quickly approved her for the position, and she took office in March 1990.

Makes Waves as U.S. Surgeon General

*While some may have hoped for a less outspoken sur-geon general than the often-controversial Dr. Koop, they did not always get it in Novello. She caused a stir more than once during her three years in office, expressing particular concern about the health problems of minorities, children, teens, and women. Among the issues she addressed were the AIDS crisis, domestic violence, decreasing rates of **immu-nization** against common infectious diseases, injury preven-tion, and the lack of health insurance coverage among His-*

immunization: making the body resistant to specific diseases by introducing elements to the system that cause it to produce antibodies and other organisms that will render the disease harmless.

panic Americans. She stressed that ignoring those problems put the very future of the nation at risk.

Novello reserved her harshest words for manufacturers of cigarettes and alcohol and the advertisers they hire to promote their products. She came down hard on both groups for glamorizing smoking and drinking and making them appear harmless. She was especially disgusted by ads specifically designed to appeal to children and teens—even though it is against the law to sell the products to them. (Her main targets were the cartoon character "Joe Camel" of Camel cigarettes and beverages with a high alcohol content that nevertheless enjoyed a "soda pop" image.) In fact, condemning such advertising tactics became one of the major themes of her administration. Not surprisingly, she was very unpopular with manufacturers of cigarettes and alcohol and with the advertising industry.

On April 21, 1992, in Los Angeles, California, Novello discussed many of these issues as part of an overall look at health concerns for the 1990s. Her speech is reprinted here in part from Vital Speeches of the Day, *August 15, 1992.*

In my efforts to protect our nation's health, I have spoken out especially about the dangers associated with illegal underage drinking, smoking, AIDS, and violence. What I have learned since taking on this task has alarmed me, but at the same time, it has also taught me that my efforts cannot let up.

I promised myself when I accepted this position that my job would not be complete until I truly felt that I had "touched" the young people of this country by teaching them what I knew. I believe that our kids are smart—perhaps smarter than we were at their age—and if we will give them honest and factual information and treat them with respect, they will make good decisions. I know that I'm *far from finished,* and I will continue to speak out about these issues whenever and wherever possible. But I am here today to enlist your help....

One phrase I have continued to recite during my tenure as Surgeon General is that *our young people are our nation's most valuable resource*—I say it over and over again because I believe it myself so fervently. When we say we have hope for the future, what we are really saying is that we have hope for our children. The work we do now can ensure that our hope becomes a reality.

In the work that we do—as legislators, educators, business leaders, health care providers, and most importantly, *as parents*—our focus must be on our young people.

The America of today is far different from what it was when we were young. The challenges are different, the pressures greater, the poverty and despair more **rampant**, and the availability of drugs and alcohol more widespread. These things are tragic—and we must do everything we can to turn them around.

Alcohol

One pressure young people face that **inherently** makes my job and our hopes for the future that much more difficult to guarantee, is the pressure to *drink alcohol,* or abuse other substances.

Illegal underage drinking is one issue which I have identified to be a cornerstone of my agenda as Surgeon General.

I speak out about it whenever and wherever possible. And today, I would like to outline the problem for you as I see it, and then I'm going to *ask for your help.*

I have been working on this issue since September 1990, when I launched a "fact finding" mission on this issue. I toured the country talking to community leaders, to teachers, and to young people about the problem of illegal underage drinking.

I learned that this issue is *more **pervasive** than I originally realized*—and that it is truly the mainstream drug abuse issue plaguing most communities and families in America today.

I also learned that, in order to realize any success, we need to strengthen our prevention efforts—I've learned that *prevention works best if the message the young person gets at home is the one he gets at school, and at church, and is the one reinforced by his community and his peers.*

rampant: widespread.
inherently: by its very nature.
pervasive: widespread.

I began to learn then—and I relearn it every day—how confusing the *mixed messages* are that we send to our children about alcohol.... We've made progress in the illicit drug war because our youth have gotten consistent messages from their families, their schools, their churches, their communities, their nation—and their media.

However, we're losing the war on the underage use of alcohol because our youth receive some very mixed messages, like the advertisements and other media images that tell them "drink me and you will be cool. Drink me and you will be glamorous. Drink me and you will have fun!" Or even worse, "Drink me and there will be no consequences."

Our health message is clear—"use of alcohol by young people can lead to serious health consequences—not to mention absenteeism, vandalism, date rape, random violence, and even death." But how can that be expected to compete with the Swedish bikini team or the Bud Man?...

Police ... point out that parents do not like their children arrested for "doing what everyone else does." One official described enforcement of alcohol laws as "a no-win" situation. And another commented, "Local police have another priority—[illicit] drugs. They ignore alcohol."

And by and large, there are only **nominal** penalties against **vendors** and minors when they violate these laws. While vendors may have fines or their licenses suspended, license **revocations** are rare. The penalties against the youth who violate the laws are often not **deterrents**. Even when strict penalties exist, courts are lenient and do not apply them....

Last week, as honorary chair of Alcohol Awareness Month, I released [a] report which deals with those usually unreported consequences of teen drinking that we often do not attribute to alcohol.

Drinking and driving certainly puts many lives at risk, but an alcohol-impaired person doesn't need to get behind the wheel of a car to do harm to himself and to others. Depression, suicides, random violence, and criminal acts—such as date rape, **battery**, other forms of assault and abuse, and homicide—all have strong links to alcohol use. So do the unintentional alcohol-related injuries that result from falls, drownings, shootings, residential fires, and the like.

nominal: minor, insignificant.

vendors: sellers.

revocations: acts of taking back something.

deterrents: things that discourage or prevent a certain activity.

battery: beating.

Antonia C. Novello

This study shows that there is much more to drinking than dying. Crime is one major consequence of alcohol consumption. Approximately one-third of our young people who commit serious crimes have consumed alcohol just prior to the commission of these illegal actions....

Alcohol has also shown itself to be a factor in being a *victim* of crime. Intoxicated minors were found to provoke assailants, to act vulnerable, and to fail to take normal, common-sense precautions. Among college student crime victims, for example, 50 percent admitted using drugs and/or alcohol at the time the crime was committed.

Rape and sexual assault are also closely associated with alcohol misuse by our youth. Among college age students, 55 percent of **perpetrators** were under the influence of alcohol, and so were 53 percent of the victims.... Who can honestly tell me that alcohol is not **adversely** affecting the future of these young people?

I want to share with you another finding I find particularly shocking and revolting: among high school females, 18 percent—nearly one in five—said it was okay to force sex if the girl was drunk, and among high school males, almost 40 percent—two out of every five—said the same thing.

We found other startling links, such as:

- 70 percent of attempted suicides involved the frequent use of drugs and/or alcohol.
- And water activities—of special interest and concern with summer rapidly approaching—often result in alcohol use and danger.
- 40 to 50 percent of young males who drown used alcohol prior to drowning.
- 40 to 50 percent of all diving injury victims had consumed alcoholic beverages.

Clearly, something *must* be done about this pervasive problem confronting our youth. In focusing my efforts and those of my office on this issue of illegal underage drinking, several things are clear.

First, we all have a role to play in solving this problem. And secondly, by working together, we *can* solve it.

perpetrators: people who carry out or commit a crime.

adversely: negatively.

I have urged the alcohol industry to come to the table, to work with us, to become *a part of the solution.* I have also urged schools to make alcohol education a central part of the health curriculum from the earliest grades all the way through—and I must add, this curriculum must include teaching resistance education and risk avoidance techniques.

And, finally, I have urged families—parents and children—to talk to each other about alcohol, about distinguishing truth from fiction.

AIDS

Now, let me outline briefly for you another dangerous situation we face with regard to the issues of sexual behavior, HIV/AIDS and substance abuse, and their associated problems....

The patterns and trends of the epidemic have changed during its first decade. The number of AIDS cases among injecting drug users and men who have sex with men appears to be leveling somewhat; however, cases are rising among women and **perinatal** infected children. There is also increasing concern about the vulnerability of adolescents, since many young people with AIDS were infected with HIV as teenagers....

Quite simply, in the second decade of this disease, our focus must also include adolescents, young adults, women, and families. HIV/AIDS has changed its focus—it is no longer a disease of "them," it is now a disease of all of "us." And especially, with our young people, *HIV/AIDS is like an accident waiting to happen*—it is like putting a match next to a can of gasoline....

Let me talk about the two avenues of HIV infection in young people—drug use and unprotected sex. First, some information about drug use and HIV.

With young people, sexual transmission is the usual route of infection. The role of drug use in HIV is usually not injection drug use, or getting infected from dirty needles and works.

Instead, the role of drug use here is that *it leads to risk taking, to more frequent sexual activity, and to unprotected sex....*

As Surgeon General, I cannot just sit and wait for accidents ... to occur. I *must* act. We must teach people that first, ***abstinence is the only sure way to protect yourself*** from acquiring an

perinatal: around the time of birth.

abstinence: voluntarily and deliberately denying oneself something.

Antonia C. Novello

STD [sexually transmitted disease] or HIV. But we must also be realistic, and we must educate our youth *and their parents* about methods of protecting themselves when they are sexually active.

And when we do, *we must provide the education, the instructions, and alert them of their responsibility.* Condom availability, just for condom sake and devoid of education and instructions, is not only bad public health policy, it is a dangerous endeavor.

The need to address the issue of HIV infection among young people is immediate. The legal, ethical, social and medical challenges that you young people present to our current legal and health care systems, however, makes this a **cumbersome** process.

AIDS in young people presents many more *social* issues than I ever would have imagined. As all of you can **attest**, adolescence is a period of **profound** physiological, psychological and social change.

Many young people often feel alienated from the rest of society, and society, in turn, often finds it difficult to understand their emotions and behaviors, which are often impulsive or risky. This alienation is heightened in the presence of HIV.

The behaviors that lead to HIV infection in adolescents are often deemed socially unacceptable, and there is a temptation to stigmatize most of the adolescent population as "high risk," or "hard to reach." It is crucial for us as adults to understand—to remember—that *most* young people find themselves at times in situations that are risky for acquiring HIV, even if these situations are encountered only infrequently, for only a few minutes, a few hours, or a few weeks.

This situation demands immediate action—action which therefore needs to build on existing systems of health care services. Given that *40 percent of recent adolescent AIDS cases are linked to sexual contact,* and because there are behavioral and physiologic[al] relationships between HIV and other sexually transmitted diseases (STDs), *we must provide HIV prevention education and services* at the same time we give care and information about other STDs.

More broadly, the HIV/AIDS services we provide must make sense, and they must be provided in the places where health

cumbersome: awkward, complicated, difficult.

attest: confirm, verify.

profound: intense, important.

Chance of Dying in the Next Decade and a Half, Smokers vs. Ex-Smokers vs. Lifetime Nonsmokers

50%

40%

30%

20%

0%

MEN   WOMEN

SMOKERS – Persons aged 55-59 who were smoking 1 pack or more of cigarettes per day and continued to smoke.

EX-SMOKERS – Persons aged 55-59 who were smoking 1 pack or more of cigarettes per day but quit smoking at that age.

LIFETIME NONSMOKERS – Persons aged 55-59 who have never smoked cigarettes

Novello at a news conference, 1990: "Young people are flooded with images of the strong, independent Marlboro man, and told that smoking Camels will give them a "smooth character." What they aren't told is that there's nothing smooth about lung cancer and emphysema, and that your independence is restricted when you can't breathe without a respirator."

integral: central, essential.

care is sought. I often say that what we need is to provide good medicine combined with good sense, and I believe it more every day.

Also, *young people must be treated with respect,* and we need to *foster an atmosphere of trust* between them and the health care provider.

We must work to provide HIV prevention education immediately—and not in isolation, but as an **integral** element of a comprehensive health curriculum that also provides education about sexuality and drug abuse. A dialogue between young people and their parents is critical to such education, and all views should be acknowledged and accommodated.

Smoking

Allow me now to discuss smoking. The Office of the Surgeon General will always be involved in trying to convince the American public of the dangers of tobacco....

Of special concern to me is the new generation of smokers—our young people who are not receiving an honest picture of what smoking actually does to their lives.

I believe in the power of a free market and the importance of advertising in making a free market operate. Advertising that is honest and gives the facts about a product is not only necessary, but good for consumers and producers alike. However, there are times when the power of advertising must be voluntarily restrained because of its great potential to influence.

Young people are flooded with images of the strong, independent Marlboro man, and told that smoking Camels will give them a "smooth character." What they aren't told is that there's nothing smooth about lung cancer and emphysema, and that your independence is restricted when you can't breathe without a respirator.

Calling for the voluntary withdrawal of a successful advertising campaign is not a traditional role of the Surgeon General, yet, it is the only responsible position that I can take regarding advertisements that mislead our youth into making decisions that will adversely affect their health.

Let me tell you about some recent research published in the *Journal of the American Medical Association* and the CDC's [Center for Disease Control's] *MMWR*. This research has shown that: approximately *30 percent of 3-year-olds, and 91 percent of 6-year-olds correctly identified "Old Joe" with a picture of a cigarette.* This is a shocking finding, indicating the power of advertising has reached the very young. Did you even imagine that 6-year-olds—yes, even 6-year-olds—are as familiar with "Old Joe" as with Mickey Mouse?

As a pediatrician, public health official, and responsible citizen, I am appalled at these findings.

Let's look at these findings more closely. The researchers found that, by 3 years of age, children understand both the content, and for whom, commercials are made. Of course, R.

J. Reynolds and the other tobacco companies stubbornly insist that they don't want children to smoke ... that their advertising does not target kids ... that their ads are aimed only at making adults switch brands.

While cigarette companies claim that they do not intend to market directly to children, the reality is that this argument is **irrelevant** if advertising affects what children know and believe.

Old Joe Camel recognition results from **ubiquitous** everyday exposure—from billboards, to movies, t-shirts, posters, promotional activities during sporting events, video arcade games, toys and candy.

Even many in the advertising industry recognize that these ads go too far. A recent *Advertising Age* editorial argued that "Old Joe Must Go." These ads are deplorable—they have to stop. If we do not push for this marketing tactic to change, then our tolerance might open the floodgates for a tide-wave of media campaigns that will attempt to duplicate these tactics—not just for cigarettes, but alcohol and other products as well.

These copy-cat antics are already **prevalent.** For example, Camel is not the only brand to prey upon our susceptible youth—it has just become the most obvious one. The strong, rough, independent Marlboro cowboy is another, earlier example. His appeal to young people is obvious....

Of course, in one way or another all cigarette manufacturers promote images of youth and fun, glamour and **affluence**, independence and achievement, and rugged spiritedness. They promote these images with the full knowledge that nearly 90 percent of smokers become regular smokers before they turn 21.

That is why tobacco manufacturers spend incredible amounts of money—3.6 billion dollars each year in advertisement and promotion to be exact—to expose children and adolescents to their messages touting peer acceptance and the social rewards of smoking.

Surveys before 1988 indicated little preference for Camels among young people. Recent surveys show that in some communities in America, one-fourth or more of young smok-

irrelevant: unimportant; without bearing on the issue under discussion.

ubiquitous: widespread.

prevalent: widespread.

affluence: wealth.

ers are now buying Camel. Indeed, the major source of Camel's recent market-share increase appears to have come from younger smokers.

It's time for the tobacco industry to stop preying on our nation's youth. It's time that cigarette companies act—voluntarily and responsibly—to help the nation achieve a key Healthy People 2000 objective: to eliminate or severely

Novello standing next to a nine-story billboard of "Old Joe Camel": "Did you even imagine that 6-year-olds—yes, even 6-year-olds—are as familiar with "Old Joe" as with Mickey Mouse?"

restrict all forms of tobacco product advertising and promotion to which youth younger than 18 are likely to be exposed.

So I have been making this appeal on behalf of the very future of this country: our youth. In years past, R. J. Reynolds would have had us walk a mile for a Camel. The time has come that we all invite "Old Joe" Camel himself to take a hike!...

99

Novello left her post as U.S. surgeon general in June 1993, five months after President George Bush left office. Her activities since then have included serving as the special representative for health and nutrition for UNICEF, the United Nations organization devoted to children and their needs.

Sources

Books

Notable Hispanic American Women, Gale, 1993.

Periodicals

Hispanic, "Dr. Antonia Novello: The Right Stuff," January/February 1990, p. 20; "Beyond Nursing," October 1991, p. 15.

Newsweek, "Surgeon General: Abortion Foe," October 30, 1989, p. 84.

New York Times, November 5, 1991, p. A16; November 6, 1991, p. A25.

People, "Butt Out, Guido Sarducci! Surgeon General Antonia Novello, Your Sister-in-Law, Wants Everyone to Quit Smoking," December 17, 1990, pp. 109–10.

Saturday Evening Post, "Antonia Novello: A Dream Come True," May/June 1991.

Vital Speeches of the Day, "Health Priorities for the Nineties: The Quest for Prevention," August 15, 1992, pp. 666–72.

Federico Peña

1947–

Mexican American attorney and politician

In late 1992, former Denver, Colorado, mayor Federico Peña reluctantly stepped into the national political spotlight when he agreed to serve as President Bill Clinton's secretary of transportation. During his four years in that position, he often found himself in the middle of controversy, most notably in the wake of several disastrous airline accidents that shook the public's confidence in the safety of air travel. Peña also had to cope with massive budget cuts and pressures to reorganize the department to make it more streamlined and efficient. Through it all, he never abandoned his goals "to build bridges, not bureaucracy, and move people, not paper." After serving a hectic term heading the Department of Transportation, Peña agreed in late 1996 to another stint in Clinton's cabinet—this time as secretary of energy. His new post promised to be as challenging as the last, with urgent issues of nuclear waste disposal, pollution, nuclear disarmament, and a mandate to downsize facing Piña from the outset.

"WE NEED TO SEE TRANSPORTATION AS MORE THAN THE ENGINE OF ECONOMIC GROWTH AND TECHNOLOGY, BUT AS AN INTEGRAL PART OF ALL OUR POLICY GOALS—EVEN WELFARE AND HEALTH-CARE REFORM AND URBAN REDEVELOPMENT."

Early Life

Peña's family has roots in Texas that go back some two hundred years. His father earned a good living as a broker for a cotton manufacturer, so the six Peña children enjoyed a comfortable life growing up in the city of Brownsville. After graduating with honors from high school, Federico— or Fred, as he was known to his fellow students—attended the University of Texas at Austin. He received his bachelor's degree in 1969 and his law degree in 1972.

Later that year, Peña moved to Denver, Colorado, the home of his older brother, Alfredo, who was also a lawyer. In 1973, the two brothers formed their own partnership. Peña quickly became familiar with the local Hispanic community through his involvement in various activities. He was, for example, a staff attorney for the Mexican American Legal Defense and Educational Fund (MALDEF), a Latino civil rights group, and a legal advisor to the Chicano Education Project.

Enters Politics

Peña's introduction to the world of politics came in 1978, when he ran for and won a seat in the Colorado House of Representatives. He served in that capacity with distinction for two terms. During his first term, he earned praise from the Colorado Social Action Committee as outstanding Democratic freshman. And during his second term, he was elected to the prestigious minority speaker's post.

In 1982, Peña decided to run for mayor of Denver. Local observers didn't think he had much of a chance to win against his opponent who had held the office for fourteen years. There was not a large Hispanic community in Denver to turn to for support. (At the time, about 18 percent of Denver's population identified themselves as Hispanic.)

Peña successfully appealed to a wide variety of people. He created an alliance that included not only Hispanics but also blacks, Asian Americans, labor groups, environmentalists, feminists, the homosexual community, and young white professionals. Several thousand of his supporters volunteered to conduct massive voter registration drives on his behalf. Thanks to their help and a campaign message that

*stressed an exciting new future for Denver under his leader-
ship, Peña came out on top in both the primary election in
May 1983 and in the regular election the following month.*

Hard Times in Denver

*Not long after Peña took office, circumstances beyond
his control forced him to scale back his ambitious plans for
the city. A sharp downturn in the oil, mining, and high-
technology industries hit Denver especially hard. Unemployment soared and real estate prices took a nosedive.*

*By the time the 1987 mayoral race got under way,
Peña's popularity had taken a beating, too. No one expected him to be reelected. But in the last month or so of the
campaign, he started to take a harder line against his
opponent. Slowly but steadily, he moved up in the polls. On
election day, Peña won with fifty-one percent of the vote.*

*Peña's second term got off to a shaky start when Den-
ver was hit with a blizzard and ice storm in December
1987. The city was virtually crippled for weeks after the
storm. Some streets were still difficult to drive on well into
February 1988. Disgusted residents launched a recall effort
they hoped would give the people of Denver a chance to
vote Peña out of office. They ended up just a couple of
thousand signatures short of the total needed to force a
special election.*

A New Course for Denver

*Over the next few years, however, Peña was finally able
to make some headway with his plans to turn Denver into
a "world-class" center for commerce and trade. For example, he won the public's approval for a new convention center and supervised its construction. This was a major victory
for Peña, because residents had overwhelmingly rejected
the idea of building a convention center when he proposed
it during his first term as mayor. Peña also improved local
parks and recreation areas; attracted a new major league
baseball franchise, the Colorado Rockies; obtained funding
to build and repair roads, bridges, libraries, and other public facilities; and fixed up aging neighborhoods. In addition,*

he significantly reduced air pollution in the Denver area by actively promoting the use of alternative fuels.

Peña's biggest project was building the city's new airport. He wanted it to be one of the largest and most creatively designed complexes of its kind in the world. He imagined a facility full of technological advances that would make air travel more efficient. Many people, however, complained that such an airport was too expensive, too fancy, and too far from downtown (eighteen miles). Peña assured Coloradans that it was necessary "to create jobs, stimulate the local economy and meet future air transportation needs"—and he eventually won out over the objections. But problems surfaced during the airport's construction, among them a computerized baggage-handling system that just wouldn't work. This and other difficulties delayed the airport's opening from late 1993 until early 1995, more than tripling its original estimated cost.

Leaves Politics

Peña decided not to run for reelection in 1991, even though he had regained his popularity with the people of Denver and was at last comfortable in his role as mayor. He withdrew from political life to spend more time with his growing family (he has two daughters) and earn a higher income than he could as a public servant. He founded Peña Investment Advisors, a corporate pension fund investment company and also served as counsel (legal advisor) to a major local law firm. In addition, Peña was a member of a state commission that developed a long-term transportation plan for Colorado.

Reenters Politics at the National Level

In 1992, after campaigning enthusiastically for Bill Clinton in that year's presidential election, Peña was invited to head the president-elect's transition team for transportation issues. Although he had told friends that he did not want a job with the new administration, he accepted Clinton's offer to become the Secretary of Transportation. As head of the Department of Transportation (DOT), Peña took on the president's goal of repairing and rebuilding the country's troubled **infrastructure**. This included everything from fixing crumbling highway bridges to revitalizing airline

infrastructure: underlying foundation or basic framework.

companies that were on the verge of going out of business. He made it through his confirmation hearings with no trouble and was sworn into office in January 1993.

On July 15, 1993, Peña appeared before an audience at the National Press Club in Washington, D.C., to discuss the Clinton administration's transportation policy as he saw it. An excerpt from his remarks is reprinted here from a copy of his speech furnished by the Office of the Secretary for Public Affairs of the U.S. Department of Transportation.

I am very, very proud to be a member of President Clinton's cabinet. We share the same philosophy of government and the same vision of why investment in transportation is central to our people's future. And much of the investment we need depends on passing the president's budget. That's obviously one reason why I support it. Another is that I understand—in my bones—what the president is trying to do.

I recall that back in 1983, when I was elected mayor of Denver, our economic boom had peaked and we were slipping into deep recession. After a long-running boom based on high oil prices, real estate development, and a flood of foreign investment, the bottom just fell out. Our unemployment rate soared to two percent above the national average; office vacancies hit thirty-one percent; **foreclosures** were skyrocketing. So were **bankruptcies.** Property values started to

foreclosures: legal proceedings that end a person's or a company's right of ownership to a piece of real estate (usually because they stopped making payments on it).

bankruptcies: legal declarations that a person or company is financially unable to pay their debts.

plummet. Our economy essentially **imploded.** Public morale was at rock bottom. The only thing Denver was "Number 1" in was in air pollution—sixty-five "bad air days" a year.

Much of this was the **legacy** of a philosophy that had been content to ride the oil boom, failing to invest in needed infrastructure like our roads and bridges. My **predecessors** practiced the kind of "don't-worry-be-happy" politics that were so popular in the 1980s. Those same political forces from the national level also cost Denver millions of federal dollars for housing, community development and other urban programs just as I was taking office....

We were forced to both cut spending and raise taxes in the teeth of the recession. Believe me, I learned a lot about bad poll numbers—fast.

But we also embarked on a whole series of investments in Denver's future. We invested in neighborhoods and small businesses; we set out to build a new convention center and a new multibillion dollar airport, both in partnership with the private sector. We passed two large new bond issues that I proposed and that the people of Denver supported, to pay for viaducts, bridges, roads, new parks and a new library.

We did it at a time when our people were suffering. They were scared. And we did it in the face of **skepticism** from some in Denver who were simply afraid of change. Others just didn't believe anymore that government could do anything right, let alone get the city's economy moving again. Our critics could always cite some reason why we shouldn't act: "We can't afford it.... We'll never finish all the jobs we set out to do." These were those who preferred gridlock and the **status quo** to taking action and bringing change.

Now, does that sound familiar?

I know you might be amazed to hear that we even ran into some doubts and criticism from members of the press!

But we brought that convention center in on time and on budget. Our new airport will open this winter. [Unforseen difficulties forced a delay in the airport opening until 1995.] People are moving back into central Denver. Office vacancies are down to twenty percent and falling; Denver's unemployment rate is now below the national average. There are more

imploded: collapsed inward on itself.

legacy: something handed down from a past generation to the present one.

predecessors: people who previously held a position now held by someone else.

skepticism: doubt, suspicion.

status quo: the existing state of affairs.

and better jobs to be had, and the number of bad air days is down from sixty-five a year to six. And most importantly, people feel more hopeful and upbeat about their city. Maybe that's why our Colorado Rockies are setting the all-time attendance record for major league baseball this year.

I just want to make two things clear to you.

The first is that investments in our people, our transportation system and our infrastructure were all crucial to Denver's turnaround.

The second is that I am not running again for mayor. I love the job I have right now.

I believe—and I know President Clinton does, too—that if we have a clear vision of the future, a willingness to make

1990 model of General Motors' electric automobile. Peña encourages innovation in tranportation: "If we invest wisely, we can spur the development of new technologies, even whole new industries, and contribute to a cleaner American environment at the same time."

partnerships and the courage to confront tough issues (even if that's not immediately popular), we can overcome and succeed beyond our fondest hopes.

Right from the beginning, President Clinton has stressed the central role that transportation and infrastructure investment can play in stimulating lasting growth, creating jobs, and reviving our national spirit. Investing in our people requires investing in transportation, because nothing touches all of our daily lives more or has a greater impact on our economy. The health of America's economy in the future depends on our making the right strategic investments now in partnership with state and local governments and the private sector—what I call "public-private-public" partnerships. If we invest wisely, we can spur the development of new technologies, even whole new industries, and contribute to a cleaner American environment at the same time.

My goals for DOT are straightforward.

First, our highest priority—this whole administration's first target—is to get our economy moving and create jobs, both immediately and in the long term, by making strategic transportation investments.

Second, these investments should be made in ways that will help clean up and even beautify our environment.

Third, we must **integrate** all modes of transportation into a seamless system for moving goods and people from coast to coast and within metropolitan communities.

Fourth, we must develop and apply new technologies that will create whole new industries.

And, fifth, we must ensure that all of our investments improve daily life by making travel safer, more convenient and more "human."

This is a vision that goes far beyond the traditional bricks-and-mortar image of the Department of Transportation.

In the brief time that we have today, I would like to focus only on two of these five goals: the application of new technologies and the "humanization" of transportation.

We are already in the midst of a revolution in transportation technologies that will transform our economy and our

integrate: coordinate; combine into a unified whole.

daily lives as much as the arrival of railroading and commercial aviation did. I can foresee American companies leading the world in a range of transportation technologies, and exporting super-sophisticated air traffic control systems, non-polluting vehicles, high-tech safety devices and components ranging from ceramic engine blocks to bridging systems made from **composite** fibers. The truth is—and most Americans are unaware of this—the early stages of this revolution are already underway. I've seen and touched and taken test drives on some of these new wonders as I've traveled around the country.

Let me cite just a few examples.

We are already beginning to use the Global Positioning System based on satellites in space to track trains and trucks here on earth and guide ships and airplanes more accurately and safely than ever before.

Texas Instruments in Dallas is developing infrared vision devices—used by our military in Desert Storm [the American military campaign to protect Saudi Arabia and liberate Kuwait from Iraqi control during the Persian Gulf War (1990-91)]—to enhance safety on our roads at night.

The first of a new generation of computerized collection devices are being used now in Oklahoma to eliminate toll booth delays.

We are well advanced on research into "intelligent" highway systems that will speed traffic flows and enhance safety. In Oakland County, Michigan, I've seen "intelligent" traffic lights that adjust to actual traffic flows and speed commuters to work while reducing pollution at the same time.

The Department of Transportation is now part of the Technology Reinvestment Project ... which will provide over $500 million in assistance to companies promoting dual-use technologies. I sought full DOT participation in this effort precisely because of the great potential for using technologies developed for defense in the transportation arena. It's only a small stretch of the imagination, for example, to conceive new composite materials like those used for the Stealth bomber being applied to coming generations of vehicles and even bridges. In fact, there is a company in California now working on a "Stealth bus."

composite: blended, combined.

The Department of Transportation is also leading the administration's push for a $1.3 billion investment in new high-speed rail corridors and technical research, including the design of a world-class, American **prototype** of a **magnetic levitation train**. We hope to **"leverage"** this initial federal stake to a total investment of over $2.5 billion by encouraging partnerships with cities, states, and private industries. Together, we will develop new high-speed rail corridors far beyond Amtrak's Northeast Corridor. In the longer term, we **envisage** growth of a new U.S. industry based on manufacturing and maintaining high-speed rail systems. Our nation, which builds the world's most advanced planes, can also build the fastest trains.

Or the best subway cars, for that matter. We are exploring the coordination of equipment purchases by local transit authorities across the United States so that we can achieve the **economies of scale** that would permit American manufacturers to compete with foreign suppliers for transit car contracts.

And we are forging an **R & D** partnership with Detroit [Michigan] for a new generation of safe, non-polluting automobiles.

All of these technologies are real. They're being **deployed** now, and they will be the seedbeds for new American industries, employing American workers, earning American wages.

New as they are, I believe these technologies are crucial to reviving an old American tradition—winning. We are determined not to repeat the mistakes of the past. We will not fail again to support the creative genius of our nation and **forfeit** technological advances to other nations.

As we Americans ride the exciting X-2000 tilt train from Sweden or the Talgo from Spain, let's remember that this technology was invented by Americans who sold their **patents** to the Europeans. As we focus on a maglev [magnetic levitation] prototype system for America, let's recall that this technology was invented by Americans—and tested in Pueblo, Colorado, over fifteen years ago—but we lost it to Japan and Germany because our government could not afford to support it.

I am committed to forming partnerships with U.S. scientists, U.S. engineers, and U.S. companies to develop and manufacture the new transportation technologies of the next century.

prototype: model.

magnetic levitation train: a type of high-speed train that is suspended just inches above a special track or guideway as it moves with the help of magnetic fields.

leverage: boost the effectiveness of something.

envisage: imagine or see.

economies of scale: savings achieved by buying something in a single large amount rather than several smaller amounts.

R & D: research and development.

deployed: set in position.

forfeit: lose, give up.

patents: legal rights to make, use, or sell something.

A solar-powered vehicle,
Yokohama, Japan, 1993

But as exciting as these technologies are, as promising for our economy's future, they must also meet another standard—humanizing our transport system and improving peoples' daily lives. We have to remember *why* we're investing in new technologies. We must remember who we serve and what values we believe in. We need to see transportation as more than the engine of economic growth and technology, but as an integral part of all our policy goals—even welfare and health-care reform and urban redevelopment.

When my good friend [Secretary of Housing and Urban Development] **Henry Cisneros** [see entry] spoke to you in April he suggested that one reason that "our cities are smoldering" is sheer isolation. Clearly, gaps in transportation have a lot to do with that.

Let me suggest to you, for example, that we won't succeed in putting any real "power" in any new **"empowerment zone"** unless we see that workers can get to work there and back home and that raw materials and finished goods can get in and out efficiently. Nor will we succeed in moving people off of welfare unless we ensure that single parents can get their kids to day-care centers on the way to work without having to take three different buses. When inner-city residents have to travel miles to shop at major supermarkets, when they cannot easily get to health clinics, then they are trapped in ways few of us can even imagine.

If we're serious about a new national health system that works, we're also going to need to find ways to bring rural people ... to health clinics. That's the only way they can get preventive care instead of being forced to turn to expensive emergency rooms for help.

Speaking of health care, how can we ignore the human agony and sheer cost of highway crashes—the fourth-leading cause of death in our country? We lost more than 39,000 lives on our highways last year. There were 300,000 hospitalizations, more than 3 million injuries in all. The total cost to our society was over $137 billion—two percent of our gross national product.

Thanks to safer vehicles, seat belts, air bags, tougher drunk driving laws and other measures, those casualties were the lowest in recent decades. So we have made progress. But can anybody doubt that to build an effective health care system we must do much, much better?

Let me assure you. We will never let up on safety in any of our transportation systems. Our roads, our airways are the safest in the world, but we will make them safer. Too many precious lives are at stake.

empowerment zone: a needy neighborhood in a major city targeted for special funding to encourage economic development and community growth.

Another part of "humanizing" transportation is simply taking account of the views of the people most affected by the decisions that we make....

We are long past the day when "experts" or "technocrats" can devise transportation projects and ram them through neighborhoods without peoples' consent. We need to weigh human needs for convenience, for quiet, for clean air, even for beauty, in all our transportation decisions. And we will. Those are just a few examples of why we need to blend human needs with the technological revolution that's underway in transportation.

Today, our country needs the vision and determination to take bold steps, some of which won't show payoffs until the next century. We must rekindle the American **entrepreneurial zeal** to take risks, even to make mistakes. We need what Franklin Roosevelt called "a bold spirit of experimentation."

President Clinton has challenged Americans to "make change our friend." I am up for that challenge.

To be sure, there will always be doubters and **naysayers**. There will be some who are simply too scared of change....

But we must begin. We will win people over the only way we can—not only with beautiful visions, but with **tangible**, step-by-step progress....

We can and will revive America's can-do spirit. And we will build a transportation system that will enhance Americans' safety and prosperity as we carry on the pursuit of happiness....

99

While in office as secretary of transportation, Peña faced a number of crises and controversies. In October 1994, for example, he caused a stir when he overruled a National Highway Traffic Safety Administration (NHTSA) recommendation for the first time in the DOT's history. At issue were as many as six million General Motors (GM) pickup trucks some consumer groups claimed had a tendency to burst into flames following side-impact collisions. The NHTSA's findings suggested that the overall risk of death in a pickup crash was

entrepreneurial zeal: enthusiasm for organizing and managing a business.

naysayers: people who oppose or reject something.

tangible: actual, real.

no greater in GM models than in those manufactured by Ford or Chrysler. Critics charged that Peña's decision to go ahead anyway with a massive recall had more to do with politics than science.

Airline troubles took up much of Peña's time as well. On several occasions, he had to find ways to help airline companies on shaky financial ground obtain tax relief and loan guarantees to head off takeovers by foreign investors. And airline safety was a particular concern, particularly because air disasters resulted in many deaths in 1994. Maintenance and inspection practices, flight crew training, air traffic control procedures, and weather monitoring all came under public scrutiny.

In response to the disturbing increase in air crash-related deaths, Peña called for a safety check of the nation's airlines and announced a "zero accident" goal. His boldest move, however, was to propose that the country's air traffic control operations no longer be supervised by the Federal Aviation Administration (FAA). Instead, he suggested that they should be run by a type of public-private partnership in an effort to improve efficiency and reduce costs.

Peña was also forced to deal with a shrinking budget. In February 1995, he submitted a plan that would cut the Department of Transportation's workforce in half and slash billions of dollars in spending from highway, rail, and aviation programs. Several months later, he proposed reorganizing the entire department. Under Peña's plan, ten DOT agencies would be combined into only three—the Federal Aviation Administration, the U.S. Coast Guard, and the Intermodal Transportation Administration (ITA). The ITA would bring together the presently separate Railroad, Transit, and Highway administrations.

With these plans in place, Peña resigned his post as secretary of transportation in December 1996. Although he planned to seek a job in the private sector, when President Clinton asked him to serve in his cabinet as secretary of energy for the president's second term, Peña agreed. The Department of Energy is responsible for the regulation, production, and conservation of energy. Upon accepting the top position, Peña again faced turmoil, particularly in the *area of nuclear waste disposal, nuclear arms testing, and nuclear weapons plant clean-ups.*

Sources

Periodicals

American Metal Market, "Peña Aims to Build 'Intelligent' Roads," January 19, 1996, p. 4.

Aviation Week and Space Technology, "Peña Calls Summit on Airline Safety," January 2, 1995, p. 26.

Business and Commercial Aviation, "Legislation: Focus on FAA Reform," May 1995, p. 29.

Detroit News, "GM Loses Plea on Pickup Trucks," November 16, 1994, p. 1C; "Peña Offers Restructuring Plan," February 3, 1995, p. 5A.

Hispanic, "Federico Peña: Quick Study," June 1993, pp. 16–21.

Nation's Cities Weekly, "Secretary Peña Promises to Bring 'New Perspective' to DOT Role," March 15, 1993, p. 6.

New Republic, "Cabinet Losers," February 28, 1994, pp. 22–29.

Newsweek, "Forget About the Experts," October 31, 1994, p. 42; "How Safe Is This Flight?" April 24, 1995, pp. 18–29; "A New Day at the FAA?" July 1, 1996, p. 46.

New York Times, "Federico Fabian Peña: Same Predicament but a Different Agency," December 21, 1996, p. 11.

Railway Age, "Keep an Eye on That 800-Pound Gorilla," April 1995, p. 12.

U.S. News and World Report, "A Taj Mahal in the Rockies," February 13, 1995, pp. 48–53.

Raul Yzaguirre

1939–

Mexican American civil rights activist and association executive

Although no single group can claim to represent the many different interests and concerns of the entire Hispanic American community, the National Council of La Raza, known simply as La Raza or NCLR comes close to filling that role. The NCLR is a Washington, D.C.-based network of nearly 200 organizations that are all working toward the common goal of obtaining civil and economic rights for Hispanics. For more than twenty years, Raul Yzaguirre has served as its president and chief spokesperson. His leadership has helped make NCLR into the largest and one of the most respected Latino advocacy groups in the United States.

Early Life

Yzaguirre's activism first took root in the poverty and discrimination he knew as a youngster growing up in the Rio Grande Valley of south Texas. He once told a reporter for Hispanic, *"Back then we had no control over our schools, our cities, or our government. Unless you wanted* to shut the world out ... you had to get involved." He was only fifteen when he organized a youth branch of the American G.I. Forum, a well-known Hispanic veterans group. In 1964, after serving four years in the U.S. Air Force Medical Corps, Yzaguirre founded the National Organization for Mexican American Services (NOMAS). What is now the National Council of La Raza sprang from a proposal he originally wrote for NOMAS.

At the time he was active with NOMAS, Yzaguirre was also pursuing his education. In 1966, he received his bachelor's degree from George Washington University in Washington, D.C. He then worked as a program analyst in the Migrant Division of the U.S. Office of Economic Opportunity for several years. After that, Yzaguirre established the nation's first Mexican American research association, Interstate Research Associates, which he built into a multimillion-dollar nonprofit consulting firm.

Officially Joins the Staff of NCLR

From the founding of the National Council of La Raza in 1968, Yzaguirre served the group as a consultant, but it was not until 1974 that he officially joined the ranks of the organization as executive director. Four years later, he was named president, the position he still held in the late 1990s.

The NCLR was originally envisioned as a group that would assist mostly Mexican Americans or "La Raza." But under Yzaguirre's leadership, the organization embraced all the Hispanic people of the Americas in its quest for strength through unity. Its large network of **affiliates** are, for the most part, community-based. Affiliates are encouraged to take advantage of the technical assistance and training offered by the main organization in the areas of economic and business development, housing, employment, health, and other fields. They also benefit from Yzaguirre's fundraising for their programs from foundations, private corporations, and government grants.

In addition, the NCLR has become involved in issues of immigration policy, citizenship, and voter registration to make sure that Hispanic Americans are able to participate in the democratic process and have a voice in matters that

affiliates: organizations that are linked to, and usually depend on, other organizations with similar interests or goals

affect their lives. In 1992, for example, the organization launched a "Know Your Rights" campaign in response to statistics that showed even Hispanics who encountered obvious discrimination in the workplace or while house-hunting were unlikely to make an official complaint. The goal of "Know Your Rights" is to educate Latinos about their civil rights and show them how to deal with the various agencies that are supposed to resolve such problems.

Attacks Media Stereotyping of Hispanics

Perhaps the most widely publicized of the NCLR's efforts, however, was its focus on the impact of negative stereotyping of Hispanics on television, in the movies, and in the news media. The subject was discussed in depth in the group's third annual State of Hispanic America *report, issued in 1994, and also became the focus of Yzaguirre's remarks at the NCLR convention that same year. "More than hurt feelings are at stake," he declared. "Our inaccurate and poor media image has a devastating effect on virtually all aspects of the Hispanic policy agenda."*

Both Yzaguirre and the NCLR report blamed the problem on the lack of Latino journalists and sources in the major media. Besides encouraging various industry groups to adopt "Latino-specific hiring and promotion goals," he suggested that Congress and the Federal Communications Commission consider taking steps to increase positive Hispanic visibility in broadcasting.

The NCLR also regularly issues studies on Hispanics in entertainment programs. These studies analyze topics such as how many television shows feature continuing Hispanic characters and whether those characters are depicted positively or negatively. A report released in 1994, for example, found that Hispanics represent only about one percent of all characters on television and that most are shown in criminal or other stereotyped roles.

Responding to the study's findings, Yzaguirre stated bluntly that "what we're seeing here is systematic slander of the entire Hispanic community." He specifically condemned the television shows Cops *and* America's Most Wanted *for their negative portrayals of Hispanics. On the other hand, he said,* NYPD Blue, The John Larroquette

Show, *and* Beverly Hills 90210 *deserved praise for depicting Latinos in a favorable light. He warned that networks and sponsors that don't take steps to mend their ways could face economic consequences.*

Concerns About Immigrant-Bashing

Discrimination and stereotyping were very much on Yzaguirre's mind when he addressed the graduating class of Mercy College in White Plains, New York, on May 31, 1994. Only a few weeks earlier—on the Mexican holiday Cinco de Mayo (May 5), in fact—a radio station in Lansing, Michigan, had aired a fake commercial for a contest in which the "prize" was a Mexican servant. (Cinco de Mayo is a festival marking the Mexican defeat of the French at the Battle of Puebla on May 5, 1862. It is observed in Mexico as well as in U.S. cities with large Mexican American populations, where it has become more of a celebration of the Hispanic presence in the United States than a victory celebration.) Yzaguirre was deeply disturbed by the cruelty and insensitivity of this supposedly "funny" routine, and it prompted him to reflect on the new wave of immigrant-bashing in the United States.

That particular topic was of great interest to his audience that day. While it began more than fifty years ago as a Catholic school for women, Mercy College has now become a center of higher education for immigrants to the United States. They arrive from all over the world, and many already have degrees from schools in their native countries. These "nontraditional" students—older and often employed full-time—attend Mercy first to learn English and the other skills they need to succeed in their new home, and then to pursue a career in the field of their choice.

Yzaguirre's words to the Mercy College graduates touched on their fears as well as their hopes. His remarks are reprinted from a copy of his text that he himself provided.

What a big day! Allow me to add my congratulations to the graduating students, to your parents, spouses, relatives,

A Norwegian tall ship sails past the Statue of Liberty in celebration of the statue's one hundredth anniversary, 1986

and friends. I have just attended my own son's graduation ceremonies, and I know from first-hand the bittersweet emotions you are experiencing.

We are participating in a rite of passage, and as in all rites of passage, there are elements of both joy and sorrow. In these rites, society—indeed, all societies—ask the participants to leave the old behind and take on new responsibilities. For some of you, the so-called "nontraditional" students, responsibility is nothing new. You have been shouldering multiple roles and responsibilities for many, many years.

Yet all of you will be asked to help shape the destiny of this great nation of ours. As members of the college-educated "elite," in the best sense of that word, you will be expected to weigh in on the monumental issues of our time.

The Know-Nothings

From 1849 until around 1860, a political party nicknamed the "Know-Nothings" gathered membership in the United States. The unusual name poked fun at the mystery surrounding the organization, since members always met in secret and replied "I know nothing" whenever they were asked about their activities and goals. The group's official name was the American party.

The Know-Nothings traced their roots to a number of smaller underground societies that all had similar beliefs and goals. These societies sprang up in response to the large wave of immigration—especially Roman Catholic immigration—that occurred between 1825 and 1855. The Know-Nothings were hostile to this immigration and the ideas and influences that arrived with the newcomers. They played on the fears of some Americans that immigrants were growing in strength and influence. To reverse that trend, they tried to prevent foreign-born citizens and Roman Catholics from holding public office.

In 1854 and 1855, the Know-Nothings were at the height of their popularity and succeeded in winning several governorships. In 1856, they nominated former President Millard Fillmore as their presidential candidate. But the Know-Nothings refused to take a stand on the issue of slavery, and as a result, they did not attract much voter support. (Maryland was the only state they carried that year.) By 1861, the party had no representatives in Congress, and it was not long until they disappeared completely from the American political scene.

One of those issues will be the matter of immigration. Mercy College, because of its history, location, and inclination, has at a very practical level responded to the challenges and opportunities that newly-arrived immigrants present to us. Because of your experiences here at Mercy, you are in a position to lead the rest of us as we wrestle with this divisive question.

America is of two minds when it comes to immigrants. On the one hand, we are proud of our immigrant heritage, symbolized by that great American icon known as the Statue of Liberty. Yet public opinion, going back as far as the early 1800s, has been decidedly against each new wave of immigrants.

Every American, including American Indians, are immigrants or descendants of immigrants. Newcomers to our land are "Americans by choice"; indeed, our very existence as a nation is based on that heritage.

Yet we are witnessing a wave of immigrant-bashing that mimics the most shameful episodes in our history. During the 1850s and through the Civil War, the so-called Know-Nothing party campaigned successfully on an explicitly racist and anti-immigrant platform, and what is **disconcerting** is that *exactly* the same rhetoric used at that time is **prevalent** today.

Just this past month, the following "contest" played on a radio station in the state of Michigan. Now try to imagine all the bells and whistles and the appropriate jingles and background music and listen to this as you would be listening to a radio program:

> Some are giving away trips to Mexico City, but we are bringing Mexico to *you!* That's right! We are giving away Mexicans—real, live Mexicans! Ay carramba!
>
> We'll be smuggling illegal aliens across the border in the wheel-well of a station van, and then we'll give one to *you!* Imagine—your own personal Mexican! They'll wash your car, clean your house, pick your crops, anything you want. Because if they don't, you'll have them deported!
>
> Adios, amigos. Be the fifth caller when you hear this sound (the sound of a mooing cow) and win a Mexican!
>
> Bathing and **delousing** of Mexicans is winner's responsibility. Station assumes no liability for infectious diseases carried by Mexicans.
>
> Celebrate Cinco de Mayo in your own home every day with your own Mexican!

How should we interpret these kinds of public remarks? Is it OK to talk about—even in jest—people owning people? Whatever the intent, we know from past history that the first step in **oppressing** a people is to dehumanize them and/or to **demonize** them.

And that is exactly what we did to the new Americans that came from Germany, from Ireland, from Italy, from China and Japan, from Hungary. And that is what we did to Jews who came from all over Europe. Anti-immigration legislation specifically aimed at these groups has either passed or nearly passed in our past.

I hasten to add that there are well-meaning Americans who believe in more restrictionist immigration policies who are neither racist nor **xenophobic.** Some Americans are

disconcerting: disturbing, troublesome.

prevalent: widespread.

delousing: removing lice from someone or something.

oppressing: crushing or persecuting through the abuse of power or authority.

demonize: make appear evil or undesirable.

xenophobic: excessively and irrationally afraid of foreigners.

honestly worried about the total population of this nation and about our collective ability to accommodate differences in culture and language. Others truly believe that immigrants cost the taxpayer additional burdens.

These are reasonable concerns that can be addressed by the facts. And the facts are that the number of foreign-born [persons] in the United States as a percentage of our population is not any higher than it has been in our past. The fact is that today's new Americans are **assimilating** *faster* than previous immigrants. The fact is that immigrants are *not* a net burden to the United States taxpayer but a net contributor, a significant contributor.

Yet we should all be worried about continued undocumented immigration and about **exploitation** of human beings—be they documented, undocumented, immigrant, or native-born.

Yzaguirre speaks out against an unfair census that undercounted Hispanic Americans, 1991

We also know that economic security fuels our worst fears and brings out our meanest instincts. During every single recession, and especially during the Great Depression, the United States **implemented** policies that should bring shame to all of us. While precise figures are hard to come by, we can confidently estimate that well over one million legal immigrants and American citizens have been illegally and unjustly **deported** during economic downturns.

Today, we are witnessing a replay of history. Politicians from both parties are **scapegoating** immigrants for our economic and social problems. Apparently there is a great deal of political capital in demonizing immigrants.

Regretfully, there are few statesmen willing to stand tall and bring reason and decency to this debate.

We need leaders like my own personal hero, President Harry Truman. He stood up to Congress and vetoed a racist immigration bill, and he sent the following message to Congress and to the American people, and let me quote:

assimilating: blending in to mainstream society.

exploitation: unfair use of another person for one's own profit.

implemented: put into effect.

deported: sent out of the country.

scapegoating: unfairly blaming.

The idea behind this policy [referring to the quota system] was, to put it boldly, that Americans with English or Irish names were better people and better citizens than Americans with Italian or Greek or Polish names.... Such a concept is utterly unworthy of our traditions and our ideals. It violates the great political doctrine of the Declaration of Independence that "all men are created equal".... It is incredible to me that, in this year of 1952, we should again be enacting into law such a slur on the patriotism, the capacity, and the decency of a large part of our citizenry.

Well, now we're here in 1994, and today we are not only slurring the decency of people, we are questioning their very humanity.

In years to come, I hope to read about an **alumnus** of Mercy College who stood up and reminded us that America is and always will be a place of opportunity, a nation of liberties, and a beacon to the world.

Thank you, have a great life, and God bless.

Sources

Periodicals

Detroit Free Press, "Hispanic Civil Rights Group Accuses Shows of Slander," September 8, 1994; "You Won't See Hispanics in Prime Time, Study Says," April 18, 1996, p. 5C.

Editor and Publisher, "State of Hispanic America," August 6, 1994, p. 11.

Grand Rapids Press (Grand Rapids, MI), "Learning America," November 19, 1995, p. A15.

Hispanic, "Know Your Rights," May 1992, p. 46; "Committed to Unity," July 1992, pp. 11–14.

alumnus: graduate.

Index

Entries on featured speakers are indicated by boldface; illustrations are marked (ill.).